# Exploring Scriptural Sources

*Aaron Milavec*

Sheed & Ward

Copyright© 1994 by Aaron Milavec

All rights reserved. No part of this book may be reproduced or transmitted in any form or by any means, electronic or mechanical, including photocopying, recording or by an information storage and retrieval system without permission in writing from the Publisher.

Sheed & Ward™ is a service of The National Catholic Reporter Publishing Company.

**Library of Congress Cataloguing-in-Publication Data**

Milavec, Aaron
    Exploring scriptural sources / Aaron Milavec.
        p.   cm. — (Rediscovered discipleship)
    Includes bibliographical references.
    ISBN: 978-1-55612-706-9
    1. Bible. N.T.—Textbooks.  2. Catholic Church—Doctrines.
I. Title. II. Series.
BS2536.M55  1994
220.6—dc20                                                                         94-25512
                                                                                                          CIP

Published by:  Sheed & Ward
                     115 E. Armour Blvd.
                     P.O. Box 419492
                     Kansas City, MO 64141

To order, call: (800) 333-7373

*Cover design by Emil Antonucci.*

# Contents

Preface for Adult Learners . . . . . . . . . . . . . . . vii
Introduction . . . . . . . . . . . . . . . . . . . . . . xiii

**Case One:**
**How Conservative Peter Became the Daring Innovator** . . . 1
   Purpose . . . . . . . . . . . . . . . . . . . . . . . 2
   Preparing Yourself to Read Luke . . . . . . . . . . . 3
   Jesus' Commitment to the Exclusion Principle . . . . . 5
   Analysis . . . . . . . . . . . . . . . . . . . . . . . 14
   Application to the Churches Today . . . . . . . . . . 23
   Further Readings . . . . . . . . . . . . . . . . . . . 24

**Case Two:**
**How Jesus Came to Be Chosen as High Priest** . . . . . . . 25
   Purpose . . . . . . . . . . . . . . . . . . . . . . . 27
   Who is Called "Priest"? . . . . . . . . . . . . . . . 29
   Jesus as Our High Priest . . . . . . . . . . . . . . . 31
   Analysis . . . . . . . . . . . . . . . . . . . . . . . 38
   Application to the Churches Today . . . . . . . . . . 46
   Further Readings . . . . . . . . . . . . . . . . . . . 47

**Case Three:**
**The Transformation Effected by Ordination** . . . . . . . . 48
   Purpose . . . . . . . . . . . . . . . . . . . . . . . 49
   Two Instances of Ordination . . . . . . . . . . . . . 50
   Analysis . . . . . . . . . . . . . . . . . . . . . . . 55
   Application to the Churches Today . . . . . . . . . . 62
   Further Readings . . . . . . . . . . . . . . . . . . . 62

**Case Four:**
**When Jesus Sided With the Women** . . . . . . . . . . . . . 64
   Purpose . . . . . . . . . . . . . . . . . . . . . . . 67
   To Whom Did Jesus Preach? . . . . . . . . . . . . . . 68
   Jesus Healing Women . . . . . . . . . . . . . . . . . 72
   The Menstruating Woman Who Touched Jesus . . . . . . 74
   The Woman Who Touched Jesus at a Banquet . . . . . . 78
   Jesus Shaming His Male Companions . . . . . . . . . . 82

    Martha's Cooking vs. Mary's Learning . . . . . . . . 85
    Analysis . . . . . . . . . . . . . . . . . . . . . . 89
    Application to the Churches Today . . . . . . . . . . 93
    Further Readings . . . . . . . . . . . . . . . . . . 94

### Case Five
### Whether the Twelve Fancied Themselves as Bishops . . . . 96
    Purpose . . . . . . . . . . . . . . . . . . . . . . 97
    An Initial World Study . . . . . . . . . . . . . . . 99
    Who is Called "Elder"? . . . . . . . . . . . . . . 100
    Elders in Jerusalem . . . . . . . . . . . . . . . . 101
    Prophets and Teachers in Antioch . . . . . . . . . 103
    Bishops and Deacons in the Pastoral Epistles . . . . 104
    The Spirit as Organizing Principle in Corinth . . . . 106
    The Failure of Paul's Model . . . . . . . . . . . . 109
    Analysis . . . . . . . . . . . . . . . . . . . . . 112
    Application to the Churches Today . . . . . . . . . 116
    Further Readings . . . . . . . . . . . . . . . . . 117

### Case Six
### Collaboration as the Hallmark of Peter's Authority . . . 118
    Purpose . . . . . . . . . . . . . . . . . . . . . 122
    Initial Word Studies . . . . . . . . . . . . . . . 123
    Peter's Failures . . . . . . . . . . . . . . . . . 124
    Peter's Authority According to Matthew . . . . . . 129
    Peter's Functioning in the Jerusalem Church . . . . 130
    Analysis . . . . . . . . . . . . . . . . . . . . . 135
    Application to the Churches Today . . . . . . . . . 140
    Further Readings . . . . . . . . . . . . . . . . . 141

### Case Seven
### The Transforming Effected by Baptism . . . . . . . . 142
    Purpose . . . . . . . . . . . . . . . . . . . . . 144
    An Initial Word Study . . . . . . . . . . . . . . 145
    The Baptism of John . . . . . . . . . . . . . . . 150
    Baptism and the Spirit . . . . . . . . . . . . . . 153
    Baptism and Community Fellowship . . . . . . . . 155
    Analysis . . . . . . . . . . . . . . . . . . . . . 157
    Application to the Churches Today . . . . . . . . . 167
    Further Readings . . . . . . . . . . . . . . . . . 168

**Case Eight:**
**Thy Kingdom Come and/or Going to Heaven?** . . . . . . 169
    Purpose . . . . . . . . . . . . . . . . 171
    An Initial Word Study . . . . . . . . . . . . 172
    The Kingdom in Jewish Expectation . . . . . . . . 177
    Where the When is the Kingdom expected? . . . . . . 178
    Delay in the Lord's Coming . . . . . . . . . . 180
    Jesus' Struggle with Evil . . . . . . . . . . . 183
    Analysis . . . . . . . . . . . . . . . . 186
    Application to the Churches Today . . . . . . . . 194
    Further Readings . . . . . . . . . . . . . 196

Appendix . . . . . . . . . . . . . . . . . 198

*In memory of Mary and her successors,
those pioneers who sit at the feet of Jesus
and actualize God's lure in our midst*


*In memory of Peter and his successors,
those collaborate and consultative leaders
who passionately forward God's cause*

# Preface for Adult Learners

Most people like to discover things for themselves and not simply to be told. Adult learners, more especially, appreciate a direct involvement in what they are learning. By taking charge of their own learning, adults invariably find that they learn more easily, more enjoyably, and more deeply. Deep learning immediately results in noticeable changes in the settled instincts whereby adults perceive, evaluate, and enjoy life. These interior changes, in their turn, provide an enlarged sense of being alive and being well in their family, in their church, in their society.

*By taking charge of their own learning, adults invariably find that they learn more easily, more enjoyably, and more deeply.*

The Case Studies within this volume were designed for and perfected by adult learners. Each Case Study was crafted to build upon and enlarge what you already know and experience about discipleship and the church. At the same time, there will be surprises: you will be exploring dimensions of the church which you have never closely examined before. Progressively, you will become fascinated with and rooted in the past—gaining a new freedom, a new discernment, and a new responsibility to live in the present. From time to time, you will even find yourself struggling to sort out how the origins and early history of Christianity square with what is going on in your church today. What kind of Christian in what kind of church, after all, does God intend?

Each Case Study will allow you to independently investigate some aspect of the early church through a direct examination of primary sources. For the first Case Study, the source will be Acts 10. Using the clues offered by Luke, "the first church historian," you will play the role of a Sherlock Holmes. Your mission will be to solve a mystery which is entitled "How Conservative Peter Became the Daring Innovator." As you move through the Case Study, you will undertake a guided investigation of the "clues" which Luke has left behind. You will puzzle over these clues. You will make hunches and test them out. In the end, you will decide to what degree you have been able to synthesize the clues in such a way as to say, "Mystery solved!"

*Each Case Study will allow you to independently investigate some aspect of the early church through a direct examination of primary sources.*

As you go, you will make notes for yourself and to yourself. Past experience demonstrates that writing with a pen in the spaces provided is best for this. Pencil smudges. Along the way, you might decide to abandon certain hunches that you have already recorded. It's easy to draw a line through such bad hunches and write in your new ones. In this way, you can later easily spot what lines of investigation you have ruled out as unsatisfactory or improbable.

During your investigation, you will sometimes get stuck. All good detectives do. When this happens, don't try to rack your brain so hard and so long that you wear yourself out. When a solution doesn't readily come, put a question mark in the margin and continue. When the moment is right, come back to the issue which you marked off for yourself with the question mark. The experience of adult learners demonstrates that it is far better to have gone through the whole Case Study in a reasonable period of time than to get hopelessly stuck somewhere in the middle.

> *It is far better to have gone through the whole Case Study in a reasonable period of time than to get hopelessly stuck in the middle.*

Why not just go to a biblical commentary? To do so would be like bringing in another detective to solve the case for you. Give yourself a crack at it first. Make up your own mind on the basis of the clues offered. If, in the end, you want to check out a trusted commentary or to consult your local pastor so as to get a second opinion, go ahead. Remember, however, that every biblical commentator (no matter how many degrees or ordinations he/she may have) is also constrained to play Sherlock Holmes and to make sense of the same clues that you have encountered. Hence, don't be shy about challenging or revising what your commentator says on the basis of your own investigations. The same, needless to say, holds true for the analysis that I have prepared at the end of each Case Study. Every solution is "true" only to the degree that it can satisfactorily account for the clues given by the sacred text.

How about working on a Case Study with a friend or a learning partner? If you are so inclined, go ahead. Some people work best when they think out loud before a "Watson" who has his/her own insights and gnawing questions to chew on. In practice, this often proves to be a much richer way to do detective work, even when it is more time consuming. In order to save time, you might want to agree with your learning partner to do a Case Study independently and then come together to compare your results. In the end, do what proves to be best for you.

> *Working on a Case Study with a learning partner, or in a group, often proves to be a much richer way to do detective work.*

How about using this Case Study in the context of a small group devoted to mutual support, faith sharing, or ecumenical dialogue? In any of these cases, the Case Study will provide a clear focus for your group and evoke incredible energy as you deliberate over the clues together. Many minds and hearts are always better than one, especially when these minds and hearts are bent upon attentively listening and sensitively negotiating difference in opinion which are bound to arise. In fact, the potential richness of any group effort expands to the degree that a diversity of viewpoints and a diversity of commitments are present.

Whether in a group or with a single learning partner, it is helpful to take some moments at the end of each session to reflect on the process. What has gone well? What needs improvement? Especially when a group is involved, each session can be closed by going around the circle and having each person take up to sixty seconds to thank one other person for what they learned from them or what they admired about them during the course of the session. For learners of all ages, especially adults, depth in learning goes along with depth in bonding. Discover what works for you and for your group. This is never time wasted.

*Depth in learning goes along with depth in bonding.*

Must these Case Studies be undertaken in the order in which they are given? Not necessarily. To some degree, each Case Study builds upon the skills and insights which have been gained earlier. This should not be taken as an absolute rule, however, since each Case Study can also stand on its own. My advice would be to begin by tackling the foundational Case One and, from that point onward, to follow the path where your interest is peaking. If, at any point, you find yourself sinking, you can always go back and try a sequential approach. Here again, you are the best guide for your own learning.

# Acknowledgments

Originally, most of these Case Studies were crafted for the adult learners in the Lay Pastoral Ministry Program at the Athenaeum of Ohio. Still others were crafted for use by the seminarians at Mount St. Mary's Seminary of the West. I am indebted to The Consortium for Higher Education Religion Studies and to the Association of Theological Schools in the United States and Canada for training me in the Harvard Case Study Method some twenty years ago. I am also indebted to the editors of Sheed & Ward for having encouraged me to take the methods which have proven so successful for my students and to make them available for a wider audience.

You may discover ways to improve these Case Studies as you use them. If so, I would personally be pleased to hear from you and to incorporate your suggestions in two ways: (a) to prepare an ungraded edition of this volume once the first run is exhausted and (b) to assist me in preparing the subsequent Case Studies which will cover the patristic, medieval, reformation, and modern experience of Christianity.

*You may discover ways to improve these Case Studies as you use them.*

Up to this point, I have already received hundreds of suggestions from those who used and improved these Case Studies during the last five years. Most especially, I want to thank Dr. Robert Obach who carefully read through each Case and made dozens of suggestions for improving their logical flow and style. Thanks also go to my wise and loving wife, Dr. Linda Milavec, who generously supported this project and helped me design the experiential components of these Case Studies. Finally, I want to thank all those students who advised me as to where I needed to clarify, deepen, and expand the Case Studies which I had designed for their use. Their names are written deep in my heart.

My home institution, the Athenaeum of Ohio, knows full well that continued excellence in education depends upon the ongoing development of its faculty. Accordingly, the timely completion of these Case Studies and their electronic counterparts would not have been possible without the sabbatical leave which my home institution granted me during the Fall and Spring Term of 1993-1994. Such faculty leaves, however, would not be possible without the continued and generous support of the people of the Archdiocese of Cincinnati along with our archbishop, the Most Rev. Daniel Pilarczyk. These people have given of their resources and of themselves to insure that the Athenaeum might benefit, not only its immediate students, but the wider Church as well for generations yet to come. My hope and prayer is those who deepen their rootedness in the early church through these Case Studies will be grateful, as I am, to those ordinary people and dedicated administrators who have made this all possible.

# Introduction

# Why Propaganda Need No Longer Pass for History

Winston Churchill once remarked, "The first casualty in every war is truth." This was the case during the Second World War as it was four hundred years earlier when Protestants and Catholics were pitted against each other in verbal and physical war. As a result, during the long years of mutual antagonism which followed the Protestant Reformation, there have been two opposing versions of what constitutes *the true church* and two versions of the history of the early church to back that up.

*There have been two opposing versions of what constitutes "the true church" and two versions of the history of the early church to back that up.*

Protestants, for their part, were persuaded that God wanted a church of simple faith and simple practices very much like that described by Luke in the Acts of the Apostles. Using the New Testament as their norm, Protestants reformed their churches so that they reflected the faith and practices of the early church. Since the papacy, indulgences, relics, devotion to the saints, purgatory, celibate priests, and seven sacraments (save for baptism and the Lord's Supper) found scarcely any place in the New Testament records, Protestants determined that these were to be scrapped. These things appeared to Protestants as so many vain human inventions which detracted from the purity and simplicity of the Gospel being rightly preached and the sacraments being rightly administered.

Catholics, for their part, were persuaded that the true church could not be anything less than what the church had become in the sixteenth century. In fact, Catholics were convinced that they could not meddle with the essential structure of the church since this was the very structure which had existed from generation to generation going all the way back to the Apostles. While papacy, relics, indulgences, etc., may not have appeared to have sufficient warrant in the eyes of Protestants, Catholics were persuaded that not everything believed and practiced by the apostolic church was written down in the New Testament. Accordingly, when Catholics wanted to know what was essential to the true church, they consulted not only the Scriptures but also the writings of the Fathers and Doctors of the Church as well.

In the light of this larger and longer tradition, the papacy, for instance, appeared to Catholics as an essential and constant ingredient in the true church. Thus, if the pope was the master of the universal Church in the sixteenth century, this was precisely because his predecessors had exercised the same dominion in the twelfth, in the sixth, in the third, in the first (century)—all in fidelity to the mandate which Christ gave to Peter when he said, "Upon this rock I will build my church" (Matthew 18:18). In parallel terms, if there were seven sacraments in the sixteenth century Church, this was precisely because there were seven and only seven being practiced in the twelfth, in the sixth, in the third, in the first (century)—all in fidelity to the expressed will and intention of Christ. Every one of the seven, therefore, could be explained by reference to some text of institution within the New Testament. In the minds of Catholics, therefore, the true church has to be the existing Roman Catholic Church because only this church had retained all the essential church structures which were originally established by Christ and his Apostles.

*Both sides engaged in propaganda wars which systematically overstated their own claims while undercutting their opponents claims.*

Neither side was able to persuade the other as to what constituted *the true church*. Accordingly, in the heat of controversy, both sides engaged in propaganda wars which systematically overstated their own claims while undercutting their opponents claims. Protestants claimed that their church submitted to the divine authority of Christ (as found in the Christian Scriptures) and not to the human authority of the papacy (which, history demonstrated, often played the role of "anti-Christ"). Catholics claimed that Christ had deliberately established the papacy for the very purpose of safeguarding the correct interpretation of the bible against the erroneous (self-willed and sometimes even "demonically inspired") interpretations insisted upon by the Protestants. On both sides, charity and truth often suffered in the zeal to defend *the true church* and to vilify its opponents.

*This has been the first generation, since the 16th century, wherein Catholic and Protestant scholars have been officially able to sit down together and to engage in collaborative biblical studies.*

In our own day, these passions have cooled. The machinery of propaganda has slowed down. Sensitive persons on both sides of the great divide have had a chance to reassess the former "enemy." As a result, this has been the first generation, since the sixteenth century, wherein Catholic and Protestant scholars have been officially able to sit down together and to engage in collaborative biblical studies. Many ordinary believers, meanwhile, have started up dialogue groups and prayer groups wherein confessional boundaries have been softened and, in some instances, even miraculously overcome. Many ordained clergy, for their part, brought their people to pray together and to act together in ways that would have been unthinkable during the time of the religious "cold war."

Stories could be multiplied here. One stands out, however, because it is so public and so symbolic. A dozen years ago, when the Crossroad Publishing Company decided to issue an illustrated biography of Martin Luther on the occasion of the 500th anniversary of his birth (1483-1983), the editors invited a Roman Catholic priest, Peter Manns, to write the text and a world-famous Lutheran theologian, Jaroslav Pelikan, to write the introduction. This reversal of things indicates how far the "cold war" had thawed: a Catholic historian was trusted to present the meaning and significance of Luther's life for both Protestants and Catholics alike. With a disarming candidness, Pelikan acknowledged that Mann's portrait of Luther rang true to his Lutheran sensibilities, and he went on to recall what a reversal of things this represents:

> *Martin Luther: An Illustrated Biography* can serve as a corrective of the distortions of Luther and his Reformation that have marred the confessional literature in English. Above all, the Luther who emerges from these pages stands out as profoundly Catholic in his devotion to the Church, to her creeds, and to her sacraments. Even when he denounced the Church for betraying the trust given to her by Christ, he was speaking in the name of that which the Church confessed and had taught him to confess. . . .
>
> Neither Roman Catholics nor Protestants will find such a Luther easy to handle. Things were so much simpler when Protestant celebrations of Reformation Day on October 31 could be devoted to a litany about such evils as Mariolatry, celibacy, papal tyranny, and the practice of chaining the Bible; or when the pamphlets available in the tract of a Roman Catholic parish could continue to portray Luther as a foulmouth, a psychopath, or even a suicide. These caricatures, which it is all too easy to caricature in turn, have now yielded on both sides to the more complex but also more accurate picture. . . .
>
> Can the man who is usually blamed or credited for tearing us apart help to bring us together? That may be too much to hope, at least for the present. But the cause can only be aided by a book about this man that dares to tell the truth (Manns: 8-9).

The distortion of history by propaganda did not start or stop with biographies of Luther. Every epoch of history has received its due amount of distortion. Let me provide an illustrative case to make my point.

Consider the whole debate as to whether two or seven sacraments were instituted by Christ for his church. In contrast to the confessional rhetoric of the past, recent studies on both sides have been able to acknowledge that every presentation of Jesus of Nazareth as "instituting" a fixed number of "sacraments" for "his" church is the result of projecting the concerns of another age upon the first

*A Catholic historian was trusted to present the meaning and significance of Luther's life.*

*The Luther who emerges from these pages stands out as profoundly Catholic in his devotion to the Church, to her creeds, and to her sacraments.*

century. If one just sits back and thinks about it for a moment, one never finds Jesus taking his disciples aside and saying, "I want to make it clear right from the very beginning how many sacraments I am instituting. . . ." In fact, the entire Christian Scriptures are entirely devoid of any listing or naming of official rites. Neither the "two" nor the "seven," consequently, can be claimed as being the definitive number of rites which Jesus wanted his church to have for all time.

*The entire Christian Scriptures are entirely devoid of any listing or naming of official rites.*

The term "sacrament" itself has a history. The New Testament did not create or use this word. Rather, it comes from the Latin term, *sacramentum*. This word was used by Romans to designate the military oath taken by new recruits at the close of their initial military training. This solemn military oath made the recruit into a "soldier" bent upon total fidelity to the cause and to the orders of one and only one man—his commanding officer. Tertullian (d. 225 CE) was the first known Church Father to have made use of this term within Christian circles and, even then, he used it exclusively to designate the seriousness with which Christians attached themselves exclusively to the Father of Jesus. With time, however, the term caught on and had a life of its own. By the time of Augustine (d. 430 CE), "sacrament" (*sacramentum*) was being used not only to designate the rite of baptism, but also the making of the sign of the cross, the receiving of ashes on the head at the beginning of the Lenten fast, the rites of Christian burial, etc. Neither Augustine nor his contemporaries felt any necessity to imagine that *the true church* had a fixed number of "sacraments" that had been "instituted by Christ."

*Neither Augustine nor his contemporaries felt any necessity to imagine that the true church had a fixed number of "sacraments."*

When the medieval theologians first raised the question as to "how many sacraments," there was wholesale confusion because no Church Father had either addressed or answered such a question. Accordingly, in his *Summa Theologica*, Thomas Aquinas (d. 1274), after having considered various opinions as to the number of sacraments, settled for the number seven on the basis of an imaginative parallel whereby the Church rites imitate key aspects of our natural life (e.g., birth=baptism, growth=confirmation, eating=eucharist, etc.). Thomas knew that he was an innovator in his day and, accordingly, he never imagined that there had been seven from the beginning or that his contemporaries who preferred to name six or nine sacraments ought to be excluded from the Church.

*The Council of Trent solemnly declared that there were seven and only seven sacraments.*

As the stature of Thomas and his *Summa* grew in importance, however, his personal professional opinion was increasingly made to serve as the official organizational position of the entire Church. Over and against the appeal of the Protestant reformers, consequently, the Council of Trent (1545-1563) solemnly declared that there were seven and only seven sacraments and that this question was not any longer open for theological discussion by anyone who calls themselves Christian. Faced with the Protestant upheaval, it became a point of honor and loyalty for Catholics to maintain their identity against the Protestants by affirming that it was "historically certain" that Christ instituted seven sacraments.

From the vantage point of history, however, it is just as inaccurate to imagine Jesus of Nazareth instituting two and only two sacraments as it is to press for seven and only seven. The time is coming and perhaps already here when Catholics and Protestants will be able to say to each other, "Jesus never made this a critical issue on his agenda; therefore, we need to seriously examine whether this issue must continue to remain the litmus test whereby one decides which is the true church." At this point, a respectful dialogue and a shared inquiry into history can begin.

*It is just as inaccurate to imagine Jesus of Nazareth instituting two and only two sacraments as it is to press for seven and only seven.*

The official dialogue which has taken place between bishops and theologians of the Catholic and Lutheran (Evangelical) Churches in Germany from 1981-1985 provides an apt instance of how, following upon shared historical and biblical studies, "important controversial questions appear in a new light" (Lehmann:182). Relative to the number of sacraments, the dialogue partners discovered that Catholics in the sixteenth century were using a broader notion of "institution by Christ" than were the Protestants in this same era. For Catholics, there was "no difference in principle being seen between Christ's institution and the action of the Holy Spirit in the church" (Lehmann:73). Protestants, on the other hand, required that "institutio means the directly demonstrable institution through Jesus Christ himself, or through an explicit divine mandate" (Lehmann:73). In the end, *both sides concluded that the sixteenth century condemnations regarding the number of sacraments can no longer be held as strictly binding upon the partner churches.* Their consensus statements read, in part, as follows:

*The Catholic and Lutheran Churches in Germany concluded that the sixteenth century condemnations regarding the number of sacraments can no longer be held as strictly binding upon the partner churches.*

> The historical process in which the number of the sacraments was fixed shows that there was considerable openness in this matter. Since for both the Catholic and the Protestant churches the institution by Jesus Christ is a constitutive aspect of the concept of sacrament, the weight of disagreement has shifted from the varying number of the sacraments to the question about their authorization and their ecclesial foundation (Lehmann:73).

> All in all, the condemnations on both sides may be viewed as not ecclesially insignificant; but largely speaking, the lines of division which they draw still obtain in their traditional vigor only if their formulations are viewed superficially. As soon as the way in which the sacraments are understood is considered, as well as the theological reasoning about the mode of their efficacy, a considerable measure of agreement emerges (Lehmann:84).

## Summary and Conclusion

Church history has been written, until now, by scholars doubling as propagandists. Catholics relied upon their respected authors and publishing houses to correctly understand "what really happened," free from Protestant bias. Meanwhile, Protestants were equally concerned to credit their "truth-sayers" over and against Catholic distortions. Given the dismantling of the "Berlin Wall" which separates us, the ideologically distorted versions of history may now safely be scrapped on both sides.

*The goal of this book is to enable both professionals and nonprofessionals to develop the necessary skills for rediscovering and reappropriating for themselves critical dimensions of the early church which have been hitherto distorted or unnoticed due to confessional polemics.*

Our settled intuitions, however, frequently betray us. So much human energy has been spent on "documenting" and "proving" that *the true church* must be this and not that as to make it impossible for most lay people to get their bearings. Even sensitive pastors, whether Catholic or Protestant, struggle with how to wisely and prudently forward the shift from propaganda to dialogue. It would be unwise, for example, for a Catholic priest to tell traditional Catholics that they can soften up on their insistence that the true church must have seven sacraments if such information would only serve to shake their Catholic identity and make them redouble their efforts to keep the faith (and the propaganda) as they have known it. The same thing holds true for a Protestant minister who would unwisely try to get traditionalists within his own congregation to lighten up on their insistence upon two and only two sacraments. On the other hand, it would be socially and historically irresponsible and an affront to the Gospel itself for any Catholic priest or Protestant minister to continue to feed into the old-time propaganda on the grounds that he or she can't risk disturbing "the identity" of his congregation.

*Rootedness in this past is the surest and the safest and the proven way for Christians to enlarge their commitment to God's cause and to his church.*

The time is ripe, consequently, for both Catholics and Protestants to go back to the sources and hear them again with open hearts and minds. This is precisely what the Case Studies that follow are all about. The goal of this book, therefore, is to enable both professionals and non-professionals to develop the necessary skills for rediscovering and reappropriating for themselves critical dimensions of the early church which have been hitherto distorted or unnoticed due to confessional polemics. More importantly, however, these Case Studies are designed to offer Christians a solid, unromanticized experience of Jesus and of the early church. Rootedness in this past is the surest and the safest and the proven way for Christians to enlarge their commitment to God's cause and to his church.

## Further Readings

Lehmann, Karl, and Wolfhart Pannenberg, eds.
> *The Condemnations of the Reformation Era: Do They Still Divide?* Minneapolis: Fortress Press, 1990.

Manns, Peter
> *Martin Luther: An Illustrated Biography.* New York: Crossroad, 1983.

---

### "Christian Scriptures" and "CE"

Throughout these Case Studies, the terms "Hebrew Scriptures" and "Christian Scriptures" will be used rather than "Old Testament" and "New Testament." Dates will also be followed by "BCE" (i.e., Before the Common Era) or "CE" (i.e., of the Common Era) rather than B.C. or A.D.

These changes in terminology are symbolic of the determination on the part of Christians to present a positive assessment of Jews and Judaism. The Catholic bishops of Vatican II declared, in part, that "the Jews still remain most dear to God because of their fathers, for He [God] does not repent of the gifts He makes nor of the calls He issues" (*Nostra Aetate*: 4). As a result, the covenant (or "testament") which God initiated with the Gentiles through Jesus Christ does not abrogate the older covenant that God made with the Jewish people. Within the context of these Case Studies, the reader will have frequent occasions to discover the points of continuity between Judaism and Christianity. Accordingly frequent reference will be made to both the Hebrew and Christian Scriptures.

---

### Note to Protestant and Orthodox Christians

The Case Studies in this book were primarily prepared for use by Catholics but had Protestant and Orthodox Christians in mind as auditors and witnesses.

Within the discovery sections neither Catholic, Protestant, or Orthodox interests are evident since the focus is properly upon hearing the clues of the text and following the agenda and concerns of the Sacred Writers. In this process, Protestants, Orthodox, and Catholics are all entering into a world which is not of their own making.

Protestant and Orthodox Christians will discover, however, that the "Analysis" after each Case Study gives somewhat greater attention to Catholic issues and Catholic experience. You, as a Protestant or Orthodox believer, might just pass over these sections. On the other hand, they might serve you as an opportunity to get better acquainted with how the early church impinges upon Catholic identity and Catholic practice. Alternately, they might stimulate you to search out, within the official sources of your own church, how your church is attempting to be responsive to present conditions and to God's future while being solidly rooted in the past.

**Case 1**

# How Conservative Peter Became the Daring Innovator

The religious enterprise is usually guided by conservative instincts. This should not come as a surprise. Whenever one discovers something of great value, the natural impulse is to preserve it for one's own enjoyment and to pass it on to one's children. Accordingly, the way of life taught by Jesus of Nazareth has been carefully passed down from generation to generation by those who gather together as "church" and understand themselves as "disciples" (i.e., followers in his way). In the words of the 19th-century hymn, we can see how both Protestant and Catholic Christians felt about holding tight to the Jesus tradition:

> Faith of our fathers living still
> In spite of dungeon, fire, and sword,
> O how our hearts beat high with joy
> Whenever we hear that glorious word!
>
> Faith of our fathers, holy faith,
> We will be true to thee till death.

While Catholic and Protestant Christians agree on the necessity of being conservative, they disagree strongly about what it is that God wants them to conserve. Catholics, for their part, have operated under the conviction that "the faith of their fathers" includes papal primacy, ordained priesthood and devotion to Mary. Catholics have traditionally clung to these things on the grounds that they were thereby preserving what had been practiced by "the one true Church" since apostolic times. Protestant Christians, for their part, have traditionally regarded these Catholic practices as human innovations which obscure the simplicity of faith which characterized "the true churches" of the apostolic period. In this frame of mind, Protestants have, to one degree or the other, removed from their churches those practices and devotions which did not seem to have any clear warrant from the Word of God (the Bible).

Once a church decides what God wants them to believe and to do, it seems that it would be a comparatively simple task to record this and to agree that nothing would ever be added or taken away.

Such a rigid conservatism would be theoretically possible in so far as every church is a human institution. However, in so far as every church is a divine institution, such a conservatism would betray its foundational purpose. This is so because the Christian churches are committed, like their founder Jesus Christ, to listening to the voice of the living God: "Today, when you hear his voice, do not harden your hearts" (Hebrews 3:7, 4:7; Psalms 95:7).

> *"Today, when you hear his voice, do not harden your hearts."*

True religion, therefore, means not only living according to the standards of excellence contained in a tradition, but also training oneself for listening to God in the present moment. Such listening to God includes entrusting oneself to the divine promptings within one's personal and collective existence even when this means altering one's religious commitments in the process. Thus, from time to time, the conservative principle has to bend in order to embrace fresh understandings of "what God wants us to be" or else fall prey to the embrace of a dead and fossilized religious tradition which stands in the way of God's purpose.

## Purpose

When the religious enterprise functions in a conservative manner, it does so in the name of fidelity to God. When the same enterprise functions prophetically, it innovates in the name of that same God. Accordingly, the purpose of the first Case Study is to probe how Acts 10 might be used as a working model to explore when, how and why church traditions sometimes need to be changed.

> *. . . from time to time, the conservative principle has to bend . . .*

Before getting started, you are invited to record your initial perceptions to three questions. By recording your spontaneous judgments now, you will be providing yourself with a declaration of your preliminary understanding of the issues. After completing the Case Study, you will then be able to reread your initial reflections and gauge to what degree you have been broadened or transformed by your inquiries. The three questions designed for this purpose are as follows:

1. Do you consider your church to have faithfully preserved all the essential elements which Jesus himself believed and practiced? \_\_\_\_ If not, state a few significant differences.

2. Regarding Jesus himself, would you characterize him as a conservative Jew who fiercely retained the essentials of Judaism throughout his whole life? _____ If not, name a few instances in which he substantially differed with the prevailing practices and beliefs of his day:




3. Regarding the Twelve, does it appear that Jesus trained them to stubbornly preserve what he taught them so that it would be passed on, neither adding or taking anything away, until the end of time? _____ Or, on the other hand, did Jesus deliberately train the Twelve to participate in his own ability to innovate so that, in different circumstances, they would know how to adapt (and, if necessary, even to reverse) the teachings that he had given them? _____ What support would you offer for your replies? _____



Let's begin. If you are so inclined, this would be the time to take your New Testament in hand, to close your eyes, and to prayerfully unite yourself with the Spirit which originally inspired Luke. For our purposes here, any translation of the New Testament will suffice, except *The Good News* or *Living Bible* (which frequently paraphrases or skips over difficult elements in the Greek text).

Translation = _____

Starting time = _____ (120 to 150 minutes needed)

## Preparing Yourself to Read Luke

Luke is unique among the Evangelists in so far as he prepared both a Gospel and its sequel, the Acts of the Apostles. Luke, within popular theology, is sometimes called the first church historian because he wrote "the first" account of the early church. It would be a full three hundred years before Eusebius (d. 342) would come along and write "the second" church history. Hence the Acts of the Apos-

*Luke is sometimes called the first church historian.*

tles has a unique place of importance among the early Christian writings.

The focus of Acts is on two apostles: Peter and Paul. At the beginning of Acts, we read that Peter thought of the Jesus Movement as entirely preoccupied with Jews, Jewish interests, and Jewish hope for the restoration of the "kingdom of Israel" (Acts 1:6). At the end of Acts, some thirty years later, the focus has shifted to Paul who has been taken as a prisoner to Rome where he boldly confirms his preoccupation with a universal Gentile mission: "[S]alvation of God has been sent to the Gentiles" (28:28).

"Gentiles" is the term used by Jews to designate non-Jews. By virtue of the covenants that God made with their ancestors hundreds of years earlier, the Jews of Jesus' day felt that their traditions set them apart from the rest of the world, that is, from the Gentiles. The Jews understood themselves as God's chosen people. As such, God took a direct interest in the offspring of Abraham and Sarah. More especially, he liberated the children of Israel from slavery, led them into the desert, fed them with mannah, and (wonder of wonder, miracle of miracles) gave them his Torah.

*Within the Jewish tradition, "torah" refers to the practical wisdom and know-how which loving parents pass on to their children.*

Within the Jewish tradition, "*torah*" refers to the practical wisdom and know-how which loving parents pass on to their children. Being created by God was a condition that all people enjoyed. Being "fathered" by God, being trained in his Torah, however, was quite another thing. And it is this latter experience that allowed Israel to realize that collectively they were God's "beloved children" whom he had called out of Egypt and trained in the desert. Thus the inspired author explains:

> Remember how Yahweh your God led you for forty years in the wilderness. . . . He humbled you, he made you feel hunger, he fed you with mannah . . . to make you understand that man [woman] does not live on bread alone but man [woman] lives on everything that comes from the mouth of Yahweh. . . . Learn from this that Yahweh your God was training you as a man [woman] trains his [her] child, . . . and so follow his ways [i.e., Torah] and reverence him (Deuteronomy 8:2-6 JB).

*This sense of being fathered by God has been distorted in English translations of the Bible.*

This sense of being fathered by God has been distorted in English translations of the Bible because the Hebrew word *torah* and the Greek word *nomos* have almost always been rendered into English as "Law" (always in the singular). The term "law" in English is bound up with our tradition of legalism and is entirely opaque to the process of parenting which dominates in the use of *torah*. When you come across the word "Law" in your Bible, therefore, you need to mentally substitute "*torah*" in order to capture what the inspired authors intended to convey.

## Jesus' Commitment to the Exclusion Principle

Having understood how "*torah*" sets Jews apart from "Gentiles," it should come as no surprise that the Gospel accounts present Jesus *as a Jew* routinely involved with Jewish interests. Thus Jesus is never presented as seeking to actively engage the Gentiles or to call them to discipleship. In his 1956 pilot study, *Jesus' Promise to the Nations*, Joachim Jeremias created quite a stir when he tried to persuade scholars that the historical Jesus had no interest in the Gentiles. Based on a careful study of key texts (esp. Matthew 10:5, 10:23, 19:28), Jeremias argued that, even for many years after Jesus' death, Jesus continued to be understood by the believing community (a) as limiting his own mission exclusively to Jews and (b) as positively prohibiting his disciples to make any overtures to non-Jews. For our purposes here, this will be referred to as the Exclusion Principle.

> *Jesus is never presented as seeking to actively engage the Gentiles or to call them to discipleship.*

Needless to say, at some point Jesus' Exclusion Principle was abandoned and the training in *torah* which Jesus had given his Jewish disciples was extended to Gentiles as well. According to Matthew's Gospel, one might get the impression that this shift was easy: all Jesus had to do was to appear to his disciples after his resurrection and say, "Make disciples of all nations [i.e., of the Gentiles]" (28:19). But was it really as easy as that? Could the Eleven, at a moment's notice, be expected to overturn their life-long training in the Exclusion Principle? It was one thing to heal a few Gentiles; it was quite another thing to offer them the *torah* which sets Jews apart from non-Jews. And, from the vantage point of the Gentiles, how could they be expected to be interested in a Jewish movement? And, even supposing they were interested, how could they ever come to think of themselves as "chosen" in the way Jews are chosen? Matthew closes his Gospel with a shocking overturning of the Exclusion Principle and leaves it up to his readers to imagine how and when this could practically come about.

> *At some point Jesus' Exclusion Principle was abandoned.*

On precisely this point, Luke's writing of Acts becomes significant. Luke appears to have offered his readers the sequel that Matthew was unwilling or unable to write. It is even unfair to say "sequel" because, according to Luke's version of things, the apostles are deliberately told "not to depart from Jerusalem" (Acts 1:4; Luke 24:49). This means that the apostles do not go "to Galilee, to the mountain to which Jesus had directed them" (Matt 28:16). Furthermore, when Luke does present Jesus as showing himself to his disciples after his resurrection, he has nothing to say about Gentiles. Even the mission statement, "You shall be my witnesses in Jerusalem and in all Judaea and Samaria [the region between Judaea and Galilee] and to the end of the earth" (1:8), can be understood as merely extending the Jewish outreach which had characterized Jesus' own mission in Galilee. The presumption of Luke's readers would be that the disciples' mission must now begin in Jerusalem (the Jewish "center of the earth") and then fan out to embrace the Jewish populations in Judaea and Samaria and, finally, in ever widening circles, spread out to embrace Jews living abroad all the way to the borders of the earth (i.e., the "civilized" earth defined by the boundaries of the Roman Empire).

> *The disciples' mission must begin in Jerusalem and then fan out to embrace the Jewish populations in Judaea and Samaria and, finally, embrace Jews living abroad.*

One has to pass through nine chapters (covering seven years of history) before Acts refers to the prospect of a Gentile outreach (Acts 9:15). Within these nine chapters, however, Luke has been patiently narrating how the circle of Galilean Jews is broken when hitherto unknown classes of persons are admitted into discipleship. Acts 2 details how the Jewish feast of Pentecost served to miraculously break the circle of Galilean Jews to admit some of the foreign-born "Jews and converts [to Judaism]" (2:11) pouring into Jerusalem from all over the Empire. Acts 6-8 details how seven Hellenized Jews are chosen as ministers for the Greek-speaking followers of Jesus and how one of them, Philip, ends up taking advantage of his forced exile by extending his message to Samaritans (Acts 8:4ff). Thus the circle was again broken, this time to admit Samaritans (the Jews who intermarried with Gentiles during the first exile, 587-537 BCE, and who were for that reason, after the exile, excluded from rebuilding the Jerusalem temple). Acts 9 details the miraculous turn-about whereby Saul, a fanatic enemy of Jesus, ends up as a zealous champion of Jesus. Once Paul received his new sight (and insight) from Ananias, he did not (as some have wrongly supposed) immediately go off preaching to Gentiles; rather, he went into the Damascus synagogue to reach out *to Jews* (9:21). Luke makes it quite clear that, even with his first missionary journey undertaken some seven years later, Paul was still bent upon exclusively addressing Jews gathered in their synagogues on the Sabbath (13:5, 14, 42).

> *From the very beginning of Acts, Luke patiently narrates how the circle of Galilean Jews is broken as hitherto unknown classes of persons are admitted into discipleship.*

The nine chapters filled with tales of the ever-widening circle, however, is leading up to a climax. Acts 9 narrates the turn-about of Paul thereby getting his readers ready to look for another turn-about. And so Luke has carefully set the stage for Acts 10 which "marks the center of the book, both in the aim of the author and in amount of material" (Kee:197). It is to these clues tucked in the center of Luke's historical narrative that our attention must now turn.

1. Read Acts 10:1-35. Traditionally this account has been interpreted as detailing the conversion of the first Gentiles. But is this where Luke's attention lies? In order to discover this for yourself, imagine that Luke is a movie director whose script is

calculated to guide the focal attention of his audience. Upon what central character does Luke dwell? _____ Why so?




2. To find out, let us begin following the drama surrounding Peter in slow motion. The camera comes in upon Peter as he is mounting the flat roof of the house in which he is lodging (10:9). What is he doing there? _____ At what hour? ____ What distracts Peter while he is praying? _____ Then, "he fell into a trance/daydream" (10:10b). What is the significance of Peter's vision/daydream (10:11-14)?




3. Peter's vision/daydream arouses his resistance even though he hears the clear command of _____ telling him to "kill and eat." Luke has this scene of resistance repeated a second and a third time. What impact does this repetition have upon the audience? What is Luke communicating about Peter?




4. Now step back from this drama and ask yourself what is behind Peter's fierce opposition to the command he received. [Need a hint? See Deuteronomy 14:3-20.]




5. From what has been said, it is clear that Peter resists the angel's command because he wants to keep kosher, i.e., to eat exclusively "clean" animals (which excludes, e.g., rabbit, pig, oysters). What does this imply regarding the training that Peter received from Jesus regarding what is to be eaten and not eaten?

6. The next scene. In 10:17 Luke presents Peter as "inwardly perplexed" while the messengers from Cornelius are arriving. Note how Luke draws out the actions taking place outside in order to again return to Peter "pondering the vision" (10:19). What impact does this have upon the audience?

All of a sudden, "the Spirit" (10:19) tells Peter to accept the invitation from Cornelius, and Peter responds without a moment's hesitation. What's going on here? How can Peter accept this invitation so readily when he, just a moment ago, so strongly opposed quite another invitation?

Note carefully the favorable impression that Luke wishes to present regarding Cornelius. Reread 10:22 and 10:2. Does this make you suspicious that Luke wants to overwhelm his audience with the fragrance of words in praise of Cornelius because there is also something odious he wishes to conceal? What is there about Cornelius that would be odious to Jews, Peter included? How could this present Peter with a compelling reason for refusing his invitation?

---

### Note on Luke's Great Omission

Luke edited and expanded Mark's Gospel account in order to create his own Gospel. In so doing, however, Luke entirely omitted certain portions of Mark's Gospel which he found objectionable.

Read, for instance, Mark 7:14-23. Here Mark presents Jesus as declaring all meats to be clean. Luke entirely suppressed this teaching as well as a string of narratives which precede and follow it. Everything from Mark 6:45 (the second crossing to the other side of the lake) to Mark 8:21 (the return from the second crossing) is silently passed over in Luke's Gospel. Scholars have called this the "great omission."

Why did Luke so massively suppress the teaching of Mark 7:14-23 in his Gospel? Most probably, Luke regarded Jesus as an entirely observant Jew when it came to foods. Furthermore, when closely examined, Mark 6:45-8:21 presents Jesus as initiating a Gentile outreach culminating in the feeding of four thousand Gentiles with the loaves of his disciples. Luke may have omitted all of this because, in Acts, he wished to detail how the disciples themselves only came to envision a Gentile outreach many years after the death of Jesus.

7. Now, by way of glimpsing how Luke has deeper designs here, go back and read Luke 7:1-10. This narrative is found only in Luke's Gospel and, surprisingly enough, it presents Jesus in a situation which remarkably parallels that of Peter in Acts 10. What are these parallels?

*Luke 7:1-10 presents Jesus in a situation which remarkably parallels that of Peter in Acts 10.*

Is the centurion in Luke 7 interested in hearing Jesus' teaching? ____ Does he hope to become a disciple? ____ Why would Jesus never have accepted a Roman soldier, much less a centurion, as a disciple?

When Jesus, the Jewish elders, and the Twelve finally approach the centurion's house, the centurion "sent friends" out with a personal message intended to dissuade Jesus from coming any closer. The message declares: "I am not worthy that you should enter under my roof" (Luke 7:7). Puzzling, isn't it? The first delegation of Jewish elders sent by Cornelius pleaded, "Come and heal" (7:3), while the second delegation of the centurion's personal friends reverses this by saying, in effect, "Don't come any closer." How do you account for this last-minute reversal?

The end of this account (Luke 7:10) makes it clear that Jesus halted where he was (perhaps an arrow-shot from the house) and did not enter the centurion's home. Why not? While Luke does not tell us directly, some scholars, aware of the gracious hospitality which prevailed at the time of Jesus, suggest that the "I am not worthy" message may have been a ploy used by the centurion to save face and/or to protect the reputation of Jesus. On the basis of what you know, how might this be the case?

*The "I am not worthy" message may have been a ploy used by the centurion to save face.*

8. Returning to Acts 10:23, note how Peter offers gracious hospitality to "the two servants and a devout soldier"—Gentiles. The next day Peter takes "some of the brethren" (10:23; "six" according to 11:12) and the ten walk together on the beach-path toward Caesarea, 35 miles away. On "the following day," they arrive. Cornelius is expecting them "together with his kinsmen and his close friends" (10:24).

Will Cornelius send out an "I am not worthy" message? Not quite. In this case "Peter entered [the courtyard]" and "Cornelius met him and fell down at his feet and worshipped him [kissed his feet?]" (10:25). Peter politely objects confessing that he is only a human being (and not some divine messenger). Then, Peter, going further than Jesus had dared to go, "entered [under his roof]" (10:27).

*Peter has moved far beyond his earlier concern over* kosher *food; he now speaks of* kosher persons.

Immediately Peter launches into a carefully reasoned explanation for his unorthodox conduct (10:28f). Note that Peter has moved far beyond his earlier concern over *kosher food*; he now speaks of *kosher persons*. Peter has taken a giant step forward! Peter explains that this is not due to any whim; rather, he is acting out of firm conviction. Who is the source of this conviction? Peter names _____. Isn't this strange? Why can't Peter say, "*Jesus* is the one who changed me around. *Jesus* has shown me that I should not call any man [woman] common or unclean"?

9. Peter has taken two leaps forward: all foods are clean (acceptable to him and to God) and all Gentiles are likewise clean (acceptable to him and to God). And now the clincher. Cornelius explains that his prayers have been answered, Peter has come, and now "we are all here present in the sight of God to hear all that you have been commanded by the Lord" (10:33). In brief, the assembled Gentiles are politely asking Peter to begin training them in *torah*! Jewish *torah*? _____ Check for yourself: How does Peter identify himself when he arrives at the home of Cornelius (10:28)?

Read Acts 10:34-43 out loud. Peter's message doesn't simply repeat what he has already been presenting to Jewish audiences.

Peter shows himself to be an innovative pastor who directly appeals to the sensibilities and interests of Gentiles. But what about the six Jewish companions that have come along with Peter? How can they be expected to respond to Peter when he says, "Truly I perceive that God shows no partiality"?

Peter's account is brutally honest. He admits it was "to Israel" (10:36) that God sent the Good News presented by Jesus. He acknowledges that it was "in the country of the Jews" (10:39) that Jesus ministered. He concedes it was "to the people [of God]" (10:42) that the disciples were commanded to preach after his resurrection. At the very end of this recital of the Exclusion Principle, however, Peter sends the ball sailing into the Gentile court by noting (a) that Jesus "is the one ordained by God to [be the final] judge" (10:42) of Gentiles and Jews alike and (b) that "everyone [Gentiles included?] who believes in him [i.e., follows his way of life] receives forgiveness of sins."

*Peter admits it was "to Israel" that God sent the Good News.*

While Peter is speaking, "the Holy Spirit fell upon all who heard the word" (10:44). The sign of this Spirit was their "speaking in tongues and extolling God" (10:46). Any reader who has followed Luke's saga from the beginning would remember that such a phenomenon happened once before, namely at Pentecost, when the apostles received the Holy Spirit. At Pentecost, the bystanders said almost exactly what is being said about the Gentiles here: "[W]e hear them telling in our own tongues the mighty works of God" (2:11). The parallel with Pentecost is unmistakable. The stage is thus carefully and deliberately set by Luke for the shocking conclusion which follows.

*Thus Luke carefully and deliberately sets the stage for the shocking conclusion which is to follow.*

10. Peter's six Jewish companions have been following him through something akin to an emotional roller coaster. First, Peter proposes that God regards no Gentile as "unclean" even though Jewish tradition says the exact opposite. Second, Peter proposes that God has no favorites even though Jewish tradition stands on the premise that the Jews alone are "God's people." Finally, Peter proposes that these Gentiles be baptized as followers of Jesus even though Gentiles have been systematically excluded from the circle of discipleship (10:47).

*Peter proposes that God regards no Gentile as "unclean" . . . that God has no favorites . . . that these Gentiles be baptized as followers of Jesus.*

Note how Luke has cleverly allowed the audience to lose touch with Peter's Jewish companions. But now they are urgently needed. Why? Couldn't Peter go ahead and baptize them himself? ____ But, if so, why does Peter turn to them (and, by innuendo, to the audience) and offer them a chance to veto his proposal by saying, "Can any one forbid water for baptizing these people?" (10:47)?

Remember that up to this point the Exclusion Principle has been strictly observed. What is the force of Peter's argument in favor of baptizing these Gentiles?

Are the six persuaded by this argument? ____ What indirect evidence does Luke offer to this effect?

*Peter finds a rude homecoming.*

11. When Peter returns to Jerusalem, he finds a rude homecoming. He may have persuaded the six who were with him at the home of Cornelius, but back in Jerusalem he is accusingly called to account for his actions. Read Acts 11:1-18. You may have noted that rumor of Peter's scandalous activity has preceded his arrival at Jerusalem. Why is it that Peter doesn't receive a hero's welcome? Why aren't the brethren saying, "Peter, you did it! You finally got the Gentile mission started! Jesus would be proud of you! Hurrah!"?

Why is it that Peter's stature/office in the Jerusalem church does not place him above the criticism of his community?

What argument does Peter use in the hope of persuading his critics that, had they been there, they too would have approved of his conduct?

12. Now step back into the twentieth century. Most people think of Paul as the great innovator, the one who initiated the mission to the Gentiles. The account of Luke, however, details Paul's turn-around regarding the importance of Jesus for Jews in Acts 9. But Paul never approached a single Gentile until Acts 13:46. After Paul's turn-around, Luke narrates Peter's turn-around in Acts 10. It is Peter who breaks the circle to admit Gentiles. Think about this for a moment. Why does Luke consider it so vital for his audience to realize that *Peter did it first?*

*Most people think of Paul as the one who initiated the mission to the Gentiles, . . . but it is Peter who breaks the circle to admit Gentiles.*

---

### Note on Matthew's Great Commission

Recall how Matthew ends his Gospel with the resurrected Jesus appearing to his disciples "on the mountain" in Galilee and commissioning them, "Make disciples of all nations" (28:19). This contrasts with Luke's account, where the circle is progressively broken until, ten years after the resurrection, Peter finally gets turned around by God and makes disciples of Cornelius and his household. So which account is to be credited? _____

If one credits both accounts, this would seemingly pose some problems. If Jesus had told Peter to "make disciples of all nations," then it would appear that he ignored it or forgot it and, according to Luke, had to rediscover it without any help from Jesus some ten years after the Ascension. On the other hand, if one credits Luke, then it must be supposed that Jesus never departed from the Exclusion Principle and never said anything about a Gentile outreach even during his post-resurrection appearances.

If Luke is to be preferred, where does this leave Matthew's account? Did Matthew, writing in the 80s, feel that his Gospel would be woefully incomplete if it did not endorse the Gentile mission? Did Matthew, accordingly, place on the lips of Jesus words which the disciples of Jesus came to endorse due to experiences some ten years after the Ascension? _____

No one knows for sure; yet, one must remember that the Gospels are first and foremost narratives directed to guide the faith and practice of Jesus' disciples. No Evangelist had an interest in history for history's sake. Hence, it would have made good pastoral sense for Matthew to present the Gentile mission as the culmination of his Gospel. Luke, for his part, impatient with quick solutions, set his hand to narrate how the circle of Galilean disciples was broken again, and again, and again until they were able to say, "Truly I perceive that God shows no partiality" (Acts 10:34).

Does this solution satisfy you? _____ If not, what alternative solution might you suggest?

13. What startling discoveries did you make while exploring Acts 10? Describe them for yourself here:

14. Did the Case Study raise any fundamental questions for you while you were completing it? If so, note them here so that you can return to them at a later moment.

Completion time = _____

Total time used on this Case = \_\_\_\_\_ minutes

Well done! You have just completed your first Case Study. Needless to say, you may judge that there are still some loose ends. Then again, only in the idealized cases does one find Sherlock Holmes neatly and methodically wrapping up all the clues. In real cases, life is sometimes far too complex to bring everything into a neat final package. Augustine (d. 430) once reflected upon his own experience in this matter as follows:

> Even if I would attempt to study them [the Scriptures] and nothing else from early boyhood to decrepit old age, with the utmost leisure, the most unwearying zeal, and greater talents than I [now] have, I should still daily find something new in them (*Letter* 137.1.3).

Hence, at this point, set your Case aside and go on to your other activities in life. Let what you have learned simmer. Then, when ready, return to take a look at the analysis which follows.

## Analysis

**1** Luke is more than a historian; he is a divinely inspired artist with a mission to persuade his audience. At every point he choreographs his words in order to deliberately guide the attention of his audience. Once he has their attention, he expects to vividly evoke the dramatic events which brought about Peter's turn-around. To be really effective, Luke's audience has to become emotionally and intellectually involved with the images in words which are being projected upon their imaginations. They have to sympathetically enter into what Peter is experiencing, to relive (at least for the moment) his resistance, his confusion, and his zeal for God. In the end, Luke wants his audience to feel emotionally exhausted because they too have passed through the grueling conversion process whereby they too can stand with Peter and say, "Truly I perceive that God shows no partiality" (Acts 10:34).

**2** The first dramatic scene features Cornelius being told by an angel (the standard "messenger of God" in Jewish literature) that "his prayers and his alms have ascended as a memorial before God" (10:4). Just before introducing Peter as a man of prayer, Luke signals to his audience that the outsider, the Gentile, the one whom many would suppose God entirely ignores, is indeed the very one whose prayer was entirely acceptable to God.

Scene Two zooms in upon a pious Jew offering his noonday prayer. But, to our disappointment, we don't hear or feel his prayer. We don't even discover that God is receiving his prayer. We get only the distraction. Here Luke is at his best. Peter may have gone up to the roof so as to catch a gentle breeze and to be alone and undistracted in his prayer, but the sweet odors of lunch being prepared over a courtyard fire rise up and distract him: "he became hungry and desired something to eat" (10:10). Luke is not intentionally shaming Peter here. Nor is Luke reflecting on the quality of Peter's prayer. Rather Luke is getting his audience ready to be surprised how, in this case at least, a momentous conversion of life can have such innocent beginnings as the sounds of cooking pots and the odors of lunch preparations. In God's world, the ordinary gives rise to the extraordinary.

*Luke prepares his audience to be surprised how a moment of conversion can have such innocent beginnings as the sounds of cooking pots and the odors of lunch preparations.*

**3** Peter's daydream invites him to a universal variety in dining. The Greek narrative clearly intends to stress this universality: "all the quadrupeds and reptiles of the earth and birds of the air" (10:12). Peter's natural revulsion to this suggestion cannot be adequately gauged if we think of Peter as manifesting a "primitive mentality" and that, scientifically speaking, we would explain the "unclean" nature of pork by noting that it was a common cause of trichinosis. Such an estimate of things is inadequate. To begin with, this hypothesis does not explain why rabbit meat should be regarded as "unclean." But even more than this, such an estimate presumes that we, as moderns, no longer divide all of God's living creatures between "clean" and "unclean." Just the contrary is the case.

*We, as moderns, might imagine that we no longer regard living creatures as "unclean."*

Imagine, for a moment, that you are picnicking at a local park. During the course of your meal, the conversation is animated, and you don't notice that a hungry ant has mounted your fork and is following its contours toward the tasty bits of potato salad clinging to its prongs. When you discover this forager, what would you do? Most people in Western society would simply pick up the fork, brush or blow the little creature off, and go on eating. But what if, during the same meal, one found that the forager was a centipede or, worse, a cockroach? Hardly anyone brought up in Western society would or could continue eating. Most would, minimally, wash the fork thoroughly in water before using it again. And, if there was even the slightest suspicion that the cockroach had touched any of the food itself, it would be entirely discarded as unfit for human consumption.

*Our gut response, registers that cock-roaches are "unclean" while ants are "clean."*

Our gut response, in this instance, has registered that cockroaches are "unclean" while ants are "clean." This viewpoint has nothing to do with science and everything to do with the way we are brought up by our parents. Why, for instance, were our parents content when, as children, we avidly watched a troop of ants breaking up and carting away small bits of a discarded gumdrop on the sidewalk while they became visibly upset when they caught us watching cockroaches with that same interest? By the time we were ten, our habitual instincts mirrored those of our parents. Accordingly, I remember fondly going to the corner candy store to buy two-inch wide strips of paper covered with little drops of candy stuck to it in neat rows. I also remember that, for a period of a year, chocolate-covered ants were sold in little red boxes. The adventuresome ate them. No one, however, could even imagine eating chocolate-covered cockroaches, no matter how "germ-free" and "sterilized" the manufacturers claimed them to be.

*The whole world retains deeply entrenched traditions of "clean" and "unclean," but every culture draws the line between them in a unique fashion.*

In other cultures, in other places, however, cockroaches are fired in butter and served as a crisp delicacy with the family meal. Singers in Japan traditionally eat earthworms to improve the mellowness of their voices. Throughout France, there are butcher shops specializing in horse meat, and snails are a favorite appetizer served in French restaurants. Meanwhile, the French have traditionally avoided eating corn (either on the cob or off) because they regard it exclusively as "animal feed." The whole world, consequently, retains deeply entrenched traditions of "clean" and "unclean," but every culture draws the line between them in a unique fashion.

**4** Returning to Acts 10, one can now better gauge the force of Peter's instinctual repulsion, "No, Lord, for I have never eaten anything which is common or unclean" (10:14). Within Judaism, moreover, the distinction between "clean" and "unclean" was perceived not only as part of the *torah* which parents pass on to their children, it was also perceived as part of the *torah*, the wisdom for living, given to the whole people of Israel by their Father in heaven (Deuteronomy 14:3-20). As far as Peter is concerned, therefore, his vision/daydream is no messenger from God but rather a "fallen angel" attempting to seduce the innocent away from the ways of God. Even if the message here might be coming with God's consent, Peter's "no" would mean that he intends to be faithful as Job was faithful when he was tempted by God (Job 1:6-12).

Luke's vivid portrayal of Peter's resistance, not once but three times, is perhaps deliberately contrived so as to allow those in his audience who feel the same revulsion as Peter to firmly identify with him as he stands up for God and for *torah*. They too would be "inwardly perplexed" as to why a pious man like Peter was given such a message when his heart and mind were turned toward his God.

*Luke's vivid portrayal of Peter's resistance allows those in the audience who feel the same revulsion as Peter to firmly identify with him as he stands up for God and for torah.*

**5** If Peter resists by claiming that he has always kept *kosher*, then this resistance points in the direction of presuming that Jesus did the same thing. Peter was intelligent. On such a sensitive issue, he would surely have taken notice if his Master had ever eaten with Gentiles; Peter would surely have remembered if Jesus had said that, under this or that circumstance, one need not keep *kosher*. Peter's resistance here is simply an echo of Jesus' resistance. To follow Jesus is to keep *kosher*. End of discussion.

Within Mark's Gospel narrative, Jesus has two feedings of the multitudes. The five thousand fed with five loaves during the first feeding were Jews on the Galilean side of the lake (Mark 8:1-10). The four thousand fed with seven loaves during the second feeding were Gentiles on the other side of the lake (Mark 8:1-10). Luke, due to his intention to spell out how the Gentile mission began in his book of Acts, had no need to retroject a ministry to Gentiles back into the life of Jesus. As a result, he entirely deleted all the material in Mark pertaining to the second crossing over "to the other side" (Mark 6:45). Luke's "great omission," consequently, gives his readers the impression that Jesus, during his lifetime, never healed the sick in Gentile "villages, cities or country" (Mark 6:56), nor declared "all foods clean" (Mark 7:19b), nor fed the four thousand Gentiles (="the dogs") with "the children's bread" (=*torah* of the Jews; Mark 7:27). Mark included these things in his Gospel narrative because, by the year 65-75 CE when he was writing, the mission to the Gentiles was an established part of the Good News. And, since his Gospel was a manual of formation, it would have been sheer negligence not to have prefigured the Gentile mission under the rubric of Jesus' excursion with his disciples "to the other side." The upshot of the "great

*The upshot of Luke's "great omission" is that Luke gives Peter no grounds to appeal to Jesus when it comes to accepting the invitation to eat of all the animals presented in his daydream.*

omission" is that Luke gives Peter no grounds to appeal to Jesus when it comes to accepting the invitation to eat of all the animals presented in his daydream. Any appeal to Jesus would have to presumably fall on the side of strict Jewish orthodoxy when it came to clean and unclean foods.

*Jesus never displayed interest in lock-step conformity. He wanted his disciples to acquire his art for discerning, what God really wants.*

**6** Nevertheless, Jesus did not train Peter to be a rigid conservative. Jesus never insisted, "I'm allowed to innovate because I'm the Messiah. But after my death, all innovation stops." Neither did Jesus insist that his disciples memorize his words or write them down in order to forestall any later confusion or deviation among his followers. Quite the contrary, Jesus never displayed interest in lock-step conformity. He wanted his disciples to acquire his art for discerning, within the complexity of everyday living, what God really wants. He wanted them to cultivate his ability for sorting out true fidelity to God from among the seductive counterfeits which can disguise themselves in the robes of orthodox religion. As a result, the Gospel accounts do not hesitate to present Jesus as sometimes acting contrary to what the traditions of his day expected of pious Jews (e.g., Mark 2:1-3:6 and par.). These exceptions were not only limited to Jesus alone, for the Gospel accounts present Jesus as defending his disciples in instances when they took the initiative in making expectations for themselves (e.g., Mark 2:23-28 and par.).

Consequently, it is quite understandable that Peter should resist suggestion within his prayer-distraction. He was being faithful both to Jesus and the *torah*. On the other hand, Jesus had trained him in the art of knowing when and how to make exceptions, therefore it is quite understandable that he should be "inwardly perplexed" (10:17). In the end, Peter is left struggling to determine whether even the *kosher* rules of Jesus had to be set aside when it came to serving God first. Then, Peter hears a knock at the gate, and life intrudes upon his confused state of mind.

*Luke is artfully and pastorally silent about certain details that could distract his readers from his focal interest.*

**7** Luke has already acknowledged that God hears and sometimes grants the petitions of pagans. How about Peter? Will he hear and grant the petition of the three Gentiles at his gate? Perhaps. To make it credible that Peter might say "yes," Luke presents Peter as receiving a flattering description of Cornelius: "an upright and God-fearing man, who is well spoken of by the whole Jewish nation" (10:22). What Luke glosses over here and in the earlier case of Luke 7 as well is the fact that Cornelius is a military officer of the Roman occupying force. Those who cooperated with the Germans occupying Norway during World War II came to be known as "quislings," traitors who came to a bad end as soon as the Germans retreated. Luke, well aware that many Romans would be reading his account, does not want to needlessly antagonize them. On the other hand, well aware that Jews would also be reading his account, Luke does not want to further inflame the Jews who have been experiencing the humiliation and brutalization of Roman occupation. Hence, Luke is artfully and pastorally silent about certain details that could distract his readers from his focal interest.

Luke knows of an instance in which Jesus heard the prayer of a centurion. Matthew (8:5-13) and John (4:46-53) record similar stories. Close inspection, however, shows that this incident in Acts has been deliberately crafted to parallel his account of the centurion in his Gospel (Luke 7:1-10). The petition of the centurion "to come and heal" in the Gospel (Luke 7:3) prepares the reader to encounter another centurion asking Peter "to come to his house" (10:22) in Acts. Moreover, in Luke and in Luke alone, the centurion makes use of the "I am not worthy" message. If, from the very start, this centurion truly believed he was not worthy, then it is difficult to understand why he would have gone through the motions of having invited Jesus to "come and heal" (Luke 7:3) in the first place. Moreover, the elders, acting on behalf of the centurion, clearly indicate to Jesus that "he is worthy" (Luke 7:4).

Yet this centurion clearly risked much for his dying slave. It must have been difficult for a Roman officer to admit that Greek physicians were inadequate to the case and that a Jewish teacher-healer might be more successful. Furthermore, when Jesus did surprise him by actually coming to the man's home, it is quite possible that only then did the centurion recognize that neither his house nor his food would be appropriate for a Jewish guest. On the other side, Jesus does not come alone, and it is possible that Jesus would be compromised in the eyes of those Jews who have come with him if he did enter "under his roof" and, in due course, partake of the nourishment provided by a Gentile. To save face and to safeguard the reputation of his approaching benefactor, therefore, the centurion asks his "friends" to take his "I am not worthy" message to Jesus. Furthermore, in order to achieve the successful healing of his slave, the centurion offers Jesus an alternative based upon his own experience as an officer: "But say the word . . ." (Luke 7:8). Jesus accepts this proposal and ends up lavishly praising the officer's "faith/trust" to the multitude of Jews who followed him.

**8** In the parallel story of Acts 10, Gentile messengers come to Peter and he offers them hospitality. There is no problem here because Gentiles have no food restrictions that could be offended by a *kosher* meal. The same holds today. Gentiles can easily accept an invitation

*It is quite possible that only then did the centurion recognize that neither his house nor his food would be appropriate for a Jewish guest.*

*Peter explains to his host, ". . . but God has shown me. . . ." A disciple of Jesus must be faithful to God and not just an imitator of Jesus.*

to dine at an orthodox Jewish home; however, orthodox Jews would not be able to accept to eat a meal prepared by even their dearest Gentile friends.

Within this understanding, Peter must quickly explain to his Gentile hosts in Caesarea, "You yourselves know how unlawful it is for a Jew . . . but God has shown me . . ." (10:28). Not Jesus. God. When did God show him? Luke doesn't say when God revealed this to Peter because Luke knows that it is important for his audience to enter into sympathy with Peter and to rediscover and reaffirm their own "reasons of the heart" which might enable them to travel with Peter. Today, we mistakenly think that everything important in religion can be told and explained. The truth is that frequently the most important things cannot be explained!

**9** The opening line of Peter's declaration is a veritable explosion: "Truly I perceive that God shows no partiality" (10:34). At this moment, Jewish election, Jewish covenants, Jewish *torah* fade into the background. Peter is affirming that God's original intention was to reach out and embrace "any one who fears him and does what is right" (10:35). Does this deny God's preferential love for Jews? Is this heresy? Can Peter continue to be a Jew after saying this? These are not easy questions to answer.

**10** When Luke portrays Cornelius and his household demonstrating the same enthusiasm for God and his message that the Jewish crowd manifested at Pentecost, Luke wants his audience to perceive this as a demonstration of the truth of Peter's declaration about the Spirit of God not having favorites. The six companions of Peter, however, may not be ready to accept the implications of Peter's declaration, namely, that the Gentiles be baptized and, as a consequence, have *equal status* within the community of those who learn and practice the ways of Jesus. Hence, Peter turns to them and seeks their approval. By doing so, Peter demonstrates that he is not a reckless innovator but a responsible pastor. To be sure, he can follow his own inspiration and go way out on the limb for God. Should he do so, however, he risks being isolated on the limb and cursing his companions because they fail to follow him. To offset this, Peter consults them. Luke, not wanting to slow his narrative down, gives us probably only the closing line of Peter's appeal (10:47). We don't hear the response of Peter's six companions. Peter must have judged it as sufficiently affirmative, however, for he does "command" that the members of Cornelius' household were "to be baptized" (10:48). And, while it is not said, one can expect that the six companions actively participated in administering the baptism to which they had

*Peter turns to six companions and seeks their approval. By doing so, Peter demonstrates that he is not a reckless innovator but a responsible pastor.*

earlier consented. Thus, when they would arrive at Jerusalem, they would be expected to defend "their actions" and not just the impetuous initiatives of Peter.

The translation of *protassō* as "command" (10:48) in the RSV can be misleading since it can be used to encourage viewing Peter as one who gives verbal orders once the consultation process comes to an end. The Greek language has a half-dozen words which are indiscriminately rendered as "command" in English. The word chosen here does not emphasize the authority of Peter's word. Rather, *protassō* suggests "making arrangements toward" a desired end (in this case, for an immersion baptism).

**11** Consider, for a moment, the rude homecoming. Prior to Peter's arrival, both "the apostles and brothers" have heard that "the Gentiles had also received the word of God" (11:1). The Jerusalem community, however, is intellectually and emotionally precisely where Peter was at the opening of Acts 10, and so they opposed Peter saying, "Why do you go to uncircumcised men and eat with them?" (11:3).

Why doesn't Peter pull rank saying, "Listen, I'm in charge here. I started this community, and I still give the orders around here. You listen to me."? To begin with, Peter is too much of a pastor in the mold of Jesus to resort to bullying the church. More to the point, however, any pastor who innovates as Peter did has to account for his conduct, even if he be "the rock" (Matthew 16:18). Remember that Peter, in the past, had trained them to keep *kosher* as part of the *torah* he received from Jesus. Now, if Peter stubbornly refuses to account for his "deviance," he will be ousted from the community for having transgressed the very tradition which *he* passed on to them. As an effective pastor, therefore, what must he do? He must listen to their complaint. He must grant its validity. And he must tell them his story with patient conviction and sufficient vividness such that, in the end, each of them might be able to say, "If I had been there, I would have done that too!"

Luke, the master storyteller, makes use of this occasion to retell his audience a slightly shorter version of what went before. In Acts 11:4-17, however, Peter is directly appealing to his audience and narrative his experience in the first person. In Acts 15, Peter will have the occasion to tell this story in capsule form once again. For the moment, however, Luke registers Peter's story and ends it with a rousing finish, "Who was I that I could withstand God?" (11:17). Note, again, Luke has tacitly appealed to the hidden foundations of their movement: they are to follow Jesus, but God first! And *if the tradition of Jesus stands in the way of God, then even this tradition must bend in order to be faithful to God our Father* whom Jesus directed his

*Peter, in the past, had trained them to keep kosher as part of the torah. . . . Now, if Peter stubbornly refuses to account for his "deviance," he will be ousted for having transgressed the very tradition which he passed on to them.*

*They are to follow Jesus, but God first!*

*"Who was I that I could withstand God?"*

disciples to heed above all else. Peter's question, "Who was I that I could withstand God?", expressed well why he did what he did.

Peter's turn-around does not mean that everyone else in the Jesus movement would do the same. Neither is Peter tempted to try to make his new perspective the new standard for the apostles and elders within the community. Rather, God works in God's own time. For the moment, the community's two responses noted by Luke suffice: (1) "they were silenced" and (2) "they glorified God" (11:18). Luke quietly passes over the fact that many were unconvinced and quietly continued to operate as though the Exclusion Principle of Jesus was still in force. When a community waits upon God and its leaders agree to use only gentle persuasion, that community has to face up to less than universal acceptance of things. But this open state of affairs cannot hold indefinitely. Acts 15:1 reports that trouble began again over this very same issue. In the end, the entire community in Jerusalem had to openly discuss and to unanimously decide on a common policy regarding the admission of the Gentiles into the community of Jesus' followers.

*Luke knew that the various local communities were in crisis. The Gentile mission had split the believers.*

**12** Stepping back, one can now appreciate something of the overall design of Acts. Luke knew that the various local communities were in crisis. The Gentile mission had split the believers. Following key apostles, most Jewish Christians at Jerusalem and elsewhere were appealing to the Exclusion Principle of Jesus as a means of opposing Paul. These Jewish Christians regarded Paul as a "Johnny-come-lately" who had no personal training under the direction of Jesus. They also resented Paul for claiming to know "entirely too much" about what God had in mind for the Gentiles. The Pauline Christians, meanwhile, were not only actively recruiting Gentiles; they seemed to be dismantling Judaism, reducing it to some essentials, and requiring that only these essentials be passed on as the *torah* for the Gentiles.

In the face of this crisis, Luke perceived that he had to strongly appeal to the sensibilities and memories of those on both sides of the rift. Thus, Peter, from the very beginning of Acts, is presented as the model pioneering pastor. Paul is hardly noticed, and, even when he does come into focus, he is first seen as a half-baked Jewish zealot openly hostile to the Jesus movement (8:1, 3). From Paul's late entry into the movement (Acts 9) to the end of the book, Luke carefully avoids dignifying Paul with the name "apostle" even though Paul claimed this dignity for himself within his letters. Luke gave enormous attention to the actions of Peter because he honestly believed that once those conservative Christians who claimed Peter on their side also reclaimed the energy of Peter's own conversion in Acts 10, they would be ready and able to reconsider their opposition to Paul and the Pauline Christians.  This is why the various breaks in the circle (first to admit foreign-born Jews, then to admit Samaritans) were presented by way of preparing the ground for Peter's turn-around and the admission of Gentiles which followed.

Peter never became a flaming advocate of a Gentile outreach; nor do we know that he ever again baptized another Gentile in his whole life.  But he takes the Jewish hard-liner Christians just far enough to get them interested in following the whole series of turn-arounds which will accompany Paul's journey of faith.  But this is a story reserved for another day.  Our story of Peter based upon Acts 10 has come to an end.

## Application to the Churches Today

If Acts 10 is part of our roots as Christians, what does this say to the churches today?  Generate a few spinoffs and write them down here:

## Further Readings for Case One

Haenchen, Ernest

> *The Acts of the Apostles: A Commentary.* Oxford: Basil Blackwell, 1971. Translated by R. McL. Wilson from 1965 German original.

Jeremias, Joachim

> *Jesus' Promise to the Nations.* Philadelphia: Fortress, 1956. Translated by S. H. Hooke from 1956 German original.

Kees, Howard Clark

> *Understanding the New Testament.* Englewood Cliffs, New Jersey: Prentice-Hall, 1965

Lee, Bernard J.

> *The Galilean Jewishness of Jesus: Retrieving the Jewish Origins of Christianity.* New York: Paulist, 1988.

Newman, John Henry

> *An Essay on the Development of Christian Doctrine.* Harmondsworth: Penguin Books, 1974. (first published in 1845)

van Buren, Paul M.

> *A Christian Theology of the People Israel: A Theology of the Jewish-Christian Reality.* San Francisco: Harper & Row, 1983. (especially Part 2, "Israel and Jesus," pp. 240-319.)

Wilken, Robert

> *The Myth of Christian Beginnings.* Notre Dame, Indiana: University Press, 1971.

# CASE TWO

# How Jesus Came to Be Chosen as High Priest

Protestant Christians who trace their roots to the Continental Reformation firmly reject the Catholic notion that "priesthood" is reserved for those select few Christians who have been be ordained by a bishop. According to these Protestant Christians, all who are baptized in Christ are baptized into his priesthood, and they all share in it the same way. Thus, there are no Christians who are "more priestly" than others, even if some happen to be ordained. Martin Luther expressed this perspective as follows:

> All of us who have been baptized are priests without distinction, but those whom we call "priests" are ministers, chosen from among us that they should do all things in our name, and their priesthood is nothing but a ministry. . . . The sacrament of ordination, therefore, can be nothing other than a certain rite of choosing a preacher in the Church (*Babylonian Captivity*).

*Protestants maintain that there are no Christians who are "more priestly" than others, even if some happen to be ordained.*

Luther had no vendetta against ordination or the clerical state. He himself was an ordained Catholic priest. For nearly a decade he functioned successfully as a pastor of a parish and as a professor of theology prior to his protest against indulgences in 1517. In fact, it was precisely because he was a conscientious pastor that he tried to alert his bishop and his colleagues to the spiritual dangers which followed upon the practice of granting indulgences to those who gave money to build a new St. Peter's Church in Rome. In 1520, when Luther wrote the words cited above, he did not have any reason to despise priests as such; neither did he intend to do away with local and regional church leadership.

Luther's problem went much deeper. The Roman Church of Luther's day was so constituted as to give the impression that the grace of Christ came to people almost exclusively through the sacraments. Thus it seemed that the ordained clergy, given their exclusive control over the sacraments, had the privilege of dispensing God's grace when and where they so willed. Father Luther, sought to defend the total gratuity of God's grace by arguing that grace was not under clerical control. Hence, Luther taught that the sacraments should not be thought of as instrumental causes dispensing God's grace (with the priest acting as mediator and agent of God in this process). Rather, for Luther, the efficacy depended upon the faith (meaning both "trust" and "submission" to God) of the minister and of the faithful alike. Only by submitting to God's expressed wish that these rites be performed and only by trusting that God was well disposed to come to our assistance through these rites could sacramental rites be understood as having any efficacy at all. According to Luther, therefore, anyone who had faith could, in an emergency situation, administer the sacraments of the church. Under normal circumstances, however, the public proclamation of the Word and the administration of the sacraments was to be reserved to ordained ministers.

> *According to Luther, anyone who had faith could, in an emergency situation, administer the sacraments of the church.*

Roman Catholic and Protestant believers alike affirm that, in case of some necessity, any baptized Christian could administer valid baptism. When it comes to the Eucharist, however, Catholics have insisted, both at the time of the Reformation and today, that only a validly ordained priest can administer this sacrament. No exceptions were allowed. When I was attending Holy Cross Grade School in Euclid, Ohio, my sixth-grade teacher explained this to me in a story which ran something like the following:

> *Catholics have insisted that only a validly ordained priest can administer the Eucharist.*

> When the priest says, "This is my body," over the host (i.e., the small wafer of unleavened bread) at Mass, it is changed. It continues to have the appearance of bread, but, in reality, it has become the sacred body of Christ. Only a priest has this power to consecrate. Anyone else could recite the words of institution a hundred times over a host and nothing would happen. The priest has only to say it once. In fact, if a priest would go into a bakery and quietly say the words of institution over all the loaves on the shelf and really mean it, all at once, every one of those loaves would become the body of Christ. No priest, of course, would do such a thing. But the truth remains that he could, by virtue of his priesthood, effect such a change if he really wanted to.

There is some degree of exaggeration in this hypothetical case of the priest in the bakery; however, within it original setting, this kind of narrative served to emphasize the importance which Catholics placed upon the ordained priest at every Mass. It also served to form the foundation whereby a Catholic lad growing up in the 50s could easily understand why the Protestant celebration of the Lord's Supper had nothing to do with the "true Mass" which Jesus instituted during the Last Supper. In simplified terms, the argument would have been that the "defective intention" and "defective rites" used by Protestants in their ordinations could not possibly have produced any "validly ordained priests." As a consequence, Protestant ministers were perceived by Catholics as merely "going through the motions" when they celebrated the Lord's Supper. True sacraments (save for the exceptional case of emergency baptism), Catholics wanted to insist, always required validly ordained priests.

Given these differences, Protestants and Catholics had their own versions of history to confirm their respective stances. Protestants, for their part, pointed out that the Gospel accounts do not show that Jesus either ordained or regarded any of the Twelve as "priests." Catholics, for their part, were persuaded that when Jesus, during the course of the Last Supper, said "Do this in memory of me," the "this" was the Holy Sacrifice of the Mass (the Eucharist) which only a validly ordained priest had the power to perform. Hence, Jesus' words implied that he did regard them as "priests" who, in the future, would perform priestly functions during the Eucharist just as he himself had done during the Last Supper.

*Protestants and Catholics had their own versions of history to confirm their respective stances.*

## Purpose

The purpose of this Case Study is to explore what the Christian Scriptures put forward regarding the "priesthood" of Jesus as well as the "priesthood" of his disciples. As a result of this study, it will become clear why both Catholic and Protestant scholars are now beginning to speak of "priesthood" in ways that were not possible before this generation and that a measure of agreement is taking place which bypasses the polemics of the past (as reflected above). One will have the occasion to discover for oneself why the Catholic notion of the "specialized priesthood" of the ordained as well as the Protestant notion of the "generalized priesthood" of all believers are creative developments rather than static repetitions of what the Evangelists themselves understood about priesthood.

*The purpose of this Case Study is to explore the "priesthood" of Jesus as well as the "priesthood" of his disciples.*

Before getting started, you are again invited to record your initial perceptions to five questions. By recording your spontaneous judgments now, you will be providing yourself with a declaration of your preliminary understanding of the issues. After completing the Case Study, you will then be able to reread your initial reflections and gauge to what degree you have been broadened or transformed by your inquiries. The five questions designed for this purpose are as follows:

1. Did the contemporaries of Jesus regard him as a "priest"? _____ What evidence from the Gospel accounts can you offer as support for your claim?

2. Did Jesus intend that his twelve disciples should be "priests"? _____ Did he, accordingly, at some moments deliberately ordain them as "priests"? _____ What evidence from the Gospel accounts can you offer as support for your claim?

3. Did the first Christians regard the Twelve as "priests"? _____ Did they regard every baptized person as a "priest"? _____ What evidence from the Gospel accounts can you offer as support for your claim?

4. When the Eucharist (Lord's Supper) was celebrated by the early Christians, was it always the case that the person presiding was regarded as "a priest"? _____ What evidence from the Christian Scriptures can you offer as support for your claim?

5. Did the Twelve ever specifically ordain anyone as a "priest"? _____ What evidence from the Christian Scriptures can you offer as support for your claim?

Now let's begin. If you are so inclined, this would be time to take your Christian Scriptures in hand, to close your eyes, and to prayerfully ask the Spirit of the Lord to guide you toward the truth that she wants you to hear therein. For our purposes here, any translation of the Christian Scriptures will suffice.

Translation = _____

Starting time = \_\_\_\_\_ (80-100 minutes needed)

## Who is Called "Priest"?

One way to begin to resolve these questions is to begin by examining a concordance in order to find out where the word "priest" appears within the Christian Scriptures. The Greek word for "priest" is *hiereus*. The word for "high priest," meanwhile, is a close derivative formed by adding a prefix to *hiereus*: *arch+hiereus* ("leading"+"priest") = *archiereus*. All in all, there are 155 occurrences of these two words scattered throughout the Christian Scriptures. Some books of the Christian Scriptures, however, make reference to "priest(s)" much more frequently than others. The following table presents a breakdown of the number of occurrences of *hiereus* ("priest") and *archiereus* ("high priest") found in various sections of the Christian Scriptures:

*There are 155 occurrences of "priest" and "high priest" scattered throughout the Christian Scriptures.*

| "priest" | "high priest" | Source |
|---|---|---|
| 03 | 25 | Matthew |
| 02 | 22 | Mark |
| 05 | 16 | Luke |
| 01 | 21 | John |
| 04 | 22 | Acts |
| 00 | 00 | Paul's Epistles |
| 00 | 00 | Pet, Jas, Jude |
| 14 | 17 | Hebrews |
| 03 | 00 | Revelations |
| 32 + | 123 = | 155 total in NT |

This table shows that a frequent reference to "priest(s)" and "high priest(s)" is to be found in each of the Gospels, in Acts, and in Hebrews (which has the highest total). Meanwhile, there is not even a single reference to "priest(s)" in any of the letters written by Paul or Peter. Does this seem odd? Given the practical nature of these letters and the variety of communities to which they were sent, how would you account for the fact that absolutely nothing regarding "priests" or "priesthood" is ever mentioned by Paul or Peter?

*There is not a single reference to "priest(s)" in any of the letters written by Paul or Peter.*

*Whom does Luke regard as "priest"?*

To resolve this puzzle, one would now have to patiently look up every single reference in the Christian Scriptures and find out who is named as priest in every instance. This would be very time consuming. To make the task more manageable, one might settle for just looking up the nine occurrences of "priest" found in Luke's Gospel and Acts. Since this record of Luke covers the key events in the life of Jesus as well as that of the early church, one could expect to find an overview of who were named "priests" and how they functioned within an expanse of sixty years (30-90 CE). Here are the references: five from the life of Jesus and four from the early church. Examine each text in your Scriptures and fill in your findings:

| Source | Are Jesus or his apostles here called "priest(s)"? | What is the "priest" doing? |
|---|---|---|
| Luke 1:5 | | |
| Luke 5:14 | | |
| Luke 6:4 | | |
| Luke 10:3 | | |
| Luke 17:14 | | |
| Acts 4:1 | | |
| Acts 5:24 | | |
| Acts 6:7 | | |
| Acts 14:13 | | |

Now draw conclusions. Why does Luke never present either Jesus or his apostles as ever being called "priests" or as functioning as "priests"? Why does Luke never designate any of those in the early church who were preaching, ordaining, baptizing as being called "priests" or as functioning as "priests"?

Someone might be tempted to think that Luke had a particular bias against the priesthood and, accordingly, he failed to mention that the Twelve were "priests." To dispel this hunch, one would have to check out what the three other Gospels say. If one did this, one would get results only marginally different from those presented by Luke (above).

Maybe Jesus and the Twelve are designated as "high priests" rather than "priests." Here again, anyone who would check this out in each of the Gospels and in Acts would find that, in every instance, the term "high priest(s)" is being used to designate the leading Jewish priest(s) associated with the Jerusalem temple. From this data, one can securely conclude that *neither Jesus nor anyone else within the early church was either regarded as or shown functioning as "a priest"* (even when baptism is being administered or the Eucharist is being celebrated.).

*Neither Jesus nor anyone else within the early church was either regarded as or shown functioning as "a priest."*

This preliminary conclusion squarely runs counter to the claims of both Catholic and Protestant Christians. According to Catholics, Jesus and the Twelve have to be "priests" because they are validly celebrating the Lord's Supper or the Eucharist. According to the Gospels and Acts, however, they are not called "priests" nor do they seemingly need to be "priests." For their part, Protestants have been claiming that everyone in the church has the dignity of "priest" by virtue of their baptism. There is one remote passage in 1 Peter 2:5 wherein the author refers to his readers as "living stones" now being used to construct "a spiritual house" (temple?) for the purpose of providing "a holy priesthood" to offer "spiritual sacrifices" acceptable to God. Then a moment later, the author directly refers to his Gentile readers as "a chosen race, a holy priesthood, a holy nation" (1 Peter 2:9). Whether or not this is metaphoric language must be decided by the context. But, even then, if some doubt remains, one has to take into account that nowhere else in the Christian Scriptures is it even hinted that all Christians are regarded as "priests." Hence, the Protestant claim for the universal priesthood of all believers as well as the Catholic claim for the special priesthood of the ordained clergy seems to be a development which took place sometime after the period in which the Christian Scriptures were framed. The following Case Study will examine this development in detail. What remains is to explore here is the unique qualities of the Letter to the Hebrews in preparing for and stimulating this development.

## Jesus as Our High Priest

In Hebrews, Jesus is named as "high priest" no less than eight times. Accordingly, it is to this small book in the Christian canon that all subsequent generations of Christians have been looking in order to understand the concept of "priesthood."

*Hebrews presents a notable exception.*

Modern scholars (and the early Church Fathers as well) have come to regard the Letter to the Hebrews as not an authentic Pauline writing but as a theological tract of unknown authorship (Hebrews 13:22-25 not withstanding). This tract is generally assumed to have been composed sometimes during the period 80-96 CE. This late date of composition helps to explain why its unique portrait of the high priesthood of Jesus does not appear in an any of the Gospel accounts nor in any of the authentic letters of Paul.

*The central point of interest in Hebrews appears to be the inadequacy of Jewish sacrifice vis à vis the new "sacrifice" and "priesthood" of Jesus.*

The central point of interest in Hebrews appears to be the inadequacy of Jewish sacrifice vis à vis the new "sacrifice" and "priesthood" of Jesus. Without reading the entire text, one can nonetheless gather some of the clues necessary to put together the substance of what the author wants to argue on behalf of Jesus' priesthood. In what follows, the clues offered by the text will be used to resolve seven central issues.

1. Was Jesus a "priest" while on earth? \_\_\_\_ Read Hebrews 8:4 in order to discover the judgment of the author. But let's dig deeper. Why was Jesus disqualified from being a "priest" while on earth? (Need a hint? Read Hebrews 7:14.)

The author of Hebrews frames his argument within Jewish tradition. According to this tradition, God selected one of the twelve tribes, the tribe of Levi, to be withdrawn from all secular occupations and to devote themselves exclusively to the work of providing suitable worship for God. In the desert, they maintained the Tent of Meeting; after the building of the temple in Jerusalem, they maintained the temple, helped worshipers properly select and prepare suitable animals for slaughter, sang in the choir, played instruments. From among these Levites, God selected Aaron and his sons as "priests" who alone were permitted to "approach the altar to serve in the sanctuary" (Exodus 28:43). Once God had made his choice clear, no others were allowed to serve as priests. Furthermore, God made this "an irrevocable ordinance for Aaron and for his descendants after him" (Exodus 28:43).

*To be God's priest, Jesus would have had to have Aaron for his great-grandfather.*

The argument of Hebrews 7:14, accordingly, is that Jesus had the wrong father, grandfather, great-grandfather, etc. To be God's priest, Jesus would have had to have Aaron for his great-grandfather (many generations removed). But, wait a second, how can we know that Jesus was not a descendant of Aaron?

For starters, Matthew and Luke both give us genealogies. Both genealogies fail to name Aaron as a great-grandfather of Jesus. Hebrews concurs: "[O]ur Lord was descended from the tribe of Judah" (Hebrews 7:14). Matthew 1:3 and Luke 3:33 confirm Judah was the great-grandfather of Jesus—not Levi.

But let's pretend. Let's imagine that Jesus felt that he did have a calling from God to be "a priest." Given Jesus' intimacy with the Father and his zeal for true religion, this would not be an unthinkable suggestion. Let's imagine further that Jesus decided to act upon his calling and went to present his case in Jerusalem before the high priest saying, "God has called me to be his priest?" What would the high priest be expected to respond?

2. After granting that Jesus could never be a priest on earth (8:4) because he had the wrong genes, Hebrews does not admit defeat. Having been excluded from the priesthood "according to the order of Aaron," Hebrews goes on to affirm repeatedly that Jesus was appointed a priest "according to the order of Melchizedek" (5:10, 6:20, 7:11, 7:17). Melchizedek was the pagan king-priest who shows up mysteriously to become the priest who offers bread and wine to the God of Abraham at the request of Abraham after the slaughter of some hostile kings (Genesis 14:17-20). Read Hebrews 6:20-7:10. What is the nub of the argument here? How does Hebrews make a case for Jesus being a true priest "according to the order of Melchizedek"?

*After granting that Jesus could never be a priest on earth, how does Hebrews make a case for Jesus being a true priest "according to the order of Melchizedek"?*

3. A real priest has to "approach the altar to serve in the sanctuary" (Exodus 28:43). But what altar and sanctuary are open to Jesus for his priestly sacrifice?

A Catholic here might be tempted to say, "The Last Supper," on the grounds that Catholic tradition calls the table upon which the Eucharist is celebrated "that altar" and refers to the space around the altar which is separated from the people by the communion rail as "the sanctuary." If one looks at all the accounts of the Last Supper in each of the four Gospels and the details which Paul provides in 1 Corinthians 11:17-34, one finds that there is not a single reference to "altar" or "sanctuary." But couldn't Hebrews argue that Jesus was a

*Hebrews fails to argue that Jesus was a "priest" during his last supper.*

"priest" during his last supper and, accordingly, the table on which they ate could be construed as "the altar" and the upper room could be construed as "the sanctuary"? No. Hebrews has already acknowledged that "if he [Jesus] were on earth, he would not be a priest at all" (8:4). Accordingly, since the Last Supper took place on earth, Hebrews did not consider that Jesus was a priest at that time. He became a priest later. When? Where? [Need a hint? Read 8:1-5.]

*Jesus is a priest only in the heavenly sanctuary.*

4. Jesus is quite unlike other Jewish priests. He is not a priest in the likeness of Aaron; he is a priest in the likeness of Melchizedek. Jesus is not a priest in the earthly sanctuary; he is a priest in the heavenly sanctuary. The latter is much better than the former since (a) the latter is "set up not by man but by the Lord" (8:2) and (b) the former is simply "a copy and shadow" (8:5) of the latter. But what "gifts and sacrifices" (8:3) can Jesus offer in this sanctuary?

Both Protestants and Catholics might be tempted to suggest here that "his death on the cross" is his sacrifice. Ever since the twelfth century popularization of Anselm's notion of redemption as centered upon making sacrifice for sins, Christians have been accustomed to think of the sin of Adam and the sins of his children as requiring a sacrifice of atonement if they are to be forgiven by God. According to this explanation of things, Jesus is spoken of as the Son of God who took on human flesh so that he could die on the cross as a sacrificial atonement on behalf of sinners. Church hymns are filled with these images. Given this nearly all-pervasive theology of the atonement in our own day, would you judge that the disciples of Jesus, following their Jewish religious instincts, would have regarded the crucifixion as a "sacrifice" to God? Why or why not?

The initial chapters of Hebrews do make reference to the sufferings of Jesus but they never call this "priestly sacrifice." The words "cross" (12:2) and "crucify" (6:6) play almost no role whatsoever in Hebrews, and even when they are used once each they do not say what medieval theology wanted them to say. Hebrew argues that Jesus is a priest in the heavenly sanctuary, not on earth where he was crucified. But, even more than this, no Jew would even remotely be tempted to think of a Roman crucifixion as "a sacrifice to God" for three important reasons: (1) Jewish tradition has made it plain that God absolutely forbids human sacrifice; (2) Jewish tradition has made it plain that no legitimate sacrifice can be offered outside of the temple at Jerusalem; (3) Jewish tradition requires that a priest do the offering. With regard to the latter, even if it would be allowed that Jesus was a priest in the likeness of Melchizedek, it still would be impossible to imagine how this priest offered himself when, for anyone who was there, it was evident that Roman soldiers pounded the nails and raised the cross. Are these soldiers to be seen as "Levites" assisting at a "human sacrifice"? No. Never. Everything about the death of Jesus on the cross fails to fit into the Jewish understanding of God and sacrifice. For Christians living in the Middle Ages, however, Anselm's theology of the vicarious atonement on the cross would have been perceived as fitting perfectly into the medieval understanding of God and sacrifice, but we have no time to develop this medieval alternative here.

*No Jew would even remotely be tempted to think of a Roman crucifixion as "a sacrifice to God."*

When the initial chapters of Hebrews make reference to the suffering of Jesus, it is by way of telling the audience what sort of qualifications and preparations Jesus had to make while on earth in order to be selected as God's high priest after he was raised an taken into heaven. To begin, Hebrews argues that a future priest must share "in flesh and blood" (2:14) and suffer the same trials and tribulations as his brothers and sisters "so that he might become a merciful and faithful high priest" (2:17). He will be merciful "for he himself has suffered and been tempted" (2:18); he has been where we are and "is able to sympathize with our weakness" (4:15); and he "can deal gently with the ignorant and the wayward" (5:2). The trials and tribulations of human life, consequently, are the training ground for one who would some day be compassionate and helpful "as a priest." But, more than "merciful," Jesus was also found to be "faithful" (3:3, 6) to God even when it was tough to do so. Thus, "he learned obedience through what he had suffered; and being made perfect he became the source of eternal salvation" (5:8, 2:10). What Hebrews wishes to emphasize is that Jesus' struggled to be faithful to God when tempted, when humiliated, when made to suffer for his fidelity; and, accordingly, that this suffering demonstrated his usefulness for others as a "source," a "pioneer" (2:10, 12:2), a "forerunner" (6:20) of what we ourselves are called to be and to do for God. In sum,

*The trials and tribulations of human life, are the training ground for one who would some day be "as a priest."*

*suffering has to do with preparing the candidate for priesthood* and does not constitute "the sacrifice" he will offer in the heavenly sanctuary.

5. In the Jewish temple, various animals and various fruits of the earth (wheat, wine, olive oil) were suitably prepared and burnt on the altar (or roasted/baked and eaten by the priests) (see, e.g., Lev 1:3-7:34). Once cannot suppose, however, that such offerings would be available in heaven. What then is "the sacrifice" that Jesus offers in the heavenly sanctuary? Read Hebrews 10:1-16.

> *Suffering has to do with preparing the candidate for priesthood and does not constitute "the sacrifice" he will offer in the heavenly sanctuary.*

The text here is not easy to understand. What Hebrews seems to be proposing is that the new high priest fulfills the prophetic expectation of a "new covenant":

> This is the covenant that I will make with the house of Israel after those days, says the Lord: I will put my Torah into their minds, and write them on their hearts, and I will be their God and they shall be my people (Jeremiah 31:33).

Hebrews cites this text at the beginning (8:10) and at the end (10:16) of his argument. Then, with his argument thus framed, the author of Hebrews goes on to show that the covenant that God made with Moses was enacted when "he took the blood of calves and goats . . . and sprinkled both the book itself and all the people" (9:19). The sprinkling of blood seals the covenant and purifies the people by blotting out their sins. But year after year, on the Day of Atonement, more animals had to be sacrificed and more blood had to be sprinkled (10:1-5). Then, "Christ came into the world" (10:5) and, without ever having offered a single sacrifice according to the Mosaic Torah, he said, "Lo, I have come to do thy will, O God" (10:7, 9). And this heartfelt adherence to the ways of God that characterized the whole life and death of Jesus is precisely what so enormously pleased God.

> *This heartfelt adherence to the ways of God is precisely what so enormously pleased God.*

According to Hebrews, once God has tasted this fidelity of Jesus, he just as quickly lost all taste for that kind of fidelity which the older covenant had always sought to attain through the offering of animals and grains upon the altar. In brief: "Sacrifices and offerings thou has not desired; . . . in burnt offerings and sin-offerings thou hast taken no pleasure" (10:5f = Ps 40:6f). From God's vantage point, consequently, *Hebrews affirms that the new kind of priest has established a new kind of sacrifice:* "I have come to do your will, O God!" This willingness of Jesus constitutes "a single sacrifice" (10:12), "a single offering [of self]" (10:14), which has the power to perfect for all time "those who are consecrated [to God]" (10:14).

6. What are the practical implications of this new mode of sacrifice which Jesus offers to God? Hebrews answers this by asking its audience to "offer to God acceptable worship" (12:28) which it immediately spells out in the details of Hebrews 13:1-6. Examine these. Then read Hebrews 13:15-16. What "sacrifices" would the followers of Jesus be expected to offer?

*Hebrews directs his audience to "offer to God acceptable worship."*

7. Here are some closing practical questions. Up to this point, Jesus alone has been repeatedly called "priest" or "high priest." Does anyone else get to be called priest? _____ Why not? (Need a hint? See Hebrews 7:23-27.)

In Hebrews, is the Lord's Supper or Eucharist referred to as a "sacrifice"? _____ Even though the whole of Hebrews makes no explicit reference to the Lord's Supper, does Hebrews at least provide a line of thinking which might enable later Christians to regard the Eucharist as "their sacrifice to God"?

If the Lord's Supper were to be considered "a sacrifice of praise" (13:15), does it then follow that those who offer it could be called "priests"? If the "priest" were considered as the one "offering the sacrifices of praise" to God, would this than mean that the presider alone at the Lord's Supper would be "the priest"? _____ Would it follow that all the faithful present also act as "priests" during the Eucharist? How so?

8. What startling discoveries did you make while exploring Case Two? Describe them for yourself here:

9. Did this Case Study raise any fundamental questions for you while you were completing it? If so, note them here so that you can return to them at a later moment?

Completion time = _____

Total time used on this Case = _____ minutes

Well done! You have completed your second Case Study. Needless to say, this case was more complex than Case One. You must be exhausted. Set everything aside, rest, and, once you are renewed, come back for the analysis.

## Analysis

Stepping back from the whole Case Study, the following short catechism has been prepared by way of exemplifying and extending the inquiries that you have made.

**1Q**: According to the evidence of the Christian Scriptures, why are the Twelve not regarded as "priests"?

**A**: At no time do the Christian Scriptures designate as "priest" any minister within the Jesus Movement. The Christian Scriptures use *hiereus* frequently (82x) but every use refers to Jewish or pagan priests. The reason for this is that the early churches shared the Jewish perspective whereby (a) only "sons of Aaron" were entitled to act as priests and (b) these priests were universally regarded as occupied with the worship of God within the context of the Jerusalem temple. Neither Jesus nor the Twelve were either "sons of Aaron" or occupied with temple worship. Hence, no one within or outside of the Jesus movement would have imagined that either Jesus or his disciples were "priests."

*No one within or outside of the Jesus movement would have imagined that either Jesus or his disciples were "priests."*

## How Jesus Came to Be Chosen as High Priest / 39

**2 Q:** According to the Christian Scriptures, under what circumstances is Jesus appropriately called "high priest"?

**A:** While all the inspired books of the Christian Scriptures, save one, are not even inclined to designate Jesus even as a "priest", the Letter to the Hebrews constitutes a singular exception. Hebrews is a theological treatise which, in part, argues that God appointed Jesus as the eternal high priest who offers the perfect sacrifice of himself in the heavenly sanctuary.

*The Letter to the Hebrews constitutes a singular exception.*

In order to sustain this claim, Hebrews had to acknowledge (a) that on earth Jesus was not a priest and (b) that the sacrifice made by Jesus had nothing to do with the burnt offerings and sin-offerings of the temple. To begin with, Hebrews presents God's choice of Jesus (whom God has raised) as akin to God's earlier unpredictable choice of Melchizedek, the "king of righteousness" (7:2). Furthermore, Hebrews promotes the prophetic critique of temple sacrifice: "Lo, I have come to do your will, O God" (10:7, 9). According to the "new covenant" (9:15) described by Hebrews, Jesus' heartfelt fidelity to God (10:7, 9, 16) is specified as the only acceptable sacrifice that serves to blot out sins. Furthermore, this fidelity is not an automatic given in the case of Jesus. It is something he came to after being tempted and made to suffer (2:18, 5:8, 12:4).

*Jesus' heartfelt fidelity to God is specified as the only acceptable sacrifice.*

**3 Q:** According to the Christian Scriptures, is the Lord's Supper considered to be a "sacrifice" which required a "priest" to officiate or celebrate?

**A:** Since neither Jesus nor his disciples were regarded as priests, it must follow that all the rites performed by Jesus and his disciples were done by them as lay persons. Even at the Last Supper, Jesus

---

### "Sacrifice" in Paul's Letters

While Paul never names anyone as "priest," he does, nonetheless, make occasional use of sacrificial language. For example, he urges Christians "to present your bodies (*sōmata*) as living sacrifice, holy and acceptable to God" (Rom 12:1). Some scholars would see this as an illusion to the eucharistic words, "This is my body (*sōma*)" (1 Cor 11:24 and Synoptic parallels), thereby reinforcing the sacrificial overtones of the Eucharist. In this same vein, Paul has a handful of texts in which he likens the bodies of Christians to a "temple of God" (1 Cor 3:16, 6:19; 2 Cor 6:16; Eph 2:19-22). At one point, Paul speaks of his own "preaching of the gospel" as his "sacrificial/priestly service" (Rom 15:15). While it is beyond the scope of this Case Study to investigate the intent of Paul, it is important to note that sacrificial language had some currency within other circles prior to the full-blown thesis of Hebrews. Interested persons should explore the *Didache* 14:1-3 and Daly, *The Origins of the Christian Doctrine of Sacrifice*.

was understood by his disciples to be a layman celebrating the Jewish Passover with his disciples. The Jewish Passover never required that a priest preside; the head of each household traditionally presided.

While the singular Letter to the Hebrews does argue that Jesus was appointed high priest, his priesthood was understood as beginning when he had entered into the heavenly sanctuary following his resurrection. Accordingly, Hebrews never has any reason to associate the Lord's Supper with the priesthood of Jesus. On the other hand, since Hebrews closes with the exhortation that Christians offer "a sacrifice of praise to God" (13:15), a small step was being taken toward that time when Christians would understand their Eucharist to be "a sacrifice" which was presided over by "a priest."

*At the Last Supper, Jesus was understood by his disciples to be a layman.*

**4 Q**: How does it come about that some or all members of the Christian community regard themselves as sharing in the priesthood of Jesus Christ?

**A**: Strictly speaking, not even Hebrews anticipated the notion that Christians somehow share in Christ's priesthood. Since Jesus never dies in heaven, he has no need of a successor; and since his priestly functions are in heaven, no one on earth is able to assist him. In sum, therefore, Hebrews works against such a notion.

However, as demonstrated in our first Case Study, religious traditions do develop as they encounter new issues and new populations. Within the early second century, for instance, Christianity had made considerable headway among the Gentile urban populations wherein sacrifices to the gods were taken for granted as a routine part of public life. Christians, having conscientiously absented themselves from such sacrifices, were suspected of dishonoring the gods and promoting a form of atheism. In the face of such accusations, Justin Martyr, writing in Rome (c. 150 CE), sought to defend the reputation of Christians by arguing (a) that the true God has no need of animal sacrifices and (b) that the Eucharist ("a meal") was considered as the perfect and pleasing "sacrifice" (of praise and thanksgiving) which Christians offered to their God. Justin Martyr didn't need to invent this idea because Christians had already been meditating and applying the notion of "sacrifice" expressed so powerfully in Hebrews to all phases of their life.

*Justin Martyr sought to defend the reputation of Christians by arguing that the Eucharist was considered as the perfect and pleasing "sacrifice."*

Once the Eucharist was routinely regarded as the pleasing sacrifice offered to God by Christians, it was only a matter of time before the question arose as to who was to be regarded as "the priest" during this sacrifice. Some fathers of the church, such as

Irenaeus (d. 200 CE) in the West and Origen (d. 254 CE) in the East proposed that the entire people of God were "priests." During the Eucharist, all those present young and old, men and women, Jews and Gentiles, were understood as offering the new covenant sacrifice to God in union with Christ, their heavenly high priest. Due to a process of development stemming largely from the Book of Hebrews, consequently, the Christians of the third century arrived at the stage where they regarded themselves as "priests" and their celebrant as "high priest" whenever they celebrated the Lord's Supper. The Jewish Passover celebrated by Jesus as a layman was thereby transformed in the imaginations of Christians by virtue of the fact that their experience of the Eucharist had entirely taken on the coloring of "sacrifice" and "priesthood"—notions entirely absent from the Jewish Passover.

**5 Q**: Does the universal priesthood of all the faithful as well as the specialized priesthood of the ordained then have no warrant in the teaching and practice of Jesus?

**A**: The universal priesthood of all the faithful as well as the specialized or ordained priesthood have no formal warrant within Jesus' teaching and practice. However, as already seen in Case One, one must expect that local pastors and local churches did not merely repeat the past but went on to extend and revise what had been passed down so as to respond to new pastoral situations. In the case of priesthood, therefore, Hebrews already represents a kind of pastoral and theological innovation whereby the Jewish tradition of priesthood was modified and extended in favor of advocating the high priesthood of Jesus in heaven. The impulse which created and inspired Hebrews did not stop there; rather, subsequent generations applied its logic to yet unforeseen pastoral cases. Out of this ferment came both the universal priesthood of all the faithful as well as the specialized priesthood. In sum, therefore, the Christian Scriptures can be perceived as witnessing a process of development, which, when taken to its limits, does provide solid grounds for regarding all Christians as "priests" sharing in the one priesthood of Jesus Christ. The same thing, of course, can be said of the specialized or ordained "priests" whom Roman Catholics regard as sharing in the one priesthood of Jesus Christ.

*Hebrews represents a kind of pastoral and theological innovation. . . .*

*Out of this ferment came both the universal priesthood of all the faithful as well as the specialized priesthood.*

**6 Q**: How did Christians during the Middle Ages entirely lose sight of their own dignity as "priest" with the result that they relied upon the ordained on earth and the Saints in heaven to be their mediators in offering their prayers to the Father?

A: During the early Middle Ages, a momentous shift in spirituality took place. Increasingly, Christians no longer felt worthy to offer themselves to the Father in union with Jesus, their heavenly high priest. Increasingly, for the same reasons, Christians no longer felt that they could address their prayers to the Father almighty, nor to his Son, who was crucified for their sins and continually reminded them of the final and terrible Last Judgment where their sins would be exposed and condemned. Accordingly, Christians began to regard the "holy priest" and their "patron saint" as go-betweens or mediators. In practice, a Christian would bring a chicken or a coin and give it to a "holy priest" in order that he might "say a Mass for his/her intentions." And, since most everyone wanted their petitions to be heard without cluttering God's attention with the petitions of others, priests found themselves committed to saying multiple Masses every day of the week. Not even the petitioner had to be present as Mass for the "holy priest" was perceived as much more eloquent and powerful in drawing down God's favor than a thousand prayers said by the unworthy petitioner.

In a similar vein, medieval Christians began to direct their private prayers and pilgrimages to a "holy saint" who had the patience to listen to the prayers of sinners and then, in a good moment, to bring these prayers to the attention of the Lord. The Saints, too, therefore, were co-opted into being "mediators." Within such a world, Christians quickly forget that they had ever been entitled to offer themselves with Christ to the Father. Now, the only reality left was the ordained "priest" who mysteriously repeated "the sacrifice of Christ on the cross in an unbloody manner" during every Mass.

> *Medieval Christians began to regard the "holy priest" and their "patron saint" as go-betweens or mediators.*

**7 Q**: Can Catholics today reclaim their dignity as priests who offer themselves to the Father in union with Jesus during every Eucharist?

A: Decidedly. To effect this, both the liturgy itself and the documents of Vatican II render an invaluable assistance.

The liturgy has always had an uncanny knack for retaining the fossilized traces of a former era. At every Eucharist, even today, the priest turns to the people and says:

> Pray, brothers and sisters, that our sacrifice may become acceptable to God the Father almighty.

One will immediately note here that the focus is upon "our sacrifice" without any mention of "Jesus' sacrifice." This is so because, following Hebrews, it is already presumed that Jesus' self-do-nation to the Father is already acceptable. But, as the pioneer of our salvation, it remains to be seen whether "our sacrifice" may now become acceptable. Thus, celebrant and people alike offer themselves as the sacrifice at every Mass saying with their high priest, "Behold, I have come to do your will, O Lord."

When I present the above story of the lost foundations of the theology and the experience of sacrifice, Catholics invariably find it appealing. But then a few are certain to ask me whether, as Catholics, they are now required to uphold the medieval notion of "sacrifice" and "priesthood" as it has come down to us. By way of answering this, I make reference to the pastors present at Vatican II who saw fit deliberately to put forward the notion of "sacrifice" and "priesthood" which prevailed during the early centuries of the church. The bishops advocated this "older Catholicism" in the following terms:

> The baptized, by regeneration and the anointing of the Holy Spirit, are consecrated to be a spiritual house and a holy priesthood, [in order] that through all the works of Christian men [and women] they may offer spiritual sacrifices. . . . Therefore all the disciples of Christ, persevering in prayer and praising God (cf. Acts 2:42-47), should present themselves as a sacrifice, living, holy and pleasing to God (*Lumen Gentium* 10).

And, in case someone mistakenly interprets what the bishops say here as referring only to those "sacrifices" other than the Eucharist, the bishops later went on to say:

> The faithful indeed, by virtue of their royal priesthood, participate in the offering of the Eucharist. They exercise that priesthood, too, by the reception of the [other] sacraments, prayer and thanksgiving, the witness of a holy life, abnegation and active charity. . . . Taking part in the eucharistic sacrifice, they offer the divine victim to God and themselves along with it (*Lumen Gentium* 10).

These words cannot be adequately understood solely within medieval categories. Only someone immersed within Patristic thought stemming out of Hebrews could frame things in this manner. Hence, as prudent pastors, the bishops of Vatican II presented Catholics with a taste for the old, the older, and the oldest orientation to sacrifice found within their 2,000-year-old tradition.

In sum, Catholics are not only permitted to recover the theology and the practice associated with the priesthood of the baptized; rather, they are positively urged to do so, both by their current liturgy and by their current pastors.

*Celebrant and people alike offer themselves at every Mass saying with their high priest, "Behold, I have come to do your will, O Lord."*

*Catholics are positively urged to recover the theology and the practice associated with the priesthood of the baptized.*

**8 Q**: What importance does all this have for ecumenical understanding between Catholics and Lutherans?

**A**: After centuries of sometimes-hot sometimes-cold mutual antagonism, Lutherans and Catholics have found a fresh start in reconciling their differences within the biblical foundations disclosed in this Case Study. While the scope of these inter-confessional discussions and mutual agreements is too vast and too complex to summarize here, the following observations are offered by way of illustration:

*Both Catholic and Lutherans are soberly reminded that Jesus and his disciples were effective and efficacious precisely as laymen.*

(a) The results of this Case Study have enabled both partners in the dialogue to set aside their hardened and oftentimes arrogant assurances that *their views and their views alone* were warranted by the Sacred Scriptures. In effect, therefore, biblical scholarship has allowed both Catholic and Lutherans to humbly acknowledge that, while their respective views on priesthood have remote beginnings within the Scriptures, their respective traditions have indeed developed in unique directions which were fashioned by pastoral needs, by controversy, and by the inspiration of the guiding Spirit functioning within both communities.

(b) The results of this Case Study further clarify that, whatever the partner churches say about priesthood and ministry today, they are soberly reminded that both Jesus and his disciples were effective and efficacious precisely as laymen responsive to that calling and anointing which comes from God. Hence, no matter what lofty designations the respective churches give to those officially ordained for the preaching of the Gospel and the administration of the Sacraments, it will always remain the case that those ordained by the churches are first and foremost called by God and remain servants of that God who is the Source and Sustainer of all ministry. As such, both the ordained and the non-ordained can never confuse institutional compliance as the sole criteria for discerning God's will. As servants of God, therefore, the ordained who are commissioned to preach the Gospel in the church will sometimes be called by God to preach the Gospel against the church (including its hierarchy). Faithfulness to God, therefore, whether as a lay person or as an ordained, can only take it cue from the lay ministry of Jesus who sometimes had harsh words for the priests of his day as well as for his own disciples. And, if our Lord is "beset with weakness" (Heb 5:2) and has "learned obedience" (Heb 5:8), it must even be presupposed that the Word Jesus received served to correct and enlarge his path as well. Hence, the one who would presume to bring the message of the Lord to others must, with even

*Catholics have sometimes overvalued the specialized priesthood of the ordained.*

greater force, have applied this same Word to himself or herself.

(c) From the vantage point of the biblical studies undertaken, many Catholics have come to recognize how Catholics have sometimes overvalued the specialized priesthood of the ordained. The pious story told to me by my sixth-grade teacher, for instance, moves toward reducing the eucharistic mystery to a magical event promoted by magical words in the mouth of the validly ordained priest. This is not Catholic theology but pious superstition which needs to be corrected by a just estimate of how God acts in history and by an informed notion of sacramental efficacy.

(d) Now that the renewal of the Catholic Church has allowed for a more biblical and more responsive specialized priesthood of the ordained, many Lutherans have found the possibility of reexamining and reaffirming a larger notion of priesthood without fear that they are thereby inviting Catholic excesses. An ordained Lutheran pastor, for instance, acknowledged during the course of dialogue that even the shared priesthood of the baptized was, in his experience, in danger of becoming an empty affirmation of faith unless it was sustained by a forthright recognition and empowerment of lay Protestants as gifted by grace and called to ministry both within the churches and within the institutions of modern society. Protestants, therefore, have found that they have something to offer and something to learn from Catholics when it comes to the theology and spirituality of priesthood.

*Lutherans have found the possibility of reexamining and reaffirming a larger notion of priesthood.*

(e) Lutherans have traditionally been highly critical of the Catholic doctrine of the "sacrifice of the Mass" because, in their eyes, it contradicted the full sufficiency of "Christ's sacrifice on the cross." Once Lutherans have discovered that Catholics have always insisted that Christ's sacrifice on the cross could be neither "continued, nor repeated, nor replaced" by the sacrifice of the Mass, the road has been opened to considering how the very term "sacrifice" does not have a single meaning within the long tradition of the church nor within the history of Catholic-Lutheran conflict. The dialogue partners thereby agreed that there never has been nor will be only one correct notion of sacrifice:

*The dialogue partners agreed that there never has been nor will be only one correct notion of sacrifice.*

> Scripture and the history of theology contain many ways of describing Christ's sacrifice and therefore also the sacrificial character of the memorial of that sacrifice which is the eucharist. The most general meaning of "sacrifice" is broader than any current in contemporary usage—or in that of the sixteenth century. Thus, according to the Second World Conference on Faith and Order (Edinburgh, 1937), "If sacrifice is understood as it was by our Lord and

His followers and in the early Church, it includes, not his death only, but the obedience of His earthly ministry, and His risen and ascended life, in which He still does His Father's will and ever liveth to make intercession for us" (*Lutherans and Catholics in Dialogue III: The Eucharist as Sacrifice*, p. 188).

Once can see in this statement how medieval notions of Christ's sacrifice (centering on his obediently dying) were moderated by Hebrews (centering on his obediently living).

*Partners in the dialogue have recognized the real presence of Christ in the Eucharist even while they express this "real presence" differently.*

(f) Going even further, both partners in the dialogue have recognized the real presence of Christ in the Eucharist (a topic which goes beyond the scope of this Case Study) even while they express this "real presence" differently. The same thing can be said for the Eucharist as a "sacrifice." While some difficulties remain, both parties of the dialogue were able to affirm the following common statement:

> By him, with him, and in him who is our High Priest and Intercessor we offer to the Father, in the power of the Holy Spirit, our praise, thanksgiving, and intercession. With contrite hearts we offer ourselves as a living and holy sacrifice which must be expressed in the whole of our daily lives (Lutherans and Catholics in Dialogue III: The Eucharist as Sacrifice, p. 188-189).

In sum, both dialogue partners have found it possible to come to a shared sense whereby every Eucharist can be affirmed as both a "sacrifice" and a "self-offering or oblation"—terms which resonate well with the citations from Vatican II in the previous question. Thanks to the mutual discovery of our radical roots, therefore, both Catholics and Lutherans have begun to take small steps together which are directed toward the time when a mutual recognition of ministry and a mutual recognition of sacraments will become possible.

Total agreement will never be possible. Catholics and Lutherans (and all other churches of Christ as well) will always be separated by diverse estimates of priesthood and diverse experiences of the Lord's Supper. None the less, official mutual recognition will someday enable the followers of Jesus within both churches to bless rather than to curse those who differ from them. In that day, the common grace, the common ground, and the common bond will entirely have healed the wounds and divisions of the past. This is our prayer; this is our hope; this is our task.

## Application to the Churches Today

On the basis of everything that has been discovered above, what application does this have to "priesthood" and "sacrifice" today? Generate a few spinoffs and write them down here and in the margins.

## Further Readings for Case Two

Brown, Raymond E.
> *Priest and Bishop: Biblical Reflections.* New York: Paulist, 1970.

Daly, Robert J.
> *The Origins of the Christian Doctrine of Sacrifice.* Philadelphia: Fortress, 1978.

Kilmartin, Edward J.
> "Sacrificium Laudis [Sacrifice of Praise]: Content and Function of Early Eucharistic Prayers." *Theological Studies,* 35:268-287, 1974.

Lathrup, Gordon W.
> "Justin, Eucharist, and 'Sacrifice': A Case Metaphor." *Worship,* 64/1:30-48, 1990.

Milavec, Aaron
> *The Pastoral Genius of the Didache.* New York: Paulist, 1995.

Osborne, Kenan B.
> *Priesthood: A History of the Ordained Ministry in the Roman Catholic Church.* New York: Paulist, 1988.
> *Ministry: Lay Ministry in the Roman Catholic Church.* New York: Paulist, 1993.

Power, David N.
> *The Sacrifice We Offer.* New York: Crossroad, 1987.

U.S.A. National Committee of the Lutheran World Federation and the [Catholic] Bishops' Committee for Ecumenical and Interreligious Affairs,
> *Lutherans and Catholics in Dialogue III: The Eucharist as Sacrifice.* Washington, D.C.: United States Catholic Conference and Philadelphia: Fortress, 1967.

# CASE THREE

# The Transformation Effected by Ordination

*Everything about the Catholic rite suggested a Cinderella-like transformation.*

Within my own Catholic upbringing, there was no more emphatic and dramatic transformation rite than the Sacrament of Ordination. Everything about the rite suggested a Cinderella-like transformation. Prior to the rite, for instance, the candidate practiced administering the sacraments using all the prescribed words and gestures of the *Sacramentary*. This was just play-acting, however. No one, not even the candidate's closest friends, would even dream of asking him to act as their priest. Following the imposition of hands by the bishop during the ordination rite, however, even total strangers eagerly sought out the "new priest" and asked for his blessing or gave him a stipend to say a Mass for their intentions. After ordination, there would never again be any play-acting. Every rite of the Church performed using the words and gestures of the *Sacramentary* now had the mysterious power of moving heaven and earth such that God himself took notice and acted through the rites of the priest.

*Southern Baptists have an entirely different disposition when it comes to the designation of their ministers.*

Southern Baptists, on the other hand, have almost an entirely different disposition when it comes to the designation of their ministers. In contrast with Catholics, the principal experience savored by Baptists is hearing the Word of God proclaimed with power. From the perspective of Baptists, anyone could rehearse and repeat rituals. Only someone in whom the Spirit of God dwells, however, could proclaim the Gospel such that the congregation senses that they have been addressed by the Lord. Accordingly, a candidate for ministry in the Baptist church does not aspire toward the laying on of hands by a bishop; rather, he or she aspires to surrender his or her whole life to be filled by the Spirit of God.

Some months ago I met a Baptist seminarian. He eagerly told me how he had been waken by the Lord in the middle of the night and been "called." The next day, he could hardly wait to contact his local minister to share this experience. Then a discernment process began which included the critical opportunity of preaching before the congregation. His expectation was that God would guide his words so as to marvelously transform the congregation through him. Praise God! This very thing came to pass.

Baptists look for a Cinderella-like transformation within the minds and hearts of the hearers when the Gospel is being rightly preached. Once a would-be preacher evokes this sign within the congregation, then he is approved by the local congregation as a preacher given to them by the Lord. In the course of time, he may enroll in a seminary program where he will receive further training; however, no laying on of hands by a bishop figures into this process at any time. For Baptists, God anoints with the Holy Spirit those whom he calls to be his ministers.

*Baptists look for a Cinderella-like transformation when the Gospel is being rightly preached.*

The Christian churches are severely divided when it comes to their understanding of ordination. Catholics maintain that ordination "is truly and properly a sacrament instituted by Christ the Lord" (Trent: DS963). Episcopalians, Lutherans, and Presbyterians practice ordination today with a solemnity that matches the Catholic rites; yet, they regard ordination as a "church ordinance" and not as a sacrament instituted by Christ. Furthermore, most Lutherans and all Presbyterians allow ordination to be conferred by presbyters or elders and do not imagine that ordinations must be reserved to bishops. Meanwhile, as we have just explained, Southern Baptists consider it inappropriate to have any ordination rite which claims to do what God is perfectly able to do without any such rite. In those local congregation where "ordination" may be practiced, this rite is perceived as merely confirming God's prior election of this person as his chosen instrument.

*Baptists consider it inappropriate to have any ordination rite which claims to do what God is perfectly able to do without any such rite.*

## Purpose

How about the early church? Did it practice ordination? By whom? Upon whom? With what effect? These are the questions which our present Case will explore. To do this, we will examine two key biblical instances in which ordinations were performed. These instances will be compared and contrasted. The overall purpose of this Case Study is to determine what understanding of ordination guided the practice of the early church. Special attention will be given to how the Spirit of God functions before, during, and after ordination rites.

*The purpose of this Case Study is to determine what understanding of ordination guided the practice of the early church.*

Before getting started, you are again invited to record your initial perceptions to three questions. By recording your spontaneous judgments now, you will be providing yourself with a declaration of your preliminary understanding of the issues. After completing the Case Study, you will then be able to reread your initial reflections

50 \ *Exploring Scriptural Sources*

and gauge to what degree you have been broadened or transformed by your inquiries. The three questions designed for this purpose are as follows:

1. Did Jesus ever personally ordain anyone? _____ Whom? _____ What evidence can you offer to support your response?

2. From what you already know, can you remember any moment in the early church when ordination was used _____ Who was ordained? _____ Who did the laying on of hands? _____ Was this a priestly ordination? _____ If not, why not?

3. When the church did develop the practice of ordination, was it understood that the Holy Spirit descends upon the candidate prior to, during, or after the rite itself? _____ If so, what does this say about the function of the rite?

Let's begin, Once again, if you are so inclined, this would be the time to take your Bible (the Hebrew and Christian Scriptures) in hand, to close your eyes, and to prayerfully unite yourself with the Spirit whom you trust to guide you to discover what is important for yourself and for your church community.

Translation = _____

Starting time = _____ (55-65 minutes needed)

## Two Instances of Ordination

Our purpose here will be to investigate the earliest instance of ordination in both the Hebrew and Christian Scriptures. In the first case, Moses is presented as laying hands upon Joshua (Numbers 27);

in the second, the Twelve lay hands upon the Seven who are traditionally understood as becoming the first "deacons" (Acts 6).

In both of these instances, the Greek verb *epitithēmi* ("lay or put upon") is used. The Greek Septuagint, literally translated, reads "and you [Moses] will lay your hands upon him" (Numbers 27:18). The RSV and NRSV renders the Greek here as "and lay your hand upon him." In this case, the RSV has interpreted the future "you will lay" as implying a mild imperative. This is acceptable. The RSV use of "hand" (in the singular) represents a literal rendering of the Hebrew text (which appears to be defective at this point). The Greek, meanwhile, clearly indicates that both hands are being applied with pressure. The text doesn't explicitly indicate on which part of his body hands were to be laid. Traditional usage, however, allows us to presume that Moses was commanded to lay his hands upon the head of Joshua. Check to see how your Bible translates the end of Numbers 27:18.

*The Greek text doesn't indicate on which part of his body hands were to be laid.*

Literally translated, Acts 6:6 reads, "and having prayed they laid upon them [the] hands." The RSV reads: "and they prayed and laid their hands upon them." In this case, the RSV decided to render the participle "having prayed" as a verb; "they prayed and . . . " This could be misleading since the Greek places the participle in the aorist tense, thereby denoting a single past action. The Greek, therefore, favors the sense that "having prayed [beforehand] they laid hands upon them."

### Note Regarding "Ordination"

The verb *epithithēmi* ("lay or lean upon") with *cheiras* ("hands") is the normal means whereby the Greek text indicates the rite of "ordination." Translators, however, are hesitant to simply render the Greek as "you [Moses] will *ordain* him" (Numbers 27:18) and as "they [the Twelve] *ordained* them" (Acts 6:6). The reason for this hesitation is that the laying on of hands does not always imply an ordination to an office.

For example, at one point the priest Aaron "lays his hands" (Leviticus 16:21) upon the scapegoat's head while reciting the sins of the people. In the Christian Scriptures, Peter and John "lay their hands" (Acts 8:17) upon the Samaritans who have been recently baptized by Philip. In both of these instances, while the same characteristic Greek phrase is used (*epitithēmi* with *cheiras*), no "ordinations" are implied.

Accordingly, most English translators have decided to translate *epitithēmi with cheiras* as "to lean hands upon"—thereby allowing the reader to decide in each case whether an "ordination" is implied. This cautious approach, meanwhile, can itself be misleading since "laying hands upon someone" may not offer many readers an adequate set of clues to signal an "ordination" even in those cases (such as Num 27 and Acts 6) where an "ordination" is implied by the original text.

*Who lays hands has to be figured out by the context and by traditional usage.*

Whose hands are represented by "the hands" has to be figured out by the context and by traditional usage. The grammatical construction favors the following parallelism:

And they [the Hellenists] chose. . . [the Seven],
whom they set before the apostles,
and . . . they laid hands upon them (Acts 6:5f).

Thus it could appear that "they" represents the Hellenists in each case. The third "they," however, could have as its subject "the apostles." Traditional usage would favor that they would be the ones to lay hands (as will be seen more clearly from the discussion below). The RSV removes the ambiguity of the Greek and leans toward allowing that the Hellenists laid hands upon the Seven:

[A]nd they [the Hellenists] chose. . . [the Seven].
These they set before the apostles,
and they . . . laid hands upon them (Acts 6:5f RSV).

The NRSV rectifies this and renders the text so as to imply (on the basis of traditional usage and not the Greek text) that only the apostles laid hands:

[A]nd they [the Hellenists] chose. . . [the Seven].
They had these men stand before the apostles,
who . . . laid their hands upon them (Acts 6:5f NRSV).

*Every translation is also an interpretation.*

From this it becomes clear how every translation is also an interpretation. If you are not using the RSV or NRSV, check to see how your Bible translates Acts 6:5f. Write it here:

1. Read the entire first text: Numbers 27:15-23. Using the clues offered by the text, fill in the chart below:

| TWO ORDINATIONS COMPARED | Num. 27 | Acts 6 |
|---|---|---|
| Who selects candidates? | | |
| On what grounds? | | |
| Who lays hands? | | |
| Upon whose head? | | |
| Is the Spirit received before/during/after rite? | | |
| What is the new identity conferred by the rite? | | |
| Who is present? | | |
| What does priest do? | | |

2. Now read Acts 6:1-7 and fill in the right-hand column in the chart above. Having done so, what conclusions can you draw? What, if anything, surprises you?

3. Now for some searching questions. Why, in the case of Moses ordaining Joshua, does the priest Eleazar not lay hands upon the candidate?

In the case of Acts 6, the text does not even draw our attention to the fact the priests may have been present during the ordination. On the basis of Case Two, it is clear that the Twelve were not regarded as "priests." In Acts 6:7b, however, Luke does allude to the fact that many temple priests did embrace the "faith" of the disciples. Hence, it is quite possible that some Jewish priests were also present at the ordination of the Seven. If so, why do these priests not lay hands upon the candidates?

*Acts 6 does not draw our attention to the fact the priests may have been present.*

4. Within the Jewish tradition, Case Two has already made it plain that only the sons of Aaron are eligible to be priests and that this priestly identity comes by virtue of having the right genes and not by virtue of any rite of ordination. What conclusion must one draw, consequently, regarding how the rite of ordination does function within the Jewish milieu of Numbers 27 and Acts 6?

5. In both cases, what is the correlation between the "new identity" which ordination confers and the already established identify of the one who lays hands?

6. Why is it essential, in both cases, that the laying on of hands not be done privately? Why must the whole community be present?

7. What must one conclude from the fact that, in both instances, the text makes it clear that the candidate has received the "Spirit of God" prior to the rite?

*Speculate why Jesus did not ordain anyone.*

8. The Gospels never present Jesus as addressing the issue of ordination. He commissioned the Twelve to go out to proclaim the kingdom, to heal, and to exorcise—the very same deeds which characterized his own ministry (Mark 3:14, 6:12f; Matt 10:1-8; Luke 9:1-3); yet, he never ordained them. Had he done so, the importance of this act would have surely been registered in the Gospels and appealed to as the reason whereby the early church practiced its own ordinations. Speculate, on the basis of what you have discovered about the nature of ordination, why Jesus not only did not but could not ordain anyone.

*Speculate why the Twelve decided to lay hands upon the Seven even though they had not received anything from Jesus on this matter.*

9. Going even further, speculate why the Twelve (without any debate or fanfare or explanation) decided to lay hands upon the Seven as a rite of "ordination" even though they had not received anything from Jesus on this matter.

As a consequence, what are the historical origins of the rite of ordination as practiced by the church?

10. What startling discoveries did you make while exploring this Case Study? Describe them for yourself here:




11. Did this Case Study raise any fundamental questions for you while you were completing it? If so, note them here so that you can return to them at a later moment?




Completion time = _____
Total time used on this Case = _____ minutes

You have now completed your third Case Study. Here again, something of the character and origins of ordination have been examined within the Jewish milieu. Needless to say, some of what contemporary churches say about ordination may differ from what the early church intended and practiced by its ordinations. This contrast will be examined shortly. For the moment, set everything aside, rest, and, once you are renewed, return for the analysis.

## Analysis

The following short catechism has been prepared by way of capturing and expanding the insights of this Case Study.

**1 Q**: According to the Christian Scriptures, what is the origin of the rite of ordination?

**A**: Even while the early church evidently practiced ordination a few short years after the death of Jesus (Acts 6), none of the Evangelists thought that this practice stemmed from some explicit mandate on the part of Jesus. Nor can it be simply presumed in the face of the complete silence of the Gospel accounts that at some time Jesus ordained the Twelve but that the Evangelists failed to mention it because it had no importance for them. Rather, had Jesus done so, it would have been decisively important and someone along the line would have appealed to what Jesus had done by way of framing the practice of the early church. Silence on this

*None of the Evangelists thought that ordination stemmed from some explicit mandate on the part of Jesus.*

point, therefore, demonstrates that it never happened. Jesus never ordained anyone.

What then was the origin of the ordinations in Acts 6? Jewish tradition. The Jewish disciples of Jesus lived in a tradition which provided them with an apt rite whereby successors could be publicly designated. Hence, when the need arose, the disciples of Jesus simply functioned as effective pastors by adopting what was already available to them in their shared Jewish tradition.

Here again, as in Case One, it must be presupposed that the disciples of Jesus were trained in the art of pastoral responsiveness. Even without any mandate on the part of Jesus, the Twelve demonstrated their genius for adapting the Jewish tradition of laying on hands. These simple pastoral origins again demonstrate that Jesus did not train his disciples to be lock-step conformists who were not permitted to go beyond what Jesus had expressly taught and done himself.

**2 Q**: What is the character of ordination as seen in the practice of Numbers 27 and Acts 6?

**A**: Ordination constitutes that public rite whereby a person's public identity is irreversibly altered.

In the first instance examined, Moses appealed to the Lord to "appoint a leader for this community . . . so that the community of the Lord may not be like a sheep without a shepherd" (Numbers 27:17). At that moment, Moses was the acknowledged shepherd of the Lord's people, but his days were numbered. In response, the Lord designated Joshua as a suitable candidate, "a man in whom the spirit/Spirit dwells," and described the appropriate rite: "Lay your hands on him" (Numbers 27:18).

Since neither Moses nor the people had any need to raise any questions regarding the nature of "laying hands," this implies that there is no question here of the Lord inventing "from scratch" a rite entirely unfamiliar to Moses and the people. In fact, the presumption of the text is that both Moses and the people already understood that this rite had the effect of transforming Joshua in the sight of the people and the priests. After the rite, Joshua was perceived as sharing in the authority and the ministry of Moses. When Moses laid hands upon him, he effectively and permanently changed Joshua's public identity in the sight of the people. The rite had expressive power which signified: "From this time forward, you who have accepted my ministry must also accept the ministry of Joshua in my name."

In Acts 6, a parallel instance presents itself. At Pentecost (Acts 2), many foreign-born Jews entered into the Jesus movement. In all probability, most of the Twelve did not speak Greek and most of the new members did not understand Aramaic; hence, in the daily distribution of the wisdom and the goods of the community, the foreign-born Jews (i.e., the Hellenists) were slighted. Luke does not go into details, but simply suggests that things got so bad that even "their widows" were neglected. Accordingly, the Twelve summoned the body of disciples and suggested that they discern among themselves "seven men of good repute, full of the spirit/Spirit and of wisdom" (Acts 6:3). Then the Twelve "laid their hands upon them," irreversibly transforming their public identity. Here, too, the rite had expressive power which signified: "You who have accepted our ministry must now accept the ministry of these seven in our name."

*The rite had expressive power which signified: "You who have accepted our ministry must now accept the ministry of these seven in our name."*

**3 Q**: Were either of these ordinations understood as conferring the "priesthood"?

**A**: No. In Case Two one discovered that the Jewish tradition of priesthood was reserved by the Lord to the sons of Aaron. Hence, within the Jewish tradition, ordination was never understood as either necessary or capable of conferring "priesthood." In both of the cases considered, a lay office is clearly conferred. Moses, who never understood himself as a priest, used ordination in order to confer upon Joshua his own identity as shepherd of the Lord's people. The Twelve did the same thing for the Seven.

*Within the Jewish tradition, ordination was never understood as capable of conferring "priesthood."*

During the second century, when the office of bishop was increasingly being understood as exercising the high priesthood,

---

### Note Regarding "Deacons"

Church tradition has viewed the Seven as "deacons" and designated Act 6 as the historical origins of the diaconate. Modern scholars, however, have been hesitant to credit these views as what Luke had in mind.

Why so? In the first place, Luke never explicitly names the Seven as "deacons." In the second place, while the term "deacon" (*diakonos*) occurs some thirty times in the Christian Scriptures, it almost never designates a specific office but rather points to "serving" as the special character of all Christian ministry. For example, Paul frequently designates himself as "a deacon" (1 Cor 3:5; 2 Cor 3:6, 6:4; Eph 3:7; Phil 1:1; Col 1:23, 25) and, in two instances, does not hesitate to designate Jesus as "deacon" (Rom 13:4, 15:8). Finally, when it comes time for Luke to specify what the Seven do, Stephen and Philip are routinely characterized as doing public preaching, healing, and exorcism (Acts 6:8-10, 8:6-13)—the very same ministries Luke designates for the Twelve.

As a result, a growing number of scholars would be more inclined to perceive the Seven as taking on the identity and ministry of the Twelve as far as the Hellenists are concerned. Raymond Brown, for instance, concludes that "they [the Seven] seem to have been the top-level administrators for the Hellenistic Christians" (1980: 326).

*When all official ministries were understood as grades of priesthood, then it would have appeared that every ordination was a priestly ordination.*

then and only then would the community have perceived that the "new identity" of the episcopal candidate included a priestly character. When, during the middle ages, all official ministries in the church were understood as grades of priesthood, then it would have appeared that every ordination was, first and foremost, a priestly ordination. The Catholic tradition which has come down to us, therefore, is simply the normative expression of medieval theology and experience.

The churches of the Reformation rejected large features of medieval piety and theology. While these churches continued to practice ordination as a "church ordinance" which irreversible designated the official preachers of the Gospel and ministers of the sacraments, they entirely rejected the priestly character of these ordinations. This is why the Protestant churches use such terms as "pastor," "elder," and "ordained minister" but never "priest."

**4 Q**: Does the laying on of hands serve to confer the Spirit?

**A**: Within the inspired texts of the Hebrew and Christian Scriptures, the reception and manifestation of the Spirit is the necessary prior condition for anyone who would be a suitable candidate for ordination. Even without ordination, therefore, the Spirit of God is the author and the source of all ministries. Every ordination rite, therefore, serves to acknowledge the charism which has already been received.

*Every ordination rite serves to acknowledge the charism which has already been received.*

In the case of Joshua, the Lord himself notes that here is "a man in whom the Spirit dwells" (Numbers 27:18). In the case of the Seven, the Hellenistic community is charged to discern among their own those who are "full of the Spirit and of wisdom" (Acts 6:3). In effect, therefore, the prior gift of the Spirit is the tangible sign that such persons are fitted for the ministry which they are about to undertake.

**5 Q**: Does this also apply to contemporary Roman Catholic ordinations?

**A**: Yes. After Vatican II, the Catholic rites of ordination were reexamined and revised so as to more aptly express and impress their essential character. Within the renewed rite of presbyterial ordination, therefore, it is evident that the gathered church petitions the Father, the source of all grace, to augment and sustain the Spirit that has *already been received*. The Prayer of Consecration which the bishop sings or prays "in a loud voice" and "with his hands extended" (rubrics) over the newly ordained clearly expresses this. According to the mind of Pope Paul VI, the key words in this prayer are the following:

> We ask you, all-powerful Father, give these servants of yours the dignity of the presbyterate. Renew the Spirit of holiness within them. By your divine gift, may they attain the second order in the hierarchy and exemplify right conduct in their lives (*Roman Pontifical* 22).

The ordaining bishop here is not using the imperial or majestic "we." Rather, he is giving voice to the shared prayer of all the presbyters who, just prior to this prayer, have laid their hands upon those being ordained and who, at the moment the bishop prays, "remain at the sides of the bishop" (rubric). The prayer acknowledges that the Father is the source and sustainer of all ministry. Accordingly, in the name of all, the bishop petitions the Father that he would give his "servants" the dignity of the presbyterate (which they did not have) and renew "the Spirit of holiness" (which they did have). To this prayer, all the faithful gather in the church give their assent by responding: "Amen!"

**6 Q**: Does a Cinderella-like transformation take place during an ordination rite?

**A**: Yes and No. As seen in the case of Num 27 and Acts 6, the rite of ordination effectively and permanently changes the public identity of the one being ordained. In effect, this is akin to a Cinderella-like transformation wherein, according to the fable, even the step-mother and sister are forced to perceive their "sister" differently as she dances in the admiration of the prince. On the other hand, the human powers (as elevated by grace) of the candidate are not perceptively increased due to the rite.

Some Catholic priests whom I know have personally confided in me that they were scared, excited, or anxious during the rite. All in all, none of them report that their powers of compassion, healing, service, theological resourcefulness, and singing in tune dramatically increased as a direct result of the rite.

My own early religious teachers were under the spell of a quasi-magical notion of priestly powers and of priestly ordination; however, they did not fail to note that a bishop ordains *only* that "man who, after a sufficient period of preparation and trial, gives signs that he has been called by God to the priesthood" (*Baltimore Catechism*). Such "signs" included not only a sound moral character and a theological training but also the Spirit-filled aptitude for priestly ministry. In effect, therefore, the exaggerated notions of my early teachers were always tacitly corrected by sound Catholic practice.

Even while the Spirit usually does not provoke sudden transformations during the rite itself, this should not obscure the fact that

*The bishop petitions the Father that he would give his "servants" the dignity of the presbyterate (which they did not have) and renew "the Spirit of holiness" (which they did have).*

*Some Catholic priests were scared, excited, or anxious during the rite.*

the whole life of an ordained minister is existentially dependent upon grace. As a consequence, every minister of the Gospel needs the urgent prayers of his community not only during the ordination rite but long afterwards. In good times and in bad, in sickness and in health, the minister needs to be open to the Spirit of God who consoles and challenges, who renews and corrects, and who enables the realization of those fresh and prophetic possibilities which are ripe for realization and which are urgently needed by the community. The graced future of every ordained minister, consequently, far exceeds the sum total of the job descriptions and expectations of both congregation and bishop. Ordained ministers are not merely public functionaries; rather, they are always, first and foremost, "servants of God" attentive to where the Spirit would lead them and their communities. "Today, when you hear his voice, do not harden your hearts" (Heb 3:7, 4:7; Ps 95:7).

*Ordained ministers are "servants of God" attentive to where the Spirit would lead them and their communities.*

**7 Q:** What are the essential elements for a valid ordination?

**A:** The Dutch Dominican, Edward Schillebeeckx, notes that three "essential elements" are required:

(1) Since the one who bears office also represents the community, the *community's consent* to the leadership of a certain candidate must be expressed in one way or another. The question which occurs in the traditional liturgy, "Do you know whether they are worthy?" is certainly a real expression of this consent, but it is in fact formalistic. . . .

(2) Reception normally takes place by the college of the already existing office-bearers *under the imposition of hands*. . .

(3) Reception into the office of the Church takes place *under the invocation of the Holy Spirit* (*epiklesis*). In this invocation of the Holy Spirit (which is concretely expressed by the laying on of hands), God is implored to send the charisma of office. . . . This act is what makes it publicly legitimate for a member of the community who is usually already charismatically gifted to act as a holder of office in the Church . . . (Schillebeeckx: 576-578).

The World Council of Churches, in its own consensus statement regarding ordination, emphasized that "the laying on of hands . . . is at one and the same time invocation of the Holy Spirit (*epiklesis*); sacramental sign; acknowledgment of gifts and commitment" (WCC: 41). Relative to the "invocation of the Holy Spirit," the WCC statement aptly highlights the dependent and proleptic aspects of every ordination:

"The Spirit blows where it will" (John 3:3); the invocation of the Spirit implies the absolute dependence on God for the outcome of the Church's prayer. This means that the Spirit may set new forces in motion and open new possibilities "far more abundantly than all that we ask or think" (Ephesians 3:20) (WCC: 42).

**8 Q**: Are there prospects today for the mutual recognition of ministry between Catholics and Protestants?

**A**: In the past, Catholics regarded their own norms for ordination as universally binding. Thus, it was quite easy for Catholics to judge Protestant ordinations as invalid on the grounds that their ordinations neglected either to use the proper rite (*defectus formae*) or to have the proper intention (*defectus intentionis*). Protestants, for their part, were prone to perceive Catholic "priests" as the vain invention of a wayward church which operated outside the norms set down in the canonical Scriptures.

Following the principles laid down in Vatican II, it is no longer possible for Catholics to judge "different from us" as always and necessarily "invalid." Meanwhile recent historical and biblical studies (such as those in this Case Study) undertaken by Protestants and Catholics alike have gone a long way toward enabling separated churches to establish shared perceptions and conviction of the essential elements involved in ordination and in ordained ministry.

Meanwhile as the Roman Catholic renewal of "priesthood" is being tempered and purified by a return to service of the Gospel and service to God's people, some Protestants have been inclined to perceive within Catholic practice a dynamic continuity with God's intention for ministry as expressed in the Christian Scriptures. In a similar vein, some Catholics have been able to understand the Reformation's separation of ministerial ordination from the notions of both "priesthood" and of "sacrament" as legitimate culturally conditioned expressions of evangelically inspired protest. Moreover, since the Catholic bishops of Vatican II decreed that "the Spirit of God has not refrained from using them [the separated Churches] as means of salvation" (*Decree on Ecumenism*, sec 3), the way is open even now for some Catholics to acknowledge that this must apply to the ordination rite and the ordained ministers within these churches as well.

*It is no longer possible for Catholics to judge "different from us" as always and necessarily "invalid."*

The official mutual recognition of ministers and of ordination rites is not yet possible. There are still legitimate and serious concerns which prevent such a mutual recognition. Those churches practicing episcopal ordination, for instance, usually have severe difficulties in recognizing ordinations conferred by presbyters, elders, or district supervisors. Likewise, those churches ordaining women usually have severe difficulties in recognizing the "fullness" of ministry in those churches where, theologically and pastorally, ordination is limited to one sex.

*There are still legitimate and serious concerns which prevent a mutual recognition of ministers.*

All those who acknowledge the same Father, Son, and Spirit, however, are being led. Acting with truth, justice, and compassion, it is enough that separated Christians remain open to a future wherein the Spirit would exceed their wildest imaginings. The disciples of Jesus once reported that they sought to hinder those who were "casting out demons in your [Jesus'] name" but "not following us" (Mark 9:38). Jesus, in his turn, taught them an ecumenical lesson which has a continued importance for us as well.

## Application to the Churches Today

On the basis of everything that has been discovered above, what does this say about "ordinations" as practiced by your church today? Generate a few spinoffs and write them down here:

## Further Readings for Case Three

Brown, Raymond E.
> *Priest and Bishop: Biblical Reflections.* New York: Paulist, 1970.
>
> "*Episkopē and Episkopos:* The New Testament Evidence," *Theological Studies* 41:322-338, 1980.
>
> *The Churches the Apostles Left Behind.* New York: Paulist, 1984.

Daube, David.
> "The Laying on of Hands," *The New Testament and Rabbinic Judaism.* London: Athone Press, 1956.

U.S.A. National Committee of the Lutheran World Federation and the [Catholic] Bishops' Committee for Ecumenical and Interreligious Affairs,
> *Lutherans and Catholics in Dialogue IV: Eucharist and Ministry.* Washington, D.C.: United States Catholic Conference and Philadelphia: Fortress, 1970.

Martos, Joseph
> *Doors to the Sacred: A Historical Introduction to the Sacraments in the Catholic Church.* Garden City: Doubleday. pp. 455-485, 1981.

McBrien, Richard.
    *Catholicism.* Minneapolis: Winston. pp. 798-811, 1980.

Milavec, Aaron
    *To Empower as Jesus Did: Acquiring Spiritual Power Through Apprenticeship.* Lewiston: The Edwin Mellen Press. Esp. pp. 24-31, 1982.

Rahner, Karl
    *The Church and the Sacraments.* New York: Herder and Herder, 1963.

Schillebeeckx, Edward
    "The Catholic Understanding of Office in the Church." *Theological Studies,* 30:567-587, 1969.

World Council of Churches
    *Baptism, Eucharist and Ministry: Faith in Order Paper No. 111.* Geneva: World Council of Churches, 1982.

# CASE FOUR

# When Jesus Sided With the Women

*The exclusion of women from ordination has been taken up in a fresh and vigorous manner because women have progressively taken significant roles in public life.*

The issue of Jesus' relation to women has come up again and again as both sides of the women's ordination issue appeal to Jesus in order to give authority to their respective positions. Even in the Middle Ages, when the new university theologians took up the issue of the exclusion of women from ordination, Thomas Aquinas, Bonaventure and Duns Scotus reexamined the Christian Scriptures and raised the question of a possible miscarriage of justice in the Church's practice of not ordaining women. In our own day, this question has been taken up within the churches in a fresh and vigorous manner because women, leaving behind the traditional seclusion of their forebears, have progressively taken significant roles in public life.

During the years prior to the Civil War, the abolitionist movement greatly impacted many Northern evangelical Protestant denominations. These churches came to perceive all class and racial divisions within the church as opposed to God's purposes. The next logical step was to perceive woman's exclusion from the ordained ministry and decision making of the churches as also opposed to God's purposes.

Rev. Antoinette Brown, a Congregationalist and a graduate of Oberlin College, was the first woman ordained. During her ordination service on 15 September 1853, Pastor Luther Lee delivered a sermon, "Woman's Right to Preach the Gospel." Before the century was over, the Free Methodist Churches, the Salvation Army, and a few Baptist congregations were ordaining women. The mainline churches, which valued the making of theological and pastoral consensus before breaking with tradition, were much slower in taking this initiative. The Lutheran Churches in Norway ordained women after 1938; in Denmark, after 1947; in Sweden, after 1953. In the United States, the United Presbyterian Church began to ordain women in 1956; the Lutheran Church in America and the American Lutheran Church (which have since united), in 1970; and the Protestant Episcopal Church, in 1976. This latter Church consecrated its first woman, Rev. Barbara Harris, as bishop in 1989.

Within Roman Catholic circles, there has been a divided response. Some Roman Catholics judged that the roles assigned to women in Genesis and in the Gospels positively precluded calling women to formal ministry. These same believers judged that those churches which ordained women would be still further removed from possible communion with the Roman Church. On the other hand, many Catholics greeted these ordinations favorably and saw in them a prophetic application of the gospel. The world-renowned Jesuit theologian Karl Rahner, for example, wrote in the early 70s to a Lutheran pastor in Bavaria as follows:

> The practice which the Catholic Church has of not ordaining women to the priesthood has no binding theological character.... The actual practice is not a dogma; it is purely and simply based on a human and historic reflection which was valid in the past in cultural and social conditions which are presently changing rapidly (cited in Stendhal: 160).

With Catholics privately and publicly divided on this issue, it was inevitable that some bishops would press Rome for some sort of definitive solution lest official silence leave open a false hope on the part of many. Thus, Paul VI assigned the issue to the Congregation for the Doctrine of the Faith (CDF) in 1975. The CDF, in turn, asked for a report from the Pontifical Biblical Commission (PBC) on this issue.

The PBC sent its final report to the CDF in June of 1976. The Commission's report concluded that, on the basis of the Christian Scriptures alone, the issue cannot be decided "in a clear way and once and for all [time]" (96). This is so, the report declared, because "the New Testament never uses the technical term *hiereus* ["priest"] for the Christian ministry" (92). But, even beyond this, the "role of leadership in the [early church] communities . . . was always held by men in conformity with Jewish custom" (95). The PBC report, consequently, did not think that decisions made within the cultural conditions prevailing in the first century ought to automatically predetermine what the church might decide would be right and proper within altered cultural circumstances.

The CDF issued its final report in October of 1976 under the title, *On the Question of the Admission of Women to the Ministerial Priesthood*. The CDF embraced significant segments of the analysis found within the PBC report; however, in contrast to the earlier report, the CDF unambiguously came to an negative conclusion: "[T]he Church, in fidelity to the example of the Lord, does not consider herself authorized to admit women to priestly ordination" (CDF: 4).

*Leadership in the [early church] communities was always held by men in conformity with Jewish custom.*

The CDF report is extraordinary in three ways:

1. The report openly acknowledges that the negative conclusion "will perhaps cause pain" (CDF: 5). In my reading of official church documents, this is the first time that I have found an expression of sensitivity directed towards those who will suffer because of a decision being made on their behalf. The report later makes mention that "some women feel they have a vocation to the priesthood" (CDF: 16). It is perhaps to these women and their supporters that the framers of the document acknowledge that their conclusion "will perhaps cause pain" (CDF: 5).

2. The CDF report never falls into the trap of supposing that either Jesus or his disciples thought of themselves as "priests." Rather, the report consistently affirms that, even though Jesus' "attitude toward women was quite different from that of his milieu" (CDF: 6), he did not, nonetheless, entrust *the apostolic charge* (CDF: 7) to any women, not even to his own mother. In like fashion, when considering the practice of the early church, the report correctly notes that the apostles had worked with certain women for the sake of the gospel; yet, "at no time was there a question of conferring *ordination* on these women" (CDF: 8). Here again, the CDF report never suggests that these early ordinations involve "priesthood" as such. Rather the surmise is that, if the "apostolic charge" of Jesus and the "ordinations" of the early church were reserved entirely to men, then it follows that the ordained ministry of the church today ought to follow the same practice.

3. The CDF report is also noteworthy in so far as it squarely acknowledges that, as culture changes, the practice of the church can and sometimes must change. The report openly acknowledges that some of the apostolic ordinances relative to women, as illustrated by the obligation of women to wear a veil on their heads (1 Cor 11:2-16), were culturally conditioned and accordingly have been changed. But then the report continues:

> However, the Apostle's forbidding of women "to speak" in the assemblies (cf. 1 Corinthians 14:34-35; 1 Timothy 2:12) is of a different nature, and exegetes define its meaning in this way: Paul in no way opposes the right, which he elsewhere recognizes as possessed by women, to prophesy in the assembly (cf. 1 Corinthians 11:5); the prohibition solely concerns the official function of teaching in the Christian assembly. For Saint Paul this prescription is bound up with the divine plan of creation (cf. 1 Corinthians 11:7; Genesis 2:18-24): it would be difficult to see in it the expression of a cultural fact (CDF: 9).

In effect, therefore, the report identifies the exclusion by Paul of women from "the official function of teaching" as not culturally determined but as theologically necessary due to "the divine plan of creation." When the report considers Jesus' exclusion of women from "the apostolic charge," the same distinction sounds through. The report even goes so far as to say that no one can prove that Jesus' exclusion of women was culturally determined precisely because Jesus was known to have opposed other "prejudices" regarding women:

> No one himself has ever proved—and it is clearly impossible to prove—that this attitude [of Jesus] is inspired only by social and cultural reasons. As we have seen, an examination of the Gospels shows on the contrary that Jesus broke with the prejudices of his time, by widely contravening the discrimination practiced with regard to women. One therefore cannot maintain that, by not calling women to enter the group of Apostles, Jesus was simply being guided by reasons of expediency (CDF: 9).

In sum, while the CDF report is remarkably sensitive to modern scholarship and to the pain it might cause; nonetheless, it's bottom line is that "Christ chose 'those he wanted' (Mark 3:13)" (CDF: 16). Accordingly, if the Roman Catholic Church continues to choose *only men* for the priestly ministry, she continues to do so, not because of any prejudice against women shaped by patriarchal patterns of culture, but solely because she is faithful to Christ.

*The Roman Catholic Church continues to choose only men solely because she is faithful to Christ.*

## Purpose

The purpose of this Case Study is not to resolve the narrow issue of women's ordination. Rather, the purpose is to develop insights regarding Jesus' interaction with women set against the backdrop of the cultural norms prevailing within his society. From these insights, one will be better equipped to gauge not just one or the other issue regarding women, but to discern something of the abiding and prophetic witness of the Gospels which brings "good news" to women—in the first-century, today, and tomorrow.

*The purpose of this Case Study is to develop insights regarding Jesus' interaction with women.*

Before getting started, you are again invited to record your initial perceptions to three questions. By recording your spontaneous judgments now, you will be providing yourself with a declaration of your preliminary understanding of the issues. After completing the Case Study, you will then be able to reread your initial reflections and gauge to what degree you have been broadened or transformed by your inquiries. The three questions designed for this purpose are as follows:

1. Do you agree with the report of the CDF when it notes that "Jesus broke with the prejudices of his time" respecting women? _____ If so, what evidence from the Christian Scriptures can you offer to support this?

2. Do you agree that, even though Jesus was counter-cultural regarding his attitude toward women, he did not choose to give women the "apostolic charge" to preach and heal in his name? _____ If he did not, why not?

3. Based on your reasoning above, do you regard this as a decision which binds his followers for all times and all places? _____ How so?

At this time, if you are so inclined, take your Christian Scriptures (New Testament) in your hands and pray that the Spirit of God may guide you in rightly understanding the truth about women in their relationship to Jesus.

Translation = _____

Starting time = _____ (120-160 minutes needed)

## To Whom Did Jesus Preach?

Each of the Synoptic Gospels presents Jesus as meeting with Jews in local synagogues in order to preach the good news of the forthcoming Kingdom of God. Mark, for instance, summarizes the early years of Jesus' ministry by saying, "And he went throughout Galilee, preaching in their synagogues" (Mark 1:39).

1. When Jesus entered into these synagogues, did he find both women and men there? _____ If so, what did the women do there? What were they not permitted to do?

Scholars today have difficulty establishing how synagogues functioned at the time of Jesus due to the scarcity of written records which have come down to us. Jesus lived in a culture which prized oral transmission and personal apprenticeships for passing on its heritage. Not even Jesus, it must be remembered, thought it necessary or advisable to write down his teaching or to have one of his disciples do so in his name.

Rabbinic Judaism (stemming from the synagogues of the Pharisees) had the same high regard for oral transmission. Accordingly, one has to wait until the year 200 CE before rabbinic Judaism produces its first official written document (the *Mishnah*). Even in the *Mishnah* one does not get a detailed set of prayers or customs governing synagogue life. As in the case of the Gospels (written between 60 and 90 CE), those things which everyone knows by personal experience don't have to be told. They only get referred to while treating of other matters.

If one would go into an Orthodox synagogue today, however, one would discover something of the conservative traditions which reach back to the formative period of rabbinic Judaism and, most probably, back to the Galilean synagogues of Jesus' day as well. Orthodox Judaism, for example, holds that only Jewish men have the obligation to learn to read and to interpret Torah and to pray three times a day. Women, given their household duties (especially relative to children), are expected to serve God by freeing their men folk for prayer and study in the synagogue. Even when women do come to the synagogue, Orthodox men and women do not study or pray together, even should they be husband and wife. According to tradition, men take the first places in the synagogue. Men alone read from the Torah. Men alone discuss and teach the Torah. Men alone lead the congregation in prayer. Women and girls take their place in the rear (or, more recently, in a balcony especially prepared for them) and observe the men searching the Scriptures and discussing what God would have them do and be. A woman, in the normal course of things, is expected to be guided in these things, not by her own insights gained through training in the synagogue, but by the di-

*Scholars today have difficulty establishing how synagogues functioned at the time of Jesus.*

*Orthodox women are expected to serve God by freeing their men folk for prayer and study in the synagogue.*

rections of her father and mother, and, once married, by the directives of her husband.

2. While Jesus is preaching or teaching in the synagogue, does he address the men alone, or does he address the women as well? _____ It would be impossible to decide this on the basis of any direct evidence. On the basis of indirect evidence, however, much can be decided.

*On the basis of indirect evidence, much can be decided.*

What indirect evidence? To begin with, examine the experience implied in the parables of Jesus. When you do so, you will note that some of the parables of Jesus directly speak to the experiences of men. For example:

The Sower (Mark 4:3-8, Matthew 13:3-8, Luke 8:5-8)
The Wicked Husbandman (Mark 12:1-11, Matthew 21:33-44, Luke 20:9-18)
The Doorkeeper (Mark 13:33-37, Luke 12:35-38)
The Fisherman's Net (Matthew 13:47-50)
The Lost Sheep (Matthew 18:12-14, Luke 15:4-7)

These five parables appeal to the tasks and experiences which traditional Jewish society associated exclusively with men. Women could observe men doing these things; but, by and large, they normally would not be expected to relate to these tasks since, in the normal course of events, they would rarely, if ever, have a chance to perform them.

*Jesus has a set of parables which specifically featured the experience of women.*

On the other hand, Jesus has a set of parables which specifically featured the experience of women. These would be the following:

The Yeast (Matthew 13:33, Luke 13:20f)
The Ten Maidens (Matthew 25:1-13)
The Lost Coin (Luke 15:5-10)
The Unjust Judge (Luke 18:1-8)

Here again, men could be expected to have observed women kneading yeast into dough and have witnessed the bride's maids going out with lamps to welcome the groom and his friends. However, it could be assumed that men would not be expected to relate to these roles since they would never have an occasion to assume such roles themselves.

In reading the evidence here, one must keep traditional Jewish society in mind. In contemporary society, some men do take pride in making loaves of bread from scratch. In the world of Jesus, however, the grinding of grain, the kneading of dough, and the baking of bread were the daily chores of women. In contemporary society, men and women usually arrive together at the church for a wedding. After the wedding, they go together to the reception. No one has to wait. Within traditional societies, however, the bride and her female attendants sometimes waited for hours in her home while the friends of the groom took their merry old time assembling at the groom's home for a "bachelor's party" before walking together to the bride's house where the wedding was to take place.

What does it say about Jesus that he would not only notice that the women were kept waiting but, as in the case of his parable, kept waiting for such a long time that many fell asleep and their lamps went out? The men, it must be remembered, were having a "bachelor's party" and, in their merry-making, not expected to be attentive to the women who were waiting with the bride. What does this parable, focusing as it does on women's experience, say about Jesus? To whom must it be presumed is Jesus directing such parables?

*Jesus noticed that the women were kept waiting for such a long time that many fell asleep.*

The Gospel writers implicitly recognize that Jesus told Kingdom parables using experiences which were sometimes proper to women and sometimes proper to men. This evidence indirectly testifies that Jesus wished the Kingdom to be intelligible to both women and men. Within the synagogue, therefore, it can be presumed that Jesus occasionally directly addressed those women who sat behind the men and who were, in most cases, entirely lost sight of by the men who sat around Jesus. Jesus, however, did not lose sight of them—even if he was not able to actually see them.

*It can be presumed that Jesus occasionally directly addressed those women who sat behind the men.*

Furthermore, since women's experiences continued to show up within the Gospel parables collected by and for the Jesus movement, this provides indirect evidence about the audience to which the apos-

---

### Women's Experience in Today's Church

At this point, we have noted that Jesus deliberately fashioned his message so as to make direct use of the experience proper to women. The early church did the same.

But how about the contemporary churches? Have the male ordained ministers, the male theologians, and the male catechists continued to follow the lead of Jesus? Do women having official functions in the church do any better in this domain?

Find out for yourself. Listen to them and make some sort of tally for yourself as to how often their illustrative stories capitalize on the experiences proper to women, to men, to both?

In a future edition of this book, I would like to include the informal inquiries of my readers relative to this issue. Hence, please be so kind as to share your results by writing me c/o Sheed and Ward. I thank you in advance.

tles and the communities which they left behind directed their message. What would you conclude from this evidence?

## Jesus Healing Women

3. Not only does Jesus specifically expect women to understand his message in terms of their own proper experience as women, he also intends women to be healed.

The healing narratives of Jesus sometimes appear to modern Christians as reporting "his divinely produced miracles" which are more or less divorced from "his teaching." In medieval Christianity, the healings of Jesus were at least perceived as proving his worth as a messenger of God. Thomas Aquinas, for example, proposed that "God enabled man to work miracles . . . in confirmation of the doctrine that a man teaches" (Summa Theologica III, q. 43, a. 2, co.).

*Within a Jewish horizon of understanding, a much more intimate connection exists between hearing and healing.*

When the Gospel accounts are properly reread within a Jewish horizon of understanding, however, a much more intimate connection exists between hearing and healing. It is this connection which allows Jesus to say to his disciples, "Blessed are your eyes for they see, and your ears, for they hear" (Matthew 13:16), while he accuses the Pharisees of being "blind" even when they claim that they see (Matthew 15:14; 23:16, 17, 19, 24, 26). There is not sufficient space to develop this point in detail. It suffices, for the moment, however, to recognize that the Jesus who addresses women's experience is the same Jesus who is able to bring healing to women. Hearing and seeing, seeing and healing, go hand in hand.

Matthew suggests the intimate connection between hearing and healing when he situates the Sermon on the Mount just prior to ten healing narratives. These healings are as follows:

Healing of the Leper (Matthew 8:2-4)*
Healing of the Centurion's Servant (8:5-13)
Healing of Peter's Mother-in-Law (8:14f)
Healing of the Fear During the Storm (8:23-27)
Healing of Two Gadarene Demoniacs (8:28-34)*
Healing of the Paralytic (9:1-8)*
Healing of the Woman With Flow of Blood (9:20-22)
Healing of the Ruler's Daughter Who Died (9:18-26)
Healing of Two Blind People (9:27-31)*
Healing of the Dumb Demoniac (9:32-33)*

*English translations frequently obscure the intent of the Greek original.*

Take a moment and place a check mark before any healing narrative above which could be interpreted as applying to a women.

English translations frequently obscure the intent of the Greek original because, at every point, English rules of grammar dictate that the masculine pronoun is to be used when the noun to which it refers could be either a man or a woman. To explore what this means, read the narrative of the Healing of the Leper (Matthew 8:2-4). Was the "leper" a man or a woman? _____

The RSV, for instance, says, "Jesus touched *him*" and "*his* leprosy was cleansed." The original Greek, meanwhile, begins the narrative by referring to "a leper" (lepros), a term which could equally refer to either a female or male leper. Since *lepros* happens to be a masculine noun, the remainder of the narrative uses masculine pronouns by way of achieving grammatical agreement. At no point, in the Greek text, can one decide whether "the leper" was a man or a woman. In brief, the original narrative is gender inclusive.

*At no point, in the Greek text, can one decide whether "the leper" was a man or a woman.*

The English language, in contrast, reserves masculine pronouns for males and female pronouns for females and has no way of dealing with the strange aspect of the Greek language wherein "life" (bios) requires masculine pronouns, "truth" (altheia) requires feminine, and "child" (teknon) requires a neuter pronoun. English translations, therefore, in order to be true to English rules of grammar, entirely ignore the Greek system of assigning gender to nouns and pronouns. Thus, in the illustrative case of the Healing of the Leper, while the Greek deliberately leaves open the sex of the leper, English translations (guided by the rule of giving preference to the masculine pronoun) make it appear that the "leper" was a man *and not a woman*.

On the other hand, in the second healing narrative, the servant (*ho pais*) is clearly either a male servant or a biological son of the centurion since the Greek uses the masculine article. Had it been a female servant or daughter, the Greek would have used *hē pais*. Even here, however, the RSV use of "my servant" obscures the fact that the Greek *ho pais* could equally mean "my son." In fact, given the urgency implied in the centurion's personal presence to press his petition, the surmise would be that he is beseeching Jesus to come and heal his paralyzed "son."

The third healing, involving Peter's mother-in-law, is clearly in favor of a woman. The fourth involves the stilling of the storm in favor of the Twelve who, since they are elsewhere named, are known to be exclusively men. In the next case, the "two demoniacs" (*duo daimonizomenoi*) could be of either or of both sexes. Matthew, interestingly enough, clearly altered Mark's account of a single demoniac (Mark 5:1-17) to produce "two" (Matt 8:28).

*The "paralytic" let down through the roof could be either a male or a female.*

The "paralytic" let down through the roof also could be either a male or a female. The RSV has Jesus say, "Take heart, my son, . . . " (Matthew 9:2). The Greek, however, uses "child" (*teknon*, a neuter noun), a term which can be used to designate either a daughter or a son, engendered biologically or spiritually. Since Jesus was not recognized as fathering biological children, the term of address would appear to signify that Jesus recognized the paralytic as someone who was a disciple (cf. parallel use in 1 Timothy 1:1 and Titus 1:1). Here again, therefore, the narrative is gender inclusive.

The remaining cases could be similarly analyzed. Those narratives above which have been found to be gender inclusive have been marked with an asterisk. The overall tally is as follows:

* Two narratives involve men alone.
* Three narratives involve women alone.
* Five narrative are gender inclusive.

*Matthew deliberately used gender inclusive narratives to convey the good news about Jesus.*

Up to this point, you have noted that the preaching and the healing activity of Jesus was sometimes deliberately crafted to serve the needs of women. If one were to judge the case from Matthew's ten healing narratives alone, one might even be tempted to conclude that Jesus according to Matthew's Gospel had a slight preference for women over men. No one, of course, was keeping a tally of how often Jesus assisted women, how often men. Hence, such a conclusion might have no basis in history. Nonetheless, one has to admire Matthew as having deliberately used gender inclusive narratives to convey the good news about Jesus. Unlike the case of the Orthodox synagogue, therefore, one can safely conclude that Matthew clearly intended his message for a mixed audience.

## The Menstruating Woman Who Touched Jesus

Jesus' healing of women is all the more noteworthy in view of the fact that no well-mannered Jewish woman could speak to a stranger (such as Jesus) on the streets.

*When women went out they were expected to be heavily veiled and never to speak to men in public.*

Why so? Traditional Jewish society did not sanction men and women mixing in the public forum. Even husbands and their wives did not socialize together either before or after marriage. The sphere of public life—the market place, the cafe, the synagogue—were almost exclusively the meeting places for men. Women were expected to remain in the private sphere—the courtyard—the only place where women could have free exchange with family, women-friends, and relatives. When women went out of the courtyard, they were expected to be heavily veiled and never to speak to men in public (unless, of course, they were prostitutes). Even at weddings, men danced with men and women danced with women. Anyone who travels to the Middle East and visits small villages relatively untouched by Westernization will find that these traditions still prevail there even today. The novel and film, *The Chosen*, admirably presents how this social segregation continues, in some degree, to function even to this day among Hasidic Jews in New York City.

Think for a moment. In the Gospels, strange men routinely come up to Jesus in public and make their needs knows (e.g., Matt 8:5, 9:18). Do you recall any Jewish woman who did this? _____ If so, make a note here:

Knowing that Jesus functioned in a socially segregated society forces one to redefine the conclusions arrived at above on the basis of inclusive language. The "leper" who came to Jesus in the public arena and knelt before him saying, "Lord, if you will, you can make me clean" (Matt 8:2) does not evoke any public scandal. When Jesus speaks to the Samaritan women at the well, however, his own disciples are scandalized (see John 4;27). As such, it must be supposed that first-century hearers would have presumed, *on the basis of Jewish social convention,* that "the leper" was a man.

*When Jesus speaks to the Samaritan women at the well, his own disciples are scandalized.*

Within Hellenized society, where both Jewish and Gentile women were allowed somewhat greater liberty in public (e.g., Acts 16:13-15), it might have been possible to continue to hear the narrative as gender inclusive. The Gospels, it will be remembered, were written in Greek—the language of Hellenized, chiefly urban, society. As a result, even in the first-century, one might suspect that the deliberate gender inclusiveness of Matthew's narratives would have been more evident to urban Gentiles than to traditional Jews.

4. Look over the other four linguistically inclusive healings noted above and draw a line through any of them which, given the social conventions governing Jewish women, would have to be interpreted by traditional Jews and conservative Gentiles, as applying to men alone.

5. Against this background, read Matthew 9:20-23. What significance is revealed in this woman's strategy to touch the fringe of his garment?

The narrative of the healing of the woman with the flow of blood is framed by the narrative of the healing of a young girl. The older woman had "suffered from a hemorrhage for twelve years" (Matt 9:20, Mark 5:25) while the young girl was "twelve years old" (Mark 5:42 only). If the problem encountered by the older woman is an unregulated menstrual flow (as most scholars suggest), then the original linking by "twelves" might have been calculated to suggest that the young girl was experiencing the trauma of her first period. In any case, both cases involve "touching" women regarded as "unclean."

A striking contrast is also evident. In the case of the dying girl, her father goes to Jesus and pleads with him to help his daughter. For the older woman, however, there does not appear to be any father, any husband, or any son who is sympathetic to her plight and willing to plead her cause. Mark, in his narrative, adds that (male) physicians brought in to heal her only made her worse and depleted her financial resources (her dowry? Mark 5:26). As a result, her strategy, born out of desperation, is to take matters into her own hands. Yet even she cannot risk upsetting Jesus by addressing him in public. What then? She decides to come up behind Jesus and to touch the fringe of his garment.

*For the older woman, there does not appear to be any father, any husband, or any son who is sympathetic to her plight.*

The narrative before us seems to imply that the woman had remained isolated in her courtyard for a full twelve years. With her desperation building up over the years, the narrative presumes that

---

### Note on Menstrual Impurity

According to Jewish tradition, a woman experiencing her monthly period was regarded as "unclean." This condition had nothing to do with "being dirty" and carried with it no connotation of "being morally impure." Technically this term seems to have originally functioned so as to prevent entering and defiling the tabernacle or the Temple (Lev 15:31). By extension, however, a menstruating woman was not to touch anyone or have anyone touch her since they would thereby also become "unclean." To remove this condition, a person had to bathe, wash his clothes, and refrain from human contact until sundown when the "unclean" condition departed. Even household objects could contract and communicate this condition: "Everything upon which she lies during her impurity shall be unclean; everything also upon which she sits shall be unclean" (Lev 15:20).

Any husband having sex with his when her period began "shall be unclean seven days" (Lev 15:24), i.e., during the entire duration of her period. During this period, a man would effectively be unable to conduct business or mix with other men. Any man having untentional intercourse with a menstruating woman was to be executed (Lev 18:19; 20:18).

And, "if she has a discharge beyond the time of her impurity, all the days of her discharge shall continue in uncleanness" (Lev 15:25). In effect, such a woman was expected to remain in her home and keep her impurity to herself. If and when the flow stopped, "she shall count seven days and after that she shall be clean" (Lev 15:28). Then, to be sure, she had piles of contaminated clothing and linens to wash.

once she hears of Jesus (Mark 5:27 only) she decides to risk everything by going outdoors. But, even in the streets, she must have had to evade detection by any of the men folk who might recognize her and quickly order her home. As a further complication, it might be presumed that she had largely lost her sense of how the village outside of her courtyard was laid out and that she had no precise knowledge of where Jesus would be and how she was to recognize him in a crowd.

Only a prostitute or an uncouth Canaanite women (who gets the silent treatment when she addresses Jesus in Matt 15:22) would be sufficiently shameless as to address a strange man in public. Hence, she cannot inquire of any man as to where Jesus is. Women, meanwhile, cannot be expected to be out in the streets and, if they are, they are more often than not in the company of a male from their household. We can only imagine, therefore, that she knew how to keep her panic down and to read the clues necessary for her to single out Jesus such that she could "touch the fringe of his garment" (Matt 9:20). But why the fringe?

*Only a prostitute or an uncouth Canaanite women be sufficiently shameless as to address a strange man in public.*

Mark's narrative fails to mention "the fringe." In Mark's account the woman simply "touched his garment" (Mark 5:27). Needless to say, neither Mark nor Matthew wanted their narrative to encourage the notion that "his garment" had magical properties. The Jewish tradition severely penalized the practice of magic and regarded it as an abomination akin to human sacrifice (see, e.g., Deut 18:10-14, 2 Kgs 17:17, 2 Chron 33:6). Moreover, the early disciples of Jesus had no interest in securing any of his garments for the sake of "healing powers" associated with them. Matthew, accordingly, may have altered Mark to read "touched the fringe of his garment" (Matt 9:20) in order to offset such a misunderstanding. Yet, more than this, the "fringe" has a powerful religious significance which Matthew expected his readers to grasp.

*The woman is reaching out to touch "the tassel" which reminds Jews of God's Torah.*

The impact of Matthew's account is to convey to Jewish ears that the woman is reaching out to touch "the tassel" which reminds Jews of God's Torah. Far from wanting to avoid the commandments

### Note on the Significance of "Tassel"

When the Greek text is carefully examined, it reveals that the woman touched "the fringe (*kraspedon*) of his garment" (Matt 9:21). The Greek term, *kraspedon*, refers to the "little fringe" or "tassel" (*zizit* in Hebrew) which hangs from any one of the four corners of the garment which male Jews traditionally wear. Any Jew hearing this narrative at the time of Jesus would have known that these tassels were prescribed by the Lord himself on Mt. Sinai: "[T]ell them to make fringes on the corners of their garments throughout all generations . . . so that when you see it, you will remember all the commandments of the Lord and do them" (Num 15:38, also Deut 22:12, Zech 8:23).

of God or to overturn them (see Matt 5:17), therefore, she precisely reaches out to embrace them *as they are worn and interpreted by Jesus* as the source leading to her "healing."

The Greek term used twice here, namely *sozein*, conveys both temporal deliverance and spiritual salvation at the same time. First, she uses it: "I will be *saved*" (9:21). Later, Jesus confirms her hope using the same term, "Your faith/trust has *saved* you" (9:22). The tacit interplay of "tassel," "Torah," and "healing" are subtle but unmistakable. Matthew's revision of Mark not only offsets a potential misunderstanding, it also promotes Matthew's insistence that this "Daughter [of Israel]" (Matt 9:22) had suffered for twelve years without relief until she reached out and touched the tassel/Torah worn by Jesus (see Matt 11:25-30, 23:1-4).

> *The tacit interplay of "tassel," "Torah," and "healing" are subtle but unmistakable.*

The fact that Jesus does not say, "I have saved you," could be taken to mean that Jesus doesn't want to demean her heroic efforts by making her dependent on yet another man. A women in her condition had already suffered too much from the shame and the shunning and the inaction of those men closest to her. Furthermore, some importance must be given to the fact that Jesus doesn't say, "Your faith has saved you this time, but, next time, when you have your period, for God's sake, don't presume to go about in public touching men." Jesus' silence on this point has great implications not only for this woman but for all other women who have touched the "tassel" of Jesus.

> *Jesus doesn't say, "Your faith has saved you this time, but, next time, don't presume to go about in public touching men."*

Step back from this narrative for a moment. What does this say about the community to which Matthew tells and retells this story? What applications might the women within the community of Matthew be making to themselves on the basis of this narrative? What applications might the men be making? Be daring in your thinking. Let the story speak to you.

## The Woman Who Touched Jesus at a Banquet

6. Another case of a woman touching Jesus is offered by Luke 7:36-50. Read it, mull it over, and note what you discover about Jesus' therein:

> *One can assume that only men were invited.*

In this case, an uninvited woman barges in on a dinner party. Given prevailing social customs, one can assume that only men were invited. In most instances, men did not eat with their wives even when they were alone. Rather, the wife customarily served supper to her husband and his sons who were over twelve; and, after they had finished, she fed herself, her daughters, and the children. When company came, the same practice prevailed. The wife of the host would never be expected to join in the table conversation with men (unless her husband was influenced by Hellenistic customs and had hired servants or slaves assigned to prepare and serve the meal in his wife's place.

For Luke, moreover, this is not just a women who fails to recognize her rightful place; this is "a woman who is wayward in the city" (Luke 7:37 literal tr.). Now that one of "these women" has barged into his home; Simon immediate thought must have been to have her removed quickly and quietly without alarming his dinner guests. Given the fact that the men are "reclining" (7:36 RSV mistranslates this as "sat") at table, the supposition might be that Simon is moderately well to do and that this is something of a formal dinner in Jesus' honor. Simon, therefore, would have had a vested interest in not allowing this woman to disturb Jesus who, by this time, has gained a reputation of being a distinguished teacher and prophet. Before she can be stopped, however, she goes right to where Jesus is reclining (perhaps on cushions or on a flat couch) and begins anointing his feet.

*Simon had a vested interest in not allowing this woman to disturb Jesus.*

During a formal dinner, a slave would ordinarily be assigned such a task, and the guest of honor might be expected to have his feet anointed first. What surprises Simon, however, is that Jesus doesn't cringe. Maybe this is why he allows her to quietly continue. While she does so, however, Simon is forced to imagine that Jesus must be entirely oblivious of "what sort of woman this is who is touching him" (7:39) and, furthermore, that such an uninsightful individual could hardly have the gift of prophecy. What insight does Simon think he has about this women which Jesus appears to lack? "What sort of woman" is this? And what do you suppose is Simon's emotional response upon seeing this woman "touching" Jesus?

*Simon is forced to imagine that Jesus must be entirely oblivious of "what sort of woman this is."*

Luke probably wants his hearers to surmise that this brazen woman is a prostitute. As often happens in polite society, however, he resorts to using a euphemism: "a wayward woman in the city" (Luke 7:37). Then, as now, a "wayward" (hamartlos) women is not just a "sinner" (following the RSV), but, invariably a "fallen" or "loose" woman, with sexual connotations. Luke's association of her

*Simon's fixation on her "touching" Jesus is also revealing.*

waywardness with "the city" probably points to the moral corruption of urban centers where most prostitutes congregate. Furthermore, Simon's fixation on her "touching" Jesus also suggests this identification. It can be imagined that Simon deliberately went out of his way to avoid prostitutes whenever he spotted them (e.g., wearing bright colors and displaying their hair uncovered) in the city. Should a prostitute have approached him, Simon, being a religious man, would have most probably drawn away in disgust. He may have even cringed at the though of have one of these woman "touching" his body.

While all this is taking place, Jesus is seemingly so unperturbed as to resume the dinner conversation. He gets his hosts attention, and Simon responds by acknowledging him as "Teacher" (7:40). But he is probably thinking, "What could this man possibly teach me?" At this point, ironically, Jesus artfully offers him a lesson delicately framed as a parable. During this entire time, the prostitute continues with her tears and her anointing in the background.

The content of the parable demonstrates (perhaps even to Simon) that Jesus was, all along, quite aware of "who and what sort of woman this is" (7:39). Then Jesus, for the first time, directly addresses the woman. In so doing, we discover more about the woman than we knew before. Note your observations and conclusions here:

*The tears of the woman are probably tears of gratitude.*

The tears of the woman may, in the first instance, appear to be tears of repentance. However, upon reflection, Luke probably wants us to understand them to be tears of gratitude. Assume, just for the moment, that this woman had heard Jesus teach or preach at some earlier point and, as a result, came to repentance. This would help explain how and why she knows Jesus. It would also help explain her deliberate preparations in securing a costly "alabaster flask of ointment" (7:37)—a gift of gratitude—before going out to find Jesus. Moreover, Jesus' parable speaks in terms of "love" (*agapaō*) which is motivated by gratitude for "debts" (a common metaphor for "sins") already forgiven. Finally, Jesus' own words to her, "Your sins have been forgiven" (7:48 and 7:47), using the past perfect tense (which the RSV mistranslates in both places as "are forgiven") also suggests that Jesus is referring to a earlier act of repentance and forgiveness.

Jesus' interaction with this woman closes with him saying to her, "Your faith has saved you; go in peace" (7:50). These are exactly Jesus' words to the woman who had the hemorrhage (Mark 5:34, Luke

8:48). In this case, however, he does not call her "Daughter [of Israel]"—and maybe for a reason. Think for a moment of Jesus' final words to the woman caught in adultery: "Go, and do not sin again" (John 8:11). Why doesn't Jesus caution this prostitute in the same words?

Given all the self-righteous anger that Christians have poured out upon prostitutes over the centuries, it seems incredible that Jesus never said a single harsh word to a prostitute nor, as in the case of this woman here, does he presume to be able to say, "Go, and do not sin again." The harsh reality is that, in Jesus' day, many women were caught up in prostitution and, given the existing social structures, their choices were either to sell their bodies to men or to allow themselves and those tho depended upon them (e.g., underage children) to starve. It's not a pretty picture. But, then again, Jesus had to face up to the real evil existing in his day. And the real evil was not this women who was herself a victim of a system. . . .

*Jesus never said a single harsh word to a prostitute.*

Jesus closing words to the woman assure her that she can go in peace because her "faith" has saved her. Just maybe this means that "her faith" has been strong enough to fight her way out of prostitution. On the other hand, just maybe she knows with a cold certainty that she has no viable alternative to prostitution. What then could the words of Jesus mean to her?

---

### Note on Erotic Connotations in Luke

Jesus says to Simon that the wayward woman "has wet my feet with her tears and wiped them with her hair" (7:44) and "has not ceased to kiss my feet" (7:45).

Normally a slave would dry someone's feet with a towel (as Jesus does in John 13:5). This woman has, at some point, uncovered and unbound her own hair for this purpose. As for the kisses, even a slave might devoutly kiss his/her master's feet. The verb *kataphileō* used here, however, suggests a fervent or even passionate kissing.

Both of these actions taken together have erotic overtones and probably represent the kind of actions which a prostitute might have undertaken for her favored clients both for their relaxation and as a mild form of foreplay. It is hard to imagine that any woman other than an experienced prostitute would have been able to act as this woman acted in the company of other men.

Luke, who has the tendency to suppress strong emotion and shocking actions when he takes over Mark's material, apparently feels no hesitation to allow for erotic overtones here. Possibly Luke judges that the excessiveness of this show of gratitude is amply justified by the forgiveness of sins which Jesus occasioned in her life.

## Jesus Shaming His Male Companions

When men ate together in the ancient world, this denoted that they shared a bond that pledged them to protect and defend each other. Luke, who is the only Evangelist who dares to note that Jesus accepted dinner invitations with the Pharisees (also 11:37 and 14:1) is also the only Evangelist to note that "some Pharisees came" (13:31) and warned Jesus regarding a plot by Herod to have him killed. Dining and defending go hand in hand.

Jesus, however, in the narrative just considered, fails to play his expected role towards Simon, his host. Instead of honoring him and his sensibilities and scolding the woman for her bad timing and bad taste, Jesus turns the tables in favor of the woman. In so doing, Jesus shames his host. How so? Be specific.

*Shaming and saving face are key elements within Luke's narrative.*

Shaming and saving face are key elements within Luke's narrative. These must be correctly understood, however, against the backdrop of the protocols of hospitality which prevailed in the world of Luke. These might be summarized as follows:

Once the invitation is accepted, the roles of the host and the guest are set by the rules of custom:

(a) The guest must not ask for anything. . . .
(b) The host provides the best he has available. . . .
(c) The guest is expected to reciprocate immediately with news, predictions of good fortune, or expressions of gratitude for what he has been given, and praise the host's generosity and honor (Matthews: 15).

---

### Note on Ancient Prostitution

[I]n antiquity most prositutes were impoverished unskilled women. Found mostly in the cities [cf. Luke 7:37a], they often lived in brothels or houses connected with a temple. Prostitutes usually were slaves, daughters who had been sold or rented out by their parents, wives who were rented out by their husbands, poor women, exposed girls, the divorced and widowed, single mothers, captives of war or piracy, women bought for soldiers—in short, women who could not derive a livelihood from their position in the patriarchal family or those who had to work for a living but could not engage in "middle"- or "upper"-class professions. In Palestine, torn by war, colonial taxation, and famine, the number of such women must have been great (Fiorenza: 128).

Jesus' conduct is quite reprehensible relative to (c). He praises the woman washing and kissing and anointing his feet while shaming his host for failing to make provisions for such things. The point of comparison is that Simon comes off far short of this prostitute when it comes to the rubrics of hospitality. What is even more galling it that Jesus, in the company of men, choose to openly defend and honor a known prostitute at the expense of shaming Simon, his honorable host.

What does this say about the disciples of Jesus who continued to hold up to their hearers the conduct of Jesus as a model for their imitation? What does it mean for Luke's readership that this narrative is included in his Gospel? What does this narrative say to the women and the men in Luke's audience who are pledged to follow Jesus?

*Jesus, in the company of men, choose to openly defend and honor a known prostitute at the expense of shaming Simon, his honorable host.*

Matthew's Gospel, while it fails to include this narrative, does nonetheless present Jesus as shaming men in favor of uplifting the conduct of prostitutes. In Matthew's case, it is the temple priests who are shamed—not for their hospitality—but for their failure to accept the baptism of repentance preached by John the Baptizer. Jesus says to them:

> Truly, I say to you, the tax collectors and the harlots go into the kingdom of God before you [priests]. For John came to you in the way of righteousness, and you did not believe him, but the tax collectors and the harlots believed him; and even when you saw it, you [priests] did not afterward repent and believe him (Matthew 21:31f).

7. Mark includes in his Gospel a different tradition of a women anointing Jesus during a meal at Simon's house. Mark's narrative, however, is recast in an entirely different direction. Read Mark 14:3-8 and write your conclusions here:

*In Mark's narrative Jesus openly shames his own disciples while honoring the lone, voiceless woman.*

In Mark's narrative, it is the disciples of Jesus who become the antagonists of the woman. Jesus, in this case, openly shames his own disciples them while honoring the lone, voiceless woman whom he befriends. Mark's scene takes place in Jerusalem two days before his death at the home of "Simon the leper" (Mark 14:3). Scholars are divided as to whether this "Simon the leper" is to be equated with "Simon the Pharisee" in Luke's narrative. Note, too, that the objection to the women in Mark's account has nothing to do with her reputation as a wayward woman. Accordingly, the scandal in Mark's account is not her "touching" Jesus but the sheer disregard of the poor which she demonstrates by her extravagance. As a result, "some" disciples (unnamed in Mark) "reproached her" verbally (14:5). Jesus immediately jumps to her defense by shaming the mistaken priorities of the disciples. Even beyond this, Mark is here clearly signaling to his readers that this nameless woman rightly anticipates the death of Jesus while the disciples have repeatedly hardened their hearts to it (Mark 8:32, 9:32, 10:32-37).

Note carefully Mark 14:10. What might Mark be intending by associating Judas' intended betrayal with the story which has just taken place?

*According to John's account, it was "Judas Iscariot" alone who took a stand against the woman.*

Mark appears to want his readers to associate Judas' decision to betray Jesus as resulting from the shaming that "some" (14:4) of the disciples received when the woman anointed Jesus at table. Was Judas among those objecting? Mark doesn't say. According to John's account, however, it was "Judas Iscariot" *alone* who took a stand against the woman "not that he cared for the poor but because he was a thief" (John 12:6). Mark's Gospel, in contrast, wants to present the picture that the Twelve had been on a collision course with Jesus long before this episode of shaming (Weeden: 32-38).

Disciples, it must be remembered, were expected to learn from both the words and the deeds of their master in order to capture his point of view. In this case, however, they make no inquiry of Jesus as to why this women is anointing him. Their trust has been gradually breaking down. Hence, stepping out of their role as disciples, "they were aroused/indignant/angry with her" (14:5 lit.) and, by implication, with Jesus as well since he too, in their eyes, was being unmindful of the poor. Unwilling to take him on; they pour their indignation on the woman who, due to her cultural upbringing, would be expected to quietly submit to them.

In brief, when Mark says that "some" of the disciples spoke out against the woman, he is clearly signaling to his readers that the growing misapprehension and disillusionment of the disciples has reached an all-time low. A close reading of Mark's narrative leaves open two probable conclusions: (1) that Judas Iscariot was not the only disciple who was getting dangerously disenchanted with Jesus and ready to jump ship, and (2) that Jesus' habit of affirming women at the expense of men was a precipitating cause that pushed Judas over the edge and brought on the early arrest, trial, and death of Jesus.

Presume this reading of Mark is correct. What would it mean that the community of Mark continued to tell and retell a narrative wherein Jesus is portrayed as slighting his own disciples in favor of a lone women (who, again, has no voice and no name)? What does this story say to both women and men in the Jesus movement regarding how they should act?

*Jesus' habit of affirming women at the expense of men was a precipitating cause that pushed Judas over the edge.*

## Martha's Cooking vs. Mary's Learning

9. Let's look at one last account. Read Luke 10:38-42. Mull over it for a few moments. Write down the reasons why, in the light of traditional Jewish society, this narrative is explosive:

The first thing that stands out is that "Martha received him into *her* house" (Luke 10:38). The implied meaning here is that this is an unusual household wherein no male is either consulted or actively present to receive invited guests. We don't know where the husbands and the brothers are, and Luke does not take time out to tell us that they are all dead or away on business. While some early Greek manuscripts exclude the phrase "into her house," the entire absence of men in the narrative would seemingly imply that Martha was the matron in change.

*This is an unusual household wherein no male is either consulted or actively present to receive invited guests.*

Immediately, Mary is introduced as "a sister" who "sat at the Lord's feet and listened to his teaching" (10:39). The posture of sitting is a decisive clue here. What does the clue imply? [Need a hint? See Luke 2:46.]

*There would be ample reason for Martha to be fuming in the kitchen.*

Meanwhile, Martha is getting food ready for those who are discussing Torah with Jesus. Who came with Jesus? Some scholars believe Jesus is alone. To support this, they note that the opening line reads: "Now as they [Jesus and his disciples] went on their way, he [Jesus alone] entered a village; and a woman named Martha received him" (Luke 10:38). On the other hand, Luke often looses track of the disciples when, for the purposes of his narrative, they have no active role to play. Moreover, the disciples are clearly present (in active roles) before and after this story; hence, their presence can be safely presumed. It is even possible that some of "the seventy others" (Luke 10:1) sent out and welcomed back by Jesus (10:17) may also have tagged along. If this surmise is correct, there would be ample reason for Martha to be fuming in the kitchen at the fact that her sister has abandoned her to do all the food preparations.

So what could Martha do to remedy this situation? Seemingly, given his household status, she could simply order Mary to give her a hand. But she doesn't. She prefers to take her complaint to Jesus and to chew him out! "Lord, do you not care . . . ?" (10:40) Conjecture why she should do this:

*Martha seems to typify the traditional Jewish woman: as soon as a suitable man appears, she honors him with the role of setting the household in order.*

One might begin by marveling at Martha's sense of liberty in the face of a man whom she acknowledges as "Lord." Martha also seems to typify the traditional Jewish woman: who can take charge when no man is present but, as soon as a suitable man appears, she honors him with the role of setting the household in order. Going even further, Martha may be gently chiding Jesus because he, after all, is the source of the problem in allowing Mary to engage in Torah discussion with him and the other men. Here again, therefore, her expectation is that once he notices the unfair burden being placed on Martha, Jesus will set things right by promptly put Mary back "into her rightful place."

Then the surprise comes! Jesus takes the side of the woman who has neglected the requirements of hospitality and neglected to come to the assistance of another woman in distress. As an astute pastor, he acknowledges that Martha is "anxious and troubled," but this does not move him to resolve the situation by sending Mary (or even a few of the men?) into the kitchen. Rather, he sets forth a new principle: "Mary has chosen the good/better portion which shall not be taken from her" (10:42; see also 8:18).

Luke probably narrates this story by way of offering guidance to his own community which is sorely divided over the proper roles of women. Following the hints in the narrative itself, who would you suspect are the one in Luke's community calling to the men in charge to return women back to their traditional roles? How does the principle enunciated by Jesus honor the Marthas while protecting the new roles (which?) taken by the Marys?

If this were a narrative designed by Luke to address a current problem within his community, then, reconstructing the problem based on the internal logic of the text might go as follows: When conflict arose, women who were tied to their culturally defined roles (in the kitchen) appear to have been the first to approach the leading men and demand that their "sisters" (a familiar term for a female religious associate) sitting at their feet be ordered back into their proper roles (i.e., sent back into the kitchen). The voices of "brothers" is not heard or implied—suggesting that this dispute did not originate with them.

The words found on Jesus' lips (Luke 10:42) represents what Jesus would have decided had he been faced with this crisis among the women. The resolution offered reveals that nothing would be gained in trying to force all of the women out of the kitchen in order to feed them all with Torah. Meanwhile, regarding those women who have joined the men, there is little desire to send them back into the kitchen to relieve the anxiety and the burden of those who remained there. Thus, Jesus' words, "The good portion . . . shall not be taken from her" (Luke 10:42), serve to secure the innovative role of women learning to interpret Torah among the men while, at the same time, they tacitly honor the contribution of women who have retained their traditional service (*diakonia*). In sum, the ruling principle of Jesus provides sound pastoral genius at its best.

*The words found on Jesus' lips secure the innovative role of women learning to interpret Torah among the men.*

11. Putting all this together, what have been the most startling discoveries that you have made? Describe them for yourself here:

How has your mind changed regarding Jesus' relationship to women? How has you mind changed regarding the implied practice of the early church which was guided by these Jesus narratives?

12. On the basis of your understanding of these narratives, would you say that the Gospels do or do not give relevant testimony to the contemporary church which is trying to discern how to approach the issue of the ordination of women? _____ If so, build a case for yourself on the basis of these narratives and spell it out for yourself here:

13. Did this Case Study raise any fundamental questions for you while you were completing it? If so, note them here so that you can return to them at a later moment?

There are many more texts which address the role of women, but, in order to keep our inquiry manageable, they have to be set aside for future study. Our inquiry is also admittedly incomplete because it fails to even mention Paul's position relative to women. This also must form the agenda for a future study which is begun in the appendix.

Completion time = _____
Total time used on this Case = _____ minutes

You have now completed the fourth Case Study. Rest now. Set everything aside. Once you are renewed, come back to the analysis.

## Analysis

In this Case Study, you began by noting how Jesus addressed his message in terms which positively appealed to women's experience. Then you noted how Matthew's ten healing narratives embraced both men and women and how the majority of them are gender inclusive (linguistically considered). After that, you analyzed specific texts. In the first, you saw how a menstruating woman broke social and religious conventions in order to be healed by touching the tassel/Torah worn by Jesus. Next, Jesus was remembered as having, on certain occasions, fractured social expectations of male bonding and of dinner etiquette by either shaming his host or shaming his disciples—in each case for the expressed purpose of defending the activity and initiative of women harassed by male criticism. Finally, you explored a text unique to Luke wherein Mary represents those women who have neglected the kitchen in order to take their place among the men discussing Torah. Faced with the criticism of her "sister," Jesus defends this new role for women without shaming those women who prefer traditional roles.

Within this Case Study, special emphasis has been placed upon the reading of the Gospel texts against the backdrop of the society in which they originated. Only in this way can the specific relevance of particular incidents be perceived as having enormous importance for the men and women who followed Jesus in the first century. How many times, for instance, have you heard the parables of Jesus without imagining how unusual it was for an inspired trainer in Torah to make use of women's experiences? How many times have you heard the narrative of the woman with the flow of blood touching Jesus' garment or of the sinner from the city touching Jesus' feet without recognizing how shocking and scandalous their behavior was to Jesus' contemporaries? What we have done here can be applied to other Gospel narratives as well.

*Special emphasis has been placed upon the reading of the Gospel texts against the backdrop of the society in which they originated.*

The key questions guiding our inquiry have been the following: (a) How and why is the conduct being presented here in step or out of step with traditional Jewish society? (b) What does this say about the community which continues to speak approvingly of conduct that was perceived as shocking and unacceptable within larger society?

Rather than try to summarize here the material which already has been richly presented in the Case Study, my purpose will be to respond to four questions which adults completing this Case have frequently asked me. These are as follows:

**1 Q**: What impact would these narratives have on both women and men who heard them in the early assemblies?

**A** This is difficult to say. We are so far removed from them culturally, and they did not leave detailed records of this kind. One can hazard an educated guess, however. For purposes of illustration, let's limit our attention to the narrative of the women with the hemorrhage (Matt 9:20-23).

Women in the early church who heard this story must have had cause to compare themselves with her since they also knew what it was like to become "homebound" and "untouchable" for a week out of every month. These women would also have noted that Jesus never said to the woman, "Your faith has saved you this time; but, in the future, for God's sake, stay home!" Moreover, in their heart of hearts, many of them couldn't quite believe that God was quite as restrictive as their fathers and husbands had made him out to be; yet, up to this point, there had been no teacher to confirm their alternative opinions. Then, driven by desperation, some entrapment in their own life may have finally forced them to act boldly and decisively in ways which went beyond the bounds of orthodox religion. In so acting, they risked to lose or to gain everything. Through these experiences, one can imagine that they too might have rediscovered in the process what it really means to trust God by accepting that terrible freedom which God extends even to women. Having no better words, such women would say, "I have been saved." And then the full meaning of Jesus' assurance might rush upon them, "Take heart, my daughter, your faith has made you well" (Matt 9:22).

Men, meanwhile, hearing this selfsame narrative might also be expected to learn something. A man, for instance, might discover that the narrative speaks to him about how women are sometimes required to find healing for themselves in ways that go beyond what men have agreed is orthodox or permissible. For starters, men might notice that Jesus never seemed concerned whether the women who touch him or the women he visits are menstruating or not. Undoubtedly, among Jewish Galilean peasants, there were already those men who had little time or patience to keep track of "touching her" or "touching her bed" or "touching any seat she has sat on" (Lev 15:19, 20, 22). As for the enormous load of bed linens and laundry deemed "unclean" at the end of a woman's period, one can imagine that some farmers, pressed by the urgent task of sowing or harvesting, sometimes instructed their wives to "forget it."

*Women are sometimes required to find healing for themselves in ways that go beyond what men have agreed is orthodox or permissible.*

Healthy religion always knows how and when to make exceptions. Jesus, therefore, may not have been such a daring innovator as might first appear. He might just have been confirming the healthy religious sensibilities of many of his listeners who already knew how to quietly make exceptions without either fretting or fomenting revolution.

*Healthy religion always knows how and when to make exceptions.*

**2 Q**: Did Jesus ever present any kind of master plan for defining women's roles in the church and in society?

**A**: Nowhere in the Gospel accounts do we come across Jesus making general pronouncements about women: "Women ought to do this. . . . Women ought not to do that. . . ." Even in the case of the tension between Martha and Mary, Jesus does not fall into the trap of supposing that he ought to impose one solution upon all women for all time. Instead, Martha is allowed to continue, with honor, in the traditional role she has cut out for herself; yet, she has to learn to do this, at least for the moment, without Mary, her "sister." As for Mary, one cannot help but note that Jesus is not presented as having invited Mary to sit at his feet in the first place. She does this by herself. He simply accepts her initiative.

*Jesus does not fall into the trap of supposing that he ought to impose one solution upon all women.*

If this narrative offers some insight into the internal affairs of Luke's community, it would have to be in the direction of signaling that the men in change do not have a pastoral plan which covers all cases and all contingencies. Part of the "good news" is that women are free to take the initiative without seeking prior approval from the men who are in charge. Madonna Kolbenschlag admirably develops this same theme on the basis of Luke's portrait of another Mary, that of the mother of Jesus (Kolbenschlag: 82-88). On the other hand, the Martha and Mary narrative offers every reason for the men in charge to continue to honor those women who are quite content with everything as it has been.

*Women are free to take the initiative without seeking prior approval from the men who are in charge.*

Learning is liberating. Once Mary begins to hear Torah for herself "at the feet of Jesus" and then begins to acquire the art of applying it to her own life, she establishes herself as *a disciple* equal with the men. She can never go back to her former position of trusting that the men in her life entirely know and understand all those things (which were formerly beyond her grasp). More importantly, she can never go back to thinking that she need only obediently submit to masculine direction to assure herself that she is entirely in harmony with what God would have her be and have her do. If every Jewish man gained his independence and his stature before men and before God by virtue of learning to read and to interpret Torah for himself, why should this same rule not apply also to women?

*If every Jewish man gained his independence and his stature by virtue of learning to read and to interpret Torah for himself, why should this same rule not apply also to women?*

**3 Q**: If some women did sit at his feet, why did Jesus not give the apostolic charge to any of them but only to men?

**A**: Anyone who takes the time to think about the condition of women at the time of Jesus would have to admit that the Gospels represent what could be called "a quiet revolution." It would have been disastrous pastoral practice for Jesus to have called some women to join the men he was training and doubly disastrous to have sent these women out in pairs to do public preaching. Jesus had to make allowances for the settled instincts of his contemporaries and not act in ways that would have been roundly condemned as shamefully irresponsible.

What Jewish father, for instance, could have responsibly given over his daughter to be a disciple of Jesus when this would have entailed habitual association with men who were not blood relatives? And what women, even supposing she had somehow received training in Torah, could have expected to gain a hearing by addressing Jewish men in the public sphere? For such conduct, women would have been pelted with stones. . . . Such was unthinkable in Jesus' society!

Let's go on step further. Let's suppose that such a woman would limit herself to training other women privately in the courtyards. Even this, however, would have been perceived as encroaching upon the right and duty of fathers and husbands. In the Jewish society of Jesus' day, women were never taught Torah by other women and only very few were taught by anyone but their fathers or husbands.

In retrospect, therefore, one must allow that even Jesus had to exercise a certain pastorally motivated restraint. Not everything was possible or necessary. Jesus knew this. Thus, he sought to encourage and defend women who were themselves inspired to stretch the socially determined and religiously sanctioned norms of his society. As for the giving women the apostolic charge, however, this was not a possible option within his society.

The CDF report, therefore, which began this study, is admirable in what it does say about Jesus working against the social prejudices of his day. The report, however, fails to go far enough or deep enough when it comes to analyzing why Jesus would have broken some barriers concerning women and not others. Those who have done this Case Study, however, will by now have informed insights as to how the CDF report needs to be altered and supplemented to remove these deficiencies.

*Even Jesus had to exercise a certain pastorally motivated restraint.*

**4 Q**: What ramifications does the example of Jesus have when it comes to women today?

**A**: The contemporary churches, for the most part, have safely championed the rights and dignity of women only in so far as these rights and dignity have been largely secured by secular society. In effect, even the churches that have ordained women have often done so only because the real prophetic work was initiated within secular society and, only later, transposed into church circles. Seldom, in recent times, have the churches scandalized society by actions or teachings in favor of women. Yet, when the Gospels carefully examined, it would appear that Jesus not only zealously championed the cause of women but, in God's name, successfully trained and committed his followers into further bending social and religious barriers inhibiting their well-being.

*Seldom, in recent times, have the churches scandalized society by actions or teachings in favor of women.*

In our own time, some Christian women and men have again made contact with the dangerous memory of Jesus. In the light of these perceptions, some of today's women have deep suspicions regarding those patriarchal traditions which men have created for them in the name of Jesus. Their questioning has proved very stressful and disturbing to many. Have these women been deceived as was Eve (see 1 Tim 2:14)? Or have they discovered that the true voice of Jesus has been systematically muzzled on the central issue of women's equality of discipleship? It is for you, the reader, to decide.

## Application to the Churches Today

If Jesus' own practice in favor of women is part of the Gospels as shown in this Case Study, what does this say to you and to your church today. Generate some applications and write them down here and in the margins:

## Further Readings for Case Four

Atkins, Anne
> *Split Image.* Grand Rapids: Eerdsmans, 1987.

Clark, Stephen B.
> *Man and Woman in Christ.* Ann Arbor: Servant [traditional theology at its best], 1980.

Corley, Kathleen E.
> *Private Women; Public Meals: Social Conflict in the Synoptic Tradition.* Peabody: Hendrickson, 1993.

Fiorenza, Elisabeth Schüssler
> *In Memory of Her: A Feminist Theological Reconstruction of Christian Origins.* New York: Crossroad, 1984.
>
> *Discipleship of Equals: A Critical Feminist Ekklsia-logy of Liberation.* New York: Crossroad, 1993.

Harrison, Verna A.
> "Orthodox Arguments Against the Ordination of Women as Priests," *Sobornost* 14/1:6-23, 1992.

John Paul II
> "The Rights of Women," *Origins* 10 (9/18/80) 210-214, 1980.

Kolbenschlag, Madonna
> *Kiss Sleeping Beauty Good-Bye: Breaking the Spell of Feminine Myths and Models.* Toronto: Bantam Books, 1981.

Lerner, Gerda
> *The Creation of Patriarchy.* Oxford: University Press, 1986.

Matthews, Victor H.
> "Hospitality and Hostility in Judges 4," *Biblical Theological Bulletin* 21:13-21, 1991.

Pontifical Biblical Commission
> Can Women be Priests?" *Origins* 6/6:92-96, 1975.

Priests for Equality
> Toward a Full and Equal Sharing: A Pastoral Letter on Equality." P.O. Box 5243; West Hyattsville, MD 20782, 1982.

Sacred Congregation for the Doctrine of the Faith
> *Declaration on the Question of the Admission of Women to the Ministerial Priesthood.* Washington, D.C.: U.S. Catholic Conference, 1976.

Spong, Bishop
>"Women in the Episcopate: Symbol of a New Day for the Church," *Living in Sin.* San Francisco: Harper & Row. Pp. 219-225, 1988.

Sölle, Dorothee
>*Beyond Mere Obedience.* New York: Pilgrim, 1982.

Stendahl, Brita
>*The Force of Tradition: A Case Study of Women Priests in Sweden.* Philadelphia: Fortress, 1985.

Wahlberg, R. C.
>*Jesus According to a Woman.* New York: Paulist, 1975.

Weeden, Sr., Theodore J.
>*Mark: Traditions in Conflict.* Philadelphia: Fortress, 1971.

# CASE FIVE

# Whether the Twelve Fancied Themselves as Bishops

In the standard manuals used for the training Roman Catholic clergy during the first sixty years of this century, the following two theses were of key importance:

> Thesis: Christ established the Church as an hierarchical society by bestowing on the Apostles the threefold power of teaching, of ruling and of sanctifying the faithful. This thesis is historically certain, it is theologically *de fide* ["concerning faith," a technical term designating a necessary element of true faith] . . . .

> Thesis: By divine right the Apostles' successors are the bishops collectively taken, as far as the powers to teach, to rule, and to sanctify the faithful are concerned. This thesis is historically certain; it is theologically *de fide* . . . (Tanquerey: 107, 111).

During Vatican II, the bishops drafted statements which largely repeat these time-honored theses. Raymond Brown was challenged by the German Catholic theologian, Rudolph Schnackenburg to explain how it was that the bishops made wide use of the subtleties of biblical research in some areas but resort to dubious traditions when it came to characterizing the origins of the hierarchy and the apostolic succession of bishops (Brown, 1970: 47f). To begin with, the very term "hierarchy" means "rule by priests," a condition which Case Two amply demonstrated did not prevail in the early church. Moveover, nothing in the Christian Scriptures suggests that any of the Twelve apostles had "successors" unless one thinks of the replacement of Judas by Matthias (Acts 1:25f). The Twelve appear to have a permanent once-for-all-time function in so far as they are destined, in the world to come, to "sit on twelve thrones and to judge the twelve tribes of Israel" (Matt 19:28). As for their historical ministry, Brown concludes:

> The image of them [the Twelve] as carrying on missionary endeavors all over the world has no support in the NT or in other reliable historical sources. . . . As for exercising supervision, there is no New Testament evidence that any of the Twelve ever served as heads of local churches; and it is several centuries before they be-

*Nothing in the Christian Scriptures suggests that any of the Twelve apostles had "successors" . . . or served as heads of local churches.*

gin to be described as "bishops" of first-century Christian centers, which is surely an anachorism (Brown, 1980: 325).

For daring to draw such conclusions, Brown has been continuously under attack by Catholics who are afraid that he is willing to sell out to the Protestants the traditional Roman Catholic claim that its hierarchy and episcopacy are found clearly expressed within the Christian Scriptures themselves. It is to this question that our present Case Study must turn.

## Purpose

How were the early churches organized? Did major church centers have bishops in charge with presbyters and deacons immediately under their control? Was this model repeated everywhere? If not, what were its alternatives? The purpose of this Case Study is twofold: (a) to explore how the first century churches organized themselves and (b) to draw conclusions regarding the existing plurality of church organization found within the churches today.

*The purpose of this Case Study is to explore how the first century churches organized themselves.*

Before getting started, you are again invited to record your initial perceptions to three questions. By recording your spontaneous judgments now, you will be providing yourself with a declaration of your preliminary understanding of the issues. After completing the Case Study, you will then be able to reread your initial reflections and gauge to what degree you have been broadened or transformed by your inquiries. The three questions designed for this purpose are as follows:

1. Did Jesus give his disciples a specific organizational model for his church? _____ If so, what was it?

2. Do all the first century churches employ the same basic terms for designating those who are "in charge"? _____ If so, what were they?

3. A modern bishop has supreme pastoral jurisdiction within the geographical division generally known as a "diocese." What would be the equivalent to this office within the Christian Scriptures?


Once again, if you are so inclined, this would be the time to take your bible in hand, to close your eyes, and to prayerfully unite yourself with the Spirit whom you trust to guide you into discovering what is important for yourself and for your church community.

Translation = _____

Starting time = _____ (120-160 minutes needed)

---

### The Meaning of "Elder"

The Greek word, *presbyteros* appears 66 times in the Christian Scriptures and 140 times in the Septuagint. This term is normally translated as "presbyter" or "elder."

The Greek term denotes someone who has priority due (a) to age and/or (b) to rank. In the first category, the term can be used to designate the "elder" of two sons, as in the case of Esau and Jacob (Gen 25:23) or two unnamed sons in Jesus' parable (Luke 15:25). More often, however, the term is found to designate those local leaders who collectively and collaboratively guide community life and resolve juridical disputes. The older men chosen to perform this public service (*leitourgia*) receive the special respect which is due to their social standing, long experience, and wisdom. In traditional societies, wisdom came with experience, and experience came with age; hence, "elders" (*presbyteroi*) was a natural designation for these local leaders.

Even in Israel's nomadic days, the "elders" repeatedly appear as tribal leaders who exercise authority next to Moses and share his spirit (e.g. Exod 24:1, Num 11:16f). The elders represent their people, decide upon tribal strategy, and bear the shame should that strategy fail (e.g., Lev 4:15; Judg 21:16f, 8:14-16). During the period of the monarchy, "elders" are found surrounding the king, legitimating his rule, lending support and advising him at critical moments (e.g., 2 Sam 3:17f, 17:4; 1 Kgs 12:6f, 20:7f). After the end of the monarchy, the "elders" reemerged as those local leaders who collectively decide in council (*gerousia* or *synderion* or *presbyterion*) issues of public policy and of punishment (e.g., Ezra 5:9f, 6:7f; Jdt 8:10f; Acts 22:5, 30).

When encountering the term "elder" (*presbyteros*) within the Christian Scriptures, one will accordingly have to imaginatively return to the traditional association of age, experience, and wisdom for living and to link this with the long Jewish experience of "elders" functioning as mentors, leaders, and judges within Jewish society.

## An Initial Word Study

1. In Case Two, we noted that some form of the word "priest" (*hiereus*) is found in 155 places in the Christian Scriptures. At the end of our investigation, however, we concluded that no one, not even the apostles, are expressly referred to as "priests" at any time or any place. By way of review, explain in this space why the early church did not designate anyone as a "priest."

2. The following table represents the number of occurrences of presbyteros in various parts of the Christian Scriptures:

| Occurrences | Source |
|---|---|
| 13 | Matthew |
| 07 | Mark |
| 05 | Luke |
| 01 | John |
| 18 | Acts |
| 00 | Paul's authentic letters |
| 04 | Timothy and Titus |
| 03 | Peter, James, Jude |
| 02 | 2 and 3 John |
| 01 | Hebrews |
| 12 | Revelations |
| 66 | TOTAL |

Ponder this table for a few moments and jot down here some insights derived from the table data:

The authentic letters of Paul do not contain even a single instance of the term "elder." Given the fact that these letters address a variety of tough issues confronting the communities to whom they are written, how would you explain the fact that Paul never refers to anyone within these communities as an "elder"?

*The authentic letters of Paul do not contain a single instance of the term "elder."*

## Who is Called "Elder"?

3. Let's explore how the term "elder" is used within the Gospels. Each of the Synoptics has between five and thirteen occurrences of "elder." John's Gospel, in contrast, has only a single occurrence, namely, John 8:9. The text literally reads: "they went out one by one beginning with the elders." The RSV has "beginning with the eldest"—a mistranslation which was corrected in the NRSV. What is being implied here by the narrative when it relates that "the elders" had the good sense to depart first?

*The contemporaries of Jesus did not regard him or his disciples as "elders."*

Since this is the only instance of "elder" in John's Gospel, it is clear that *presbyteros* is never used to designate Jesus or any of his disciples. If one combed through the Synoptic Gospels as well, one would be confirmed in the conclusion that the contemporaries of Jesus did not regard him or his disciples as "elders." Who, then, did the Synoptics designate as "elders"? To find this out for yourself, look up the five instances of presbyteros in Luke and note "who" is designated as "elder" in each case:

| Text | Who is designated as "elder"? |
|---|---|
| Luke 7:3 | |
| Luke 9:22 | |
| Luke 15:25 | |
| Luke 20:1 | |
| Luke 22:52 | |

What generalized conclusion can you draw?

## Elders in Jerusalem

4. If there were "elders" in the Jesus movement, they might be expected to show up in the Acts of the Apostles. All in all, there are eighteen occurrences of *presbyteros* in Acts. If you had chosen to examine each of these instances and then synthesized your results, you would have something like the following:

   (a) In eight instances, "elders" are associated with the high priest (e.g., Acts 4:5, 23:14) and, in the mind of most scholars, this implies that the term *presbyteros* was used here to designate the members of the high priest's council who advised him in matters of importance and shared with him the administration of the community. The usage here is in continuity with what you discovered in Luke 20:1 and 22:52 above.

   (b) In ten instances, "elders" is used to designate a class of persons within the Jerusalem church (Acts 11:30; 14:23; 15:2, 4, 6, 22, 23; 16:4; 20:17; 21:18).

*The term presbyteros was used here to designate the members of the high priest's council.*

Examine a few of these latter texts and try to decide "who" is being designated as presbyter within this community. Write your results here:

What is evident here is that Luke does not think it necessary to explain that his use of "elders" within the Jerusalem community is somehow different from his use of "elders" respecting Jewish institutions of Jesus' day. What does this imply?

Many scholars conclude from this that the Jerusalem church used an organizational model familiar to Jews. Just as lay "elders" cooperated together in administrating the local synagogue, and just as priest "elders" grouped around the high priest to administer the affairs of the temple, so too, "elders" became the natural designation for the principal leaders within the Jerusalem community.

*The Jerusalem church used an organizational model familiar to Jews.*

If one follows this closely within Acts, three phases are evident within the Jerusalem community:

(a) Initially no "elders" are mentioned. During this phase, the pastoral initiative within the Jerusalem church is repeatedly shown to be in the hands of "the apostles."
(b) Then, without warning, funds are brought by Barnabas and Saul "to the elders" (11:30) in the Jerusalem church. Formerly, it will be noted, money was customarily brought and laid "at the apostles' feet" (5:2). A change has taken place. A few chapters later, the phrase "the apostles and elders" (15:2, 4, 6, 22, 23) is used again and again to describe the supreme decision making council of the Jerusalem church. This allows one to conclude that "elders" now share in the decision making and administration of the Jerusalem church.
(c) In the final phase, the apostles have seemingly left Jerusalem permanently, and one now finds that the direction of the community is entirely in the hands of "elders." See Acts 21:18. James here appears to be acting as president of the council of elders, although he has no official title here or in Acts 15:13.

Up to this point, the above investigations enables us to form the following conclusions relative to the organizational structures and offices evident within the Jerusalem church:

- The Jerusalem church appears to have known only the offices of "apostles" and "elders." "Bishops" and "deacons" were either entirely unknown, or, if known, of little significance in community life.
- The Jerusalem church did not have to invent either the name nor the function of "elders." This office traditionally existed as the routine way in which both the local synagogue and the Jerusalem temple formed collegial bodies for the purpose of deliberating and administrating their respective community affairs.
- Within the development of the Jerusalem church, it would appear that this task of deliberating and administering was initially in the hands of the apostles. In the course of time, however, the apostles appear to have associated "elders" with themselves in all areas of administration. Then, once the apostles departed, the "elders" alone remained as the governing council, with James appearing to function as the presiding elder.

*Once the apostles departed, the "elders" alone remained as the governing council.*

5. If one would search through all the other books of the Christian Scriptures, one would find only one instance in which the term *presbyteros* is used relative to the Twelve. See 1 P 5:1-5. Here Peter calls himself _____ Based on the context, why would you surmise that this term is used for Peter here?

## Prophets and Teachers in Antioch

6. Now look in upon the church at Antioch in which Paul spent his formative years as a follower of Jesus. See Acts 13:1-4. What ministries appear to be prized most highly in this church? What can you conclude?

Note that Barnabas is named first as "prophet and teacher" in the church at Antioch. Paul is named last. Is this order of names deliberate or accidental? _____ To find out examine Acts 11:19-26 wherein the foundation of the Antioch church is recorded. Now, what do you conclude must be the place of Barnabas in this church?

*The Antioch community appears to be under the direction of "prophets and teachers."*

Note that Acts never names any "elders" in Antioch. Only "prophets and teachers" are named, and it can be presumed that Luke wants us to understand these terms as designating the principal ministers within this community. If Luke deliberately avoids the term *presbyteros* when speaking of the church in Antioch (also Acts 15:2, 22f, 35, 40; 18:22), most scholars would take this to be an indication that here there was a different form of church organization or that, if elders did exist, they had little influence over the charismatic "prophets and teachers" (see, e.g., Burtchaell: 299-316).

---

### Note on James

During the council meeting of Acts 15, James forwards the debate by adding a scriptural proof to Peter's testimony and by drawing up the compromise resolution which carries the day. From this vantage point, he appears already to be acting as chairman of the council. This earlier instance undoubtedly prepares the reader of Acts to anticipate that James would be the chief receptionist in Acts 21 when the apostles are gone.

In even an earlier instance, Peter is presented as sending his urgent message "to James and to the brethren" (12:17), a clue that James is being singled out in some way which only Acts 15 and Acts 21 make clear.

Lest it be thought that this is James, the brother of John and one of the Twelve, recall that Luke reports that this James was beheaded by Herod (Acts 12:2). Who is this James then? Based upon evidence from Galatians, it would appear that this James was "the Lord's brother" (Gal 1:18 and 2:9; mentioned also in Mark 6:3 and Matt 13:55).

## Bishops and Deacons in the Pastoral Epistles

7. Now read Phil 1:1. Alas! Note that Paul addresses his letter "to all the saints . . . together with their bishops and deacons" (*episkopoi* and *diakonoi*). In the Christian Scriptures, where "bishops" are mentioned, there are almost always associated with "deacons." Both terms, moreover, are habitually used in the plural. If a single church had many "bishops," what does this say about the office of bishop in that community?

By the third century, the term "bishop" was being reserved for the chief pastor/teacher/celebrant within the principal urban churches. Needless to say, this was not the situation in the first century church of Philippi (or in the many other early church who had "bishops and deacons," e.g., Did. 15:1-2). The existence of many bishops within the same household community indicates that, in its origins, the office of bishop appears to have been shared by many men who exercised a shared pastoral leadership. Since Paul's letter never mentions "bishops" after his formal greeting, it is impossible to say exactly what their roles were or in what way they collaborated.

The appearance of "bishops and deacons" in Phil 1:1 has created controversy because this is the only authentic letter of Paul us-

---

### The Meaning of "Bishops"

The term *episkopos* ("bishop") occurs only four times in the Christian Scriptures and thirteen times in the Septuagint.

The Greek term points to someone who has oversight over a group of people, e.g., someone in charge of a construction site or someone supervising grape harvesters. The Septuagint, for instance, uses this very term when it presents Joseph as advising the Pharaoh "to appoint overseers (lit., "bishops") over the land, and take [and store] a fifth part of the produce of the land of Egypt during the seven plenteous years" (Gen 41:34). This term was not clearly associated with any religious office or ministry by those speaking Greek in Paul's day. Moreover, the Jewish tradition never made significant use of this term or its Hebrew equivalent (save at Qumran) to designate any specific office or function within the community.

Most scholars agree that *episkopoi* ("bishops") may have been an equivalent term for *presbyteroi* ("elders"). Acts suggests this equivalence when, in Ephesus, Paul assembled the "elders of the church" and urged them to be watchful over "the flock in which the Holy Spirit has made you guardians (lit. "bishops")" (Acts 20:28). This is the first instance in which "elders" are spoken of as functioning as "bishops/overseers"—terms, which during the course of the next hundred years, would be used interchangeably in many church contexts.

ing these terms. Some scholars, noting that Paul uses these terms only once, prefer to believe that the phrase "with the bishops and deacons" constitutes a later addition to the letter which was originally addressed only to "all the saints" (see Schweizer: 103, n. 395). If this were the case, then Philippians would take its place alongside the other authentic letters of Paul which are addressed to the entire community of saints without any special reference to any church leadership.

*The office of bishop appears to have been shared by many men who exercised a shared pastoral leadership.*

Other scholars have tried to deal with the unusual and unexpected greetings to the "bishops and deacons" by allowing that the phrase is original, but they then regard Philippians to be one of the latest Pauline epistles and a testimony to the late first-century transition within the Pauline congregations toward a fixed form of community organization (e.g., Campenhausen: 69). This latter explanation see Philippians as representing transitional phase in the direction of the Pastoral Epistles wherein "bishops and deacons" are clearly named as the principal pastors. It is to these Pastoral Epistles that our attention must now turn.

8. Thirteen letters are attributed to Paul in the Christian Scriptures. Of these, only four out of thirteen "Pauline" letters make mention of "bishops and deacons." Philippians has just been considered. The other three (namely, 1 Tim, 2 Tim, and Tit) distinguish themselves from the other writings of Paul and are commonly called the Pastoral Epistles. With almost universal agreement, the Pastoral Epistles are classed as coming very late in Paul's life or, what is more probable, they represent letters written in his name by way of sanctioning the new church order of "bishops and deacons" which had come to replace the previous church order of "apostles and teachers" which Paul had endorsed while he visited them. There are clues within the letters attributed to Paul, therefore, to distinguish between the "earlier" and the "later" mode of church organization.

*Only four out of thirteen "Pauline" letters make mention of "bishops and deacons."*

Let's examine the "later" mode in some detail. To begin with, the letters written to Timothy and Titus are evidently written to specific individuals. This departs from Paul's practice of writing to the entire community. Take a few moments and examine the opening lines of three of Paul's early letters to verify this for yourself.

The Timothy letters purport to represent the affairs at Ephesus (1 Tim 1:3) while the Titus letter pertains to Crete (Tit 1:5). In both instances, Timothy and Titus are referred to by Paul as "my true child" (1 Tim 1:2, Tit 1:4). Check this and try to decide what this preferential designation might mean:

*The Pastoral Epistles presuppose that "bishops and deacons" were to be appointed.*

But there are no clear indications as to whether Timothy and Titus do this alone or with the collaboration of others. No job description is given for the office of bishop or of deacon; yet, something of their functioning can be surmised from the careful listing of the necessary qualifications given. Examine 1 Tim 3:1-13. What can be surmised respecting the function of each of these ministers?

*Not enough information is given to decide precisely how these "elders" are related to the "bishops and deacons."*

To further complicate the state of affairs in the "later" Pauline communities, one must note that the Pastoral Epistles occasionally speak of "elders" as having functions which apparently overlap those assigned to the "bishops and deacons." In 1 Timothy, for instance, "elders" are referred to as those who "labor in preaching and teaching" (1 Tim 5:17). Earlier in the same epistle, "elders" are referred to as having laid hands upon Timothy (1 Tim 4:14). As a consequence, it is not clear whether Timothy is an "elder," "bishop," or both (see boxed note above). Timothy's principal duty is named as that of "teaching" (1 Tim 4:16). Not enough information is given to decide precisely how these "elders" are related to the "bishops and deacons" which were mentioned earlier. Scholars themselves have found no universal agreement in this matter.

Examine Tit 1:5-9 (which echoes Acts 14:23) and see whether this suggests to you that the terms "elder" and "bishop" are here being used interchangeably. In any case, note your conclusions here:

## The Spirit as Organizing Principle in Corinth

*In the nine early letters of Paul, no special class of leaders is designated.*

9. Let's return now to the nine early letters of Paul. In what we have already seen, these letters are addressed to the entire community. No special class of leaders is designated as responsible for overseeing the community. According to 1 Cor 12, Paul regards everyone is the community as having some "gift of the Spirit"; yet, this does not result in an egalitarian society for "God has appointed" some to the "higher gifts" (1 Cor 12:28, 31).

> Paul develops the idea of the Spirit as the organizing principle of the Christian congregation. There is no need for any fixed system with its rules and regulations and prohibitions. . . . The community is not understood as a sociological entity, and

the Spirit which governs it does not act within the framework of a particular church order or constitution. .... In the Church, 'freedom' is the basic controlling principle; for the Spirit of Christ, which is the giver of freedom, urges men [and women] on not to independence and self-assertion but to loving service (Campenhausen: 58).

How did this ideal work out in Corinth? Only partially. From the actual tenor of Paul's letter, one can sense that having the Spirit as the organizing principle leaves something to be desired. Consider the following:

(a) Read 1 Cor 6:2-6. Here Paul suggests that the "saints" are taking each other to civil courts precisely because they have not been able to find a "man among you wise enough to decide [grievances] between members of the brotherhood" (1 Cor 6:5). Where are the apostles and prophets here? Not to be found. This must mean that their "gifts," even while most highly prized, do not include settling disputes among the members.

(b) For another instance, read 1 Cor 14:26-33. Here the order and conduct of public prayer is at stake. Prophets are directly involved, but as part of the problem rather than part of the solution. Hence, even though the gift of prophesy is number two on Paul's list (1 Cor 12:28), the presupposition is that "the prophets" are not in change, not even of the conduct of worship. Everyone contributes (1 Cor 14:26) and everyone is expected to order things such that only "two or three prophets speak" and "others weigh what is said" (1 Cor 14:29).

*Paul at no time is tempted to appoint "bishops and deacons" or "elders."*

Despite these and other indications of a breakdown of harmony and good order within 1 Corinthians, Paul at no time is tempted to appoint "bishops and deacons" or "elders" to take charge of these areas of community life which have fallen through the cracks. Paul continues to doggedly maintain that those who have good sense will know how to regulate things to the benefit of all. This same strategy prevails in Paul's subsequent letter(s) (2 Cor.) as well.

Read carefully 1 Cor 12:27-30. Which three ministries are prized most highly by Paul?


Note that "administrators" are named in the sixth place. The Greek term used here (kupernseis) refers literally to a pilot or helmsman who has the art of guiding the course of a ship. The term is metaphorically used here and in other ancient literature by way of designating the art of governing a social body such that it arrives at its intended goal.

While Paul does not place "administrators" among the highest gifts, he does, none the less, consider them worthy to be classified among the God-given gifts to be prized by the community. There actual role or job description is not given.

*Paul does not place "administrators" among the God-given gifts to be prized.*

What appears to be the case here? (a) Are these "administrators" to be understood as exercising a recognized and permanent office within the community? _____ (b) Or are the "administrators" here understood only as exercising transitory roles which this or that member of the community might spontaneously undertake by way of organizing this or that concrete need arising within the community? _____ Explain your choice:

However one resolves the above problem, it remains clear that Paul does not call upon these "administrators" or any other office holders to bring order into the problematic areas of community life within the church at Corinth. He fully expects that the one Spirit animating all will bring a resolution to all its prevailing problems.

*Paul expects that the one Spirit animating all will bring a resolution to all its prevailing problems.*

10. In our own day, the Quakers, more than any other community, have endeavored to put Paul's model of Spirit-led community organization into practice. When Quakers meet on Sunday mornings in their Meeting Houses, for instance, no one is assigned the task of leading the community worship. In fact, there are no fixed prayers of any kind or any prayer books. All sit in silence at the designated time. All open their hearts and minds to the Spirit of the Lord. All are persuaded that they must wait upon the Spirit to lead them in worship and not resort to rites. And so, after much silence, one person shares a spontaneous prayer, another shares a concern for those who are suffering from some injustice, another leads a song of praise, another admonishes the community for a collective failing. When the designated time for closing arrives, all rise and leave. Again, no closing prayer or prayer leader is operative.

The same thing holds true when Quakers embark upon decision making. When decisions are to be made which effect the whole life of the community, everyone assembles. Open discussion, persuasion, and times of prayer enter into the process. In the end, no decision is considered binding until every single person present can say "yes" and live with the shared consequences. Such a consensual model of decision making requires much more time than simply voting and following the majority. On the other hand, while much slower, the results are much more lasting since, due to the process, all are moved by the same Spirit. There is never any danger of the majority overriding and discounting the minority.

In brief, Quakers today offer a modern-day intimation that the early Pauline churches might have worked—at least for a time—without any designated office holders and without any fixed patterns for community worship. One must be cautious of such cross-cultural comparisons, however. The Quakers of today are guided by modern instincts which are entirely distinct from those operative among the Corinthians of the first century. Maybe it is for this reason that the Corinthian model failed to persist in history while the Quakers have had a good deal of success.

*Quakers offer a modern-day intimation that the early Pauline churches worked.*

## The Failure of Paul's Model

The Pauline letters show two phases: (a) The nine early letters indicate that, during thirty to sixty years, there were no designated leaders and the Spirit was relied upon as the organizing principle; (b) The Pastoral Epistles written near the end of the first century indicate that "bishops and deacons" (with "elders") were expected to oversee the key aspects of community existence. From what you know of Paul's letter and of community organization, what would you surmise were the leading causes for the abandonment of Paul's early model and its replacement by "bishops and deacons"?

*Paul's early model was abandoned.*

After the death of the apostle Paul, the communities which he founded could no longer count upon him for any further trouble shooting or emergency interventions. Accordingly, there was an impulse to learn from and adapt for themselves corrective models of community organization which embraced stable leadership. The Pastoral Epistles testify how designated leaders responsible for coordinated the key functions of teaching and judging came to replace an earlier charismatic order which was only partially successful. One can presume that these leaders exercised supervision in the arena of community worship; yet, it is impossible to say whether they became the regular presiders at worship. In any case, the question remains as to why Paul himself did not appoint "officers" in the communities that he left behind or, if Phil 1:1 and Acts 14:23 are to be credited as authentic, why Paul held out so long before designating "bishops and

*The Pastoral Epistles testify how designated leaders came to replace an earlier charismatic order.*

deacons" as being in charge. What value or values was he trying to preserve that might have caused him to resist such a practical necessity?

11. From what has been examined above, you have become acquainted with four distinct forms of community organization within the early churches: (a) the Jerusalem model, (b) the Antioch model, (c) the Corinthian model, and (d) the Pastoral Letters model. Take a few moments to make a chart summarizing your results: Use a blank page at the end of this Case or at the end of the book for this purpose.

*Did Jesus ever designate any "offices" or "organizational plan"?*

12. Now the key questions can be put forward. Did Jesus ever designate any "offices" or "organizational plan" which was to be used by the churches founded in his name? _____ On the basis of the Christian Scriptures, how would you defend your conclusion?

Roman Catholics and other mainline churches have traditionally maintained that the apostles appointed "bishops" in the churches that they founded. To what degree can this position be maintained on the basis of the evidence in the Christian Scriptures?

*The predominant third-century model consisted of a single bishop surrounded by his council of elders.*

By the third century, the predominant model for local church organization was that of having an administrative team (*collegium*) consisting of a single bishop surrounded by his council of elders. In addition to being the principal teacher and judge, the bishop also functioned as the normal presider at the community's liturgies. Since this model turned out to be the most stable and advantageous system during this period, does it offer some support for the current organizational structures found within the Roman, Episcopal, and Methodist churches? _____ If so, how much and of what kind?

Do the Christian Scriptures offer support for the Quaker model of church order and allow, at least in theory, that a legitimate church of Jesus Christ could exist without the offices of "bishop," "presbyter," or "deacon." _____ If so, specify the support offered by the Christian Scriptures.

13. The various churches have been in conflict for centuries regarding the issue of church organization. In most cases this conflict let to an adversarial mentality which promoted a type of scholarship bent upon proving that "my church and my church alone" has the organizational structure that is divinely warranted in the Sacred Scriptures. On the basis of what you have discovered, what might be a starting point for resolving these conflicts such that each church might positively affirm its own organizational structures while leaving open room for the mutual recognition of different church orders?

14. What startling discoveries did you make while exploring this Case Study? Describe them for yourself here:

15. Did this Case Study raise any fundamental questions for you while you were completing it? If so, note them here so that you can return to them at a later moment?


Completion time = _____

Total time used on this Case = \_\_\_\_\_ minutes

Again, well done! Set everything aside, rest, and then come back to the following.

## Analysis

This Case Study has briefly examined the diversity of ministerial organization present within some of the early churches. Time and space do not permit a more exhaustive treatment. Nor have we attempted to trace how developments in the late first century gradually blossomed into a full blown and nearly universal presence of a single bishop, a pastoral team of elders/presbyters, and a group of deacons within each of the major urban churches.

Given the limitations of this study and given the fact that this Case Study was prepared with extensive commentary within the investigation itself, a systematic analysis will not be undertaken. In lieu of this, however, four questions have been prepared which draw upon the conclusions put forward by the Bishops' Committee on the Liturgy (*Study Text 3: Ministries in the Church*) and by Raymond Brown (*The Churches the Apostles Left Behind*).

**1 Q**: What exaggerations are to be avoided when using the Christian Scriptures to determine the practice and structure of ministry within the early churches?

**A**: There are two exaggerations to be avoided in reviewing the practice and structure of ministry in the New Testament:

(1) the New Testament is a unified document which presents a clear and fully developed picture of Church order and Church ministry; and
(2) New Testament ministry, inspired by the freshness of the Easter experience and animated by the promised Spirit is completely unstructured (*Study Text* 3: 17-18).

**2 Q:** What conclusions have biblical scholars arrived at when exploring the structures of ministry found in the early churches?

**A:** Biblical scholars have been pealing away the layers of history, culture, language, and theology in the New Testament in order to understand better the early Church experiences. One can only summarize some of their findings related to ministry:

- the Gospels indicate that Jesus gave his disciples few instructions about how to organize the Christian community;
- the first leaders of the Jerusalem community introduced flexible structures in order to serve the needs of all segments of the growing Church;
- the Twelve recognized that they could guide the Church in carrying out its ministry of reconciliation only by creating a flexible Church order;
- the apostles [Paul?] recognized and encouraged the variety of spiritual gifts present within the body of Christ;
- it is clear that the earliest books of the New Testament present a rich diversity of ministries for laymen and laywomen, and some of these ministries were not formalized by the laying on of hands;
- it is only in the later New Testament era when the Churches were reflecting on their traditions [and problems?] and searching for canons of belief that fixed, empirical criteria of the apostolic office [of bishop?] so familiar to us would be formulated;
- it is doubtful that a single ecclesiastical office remains today in the same form as the New Testament Churches employed it (*Study Text* 3: 18).

*Jesus gave his disciples few instructions about how to organize the Christian community.*

**3 Q:** What are the ecumenical consequences of this Case Study?

**A:** In a divided Christianity we have had a long history of using the Scriptures to prove ourselves right, whether as churches or as individuals. The greater contribution of modern NT studies, therefore, may consist in highlighting the ways in which Scripture can *challenge constructively*. A recognition of the range of NT ecclesiological diversity makes the claim of any church to be absolutely faithful to the Scriptures much more complex. We are faithful but in our own specific way; and both ecumenics and biblical studies should make us aware that there are other ways of being faithful to which we do not do justice (Brown, 1984:149).

There are Christians, of course, who still reject the existence of NT diversities. Some do so from a rigid theory of divine inspiration which discounts the human situation of the NT writ-

*The range of NT ecclesiological diversity makes the claim of any church to be absolutely faithful more complex.*

ings. . . . Others reject diversity in the NT because they project on the first century an ideal situation wherein Jesus had planned out the church, the apostles were of one mind in carrying out his directives, and the only ones who differed were the troublemakers condemned by the NT authors (Brown, 1984: 147).

**4 Q**: Did the Twelve fancy themselves as bishops?

**A**: On the basis of the investigations undertaken, one can conclude that the Twelve were not addressed by the Jerusalem community as "bishops." Nonetheless, one can fairly ask whether the Twelve functioned as "bishops" even when they were not so designated.

This study opened up with an affirmation by Raymond Brown to the effect that the Twelve never "served as heads of local churches." At the end of this study, Brown's biblical conclusion can be clarified.

> According to Acts, the Twelve did exercise a type of leadership in the Jerusalem church in the early days when that church constituted all of Christendom, and Peter was the spokesman for the Twelve. But Acts 6:2 shows Peter on behalf of the Twelve refusing administration properly understood when that became necessary because of numbers and complexity. Thus it is more correct to say that from the moment that the Jerusalem church needed precise supervision, James along with the presbyters played that role. . . . In the mid-30s, then, it would appear that the need was recognized for local supervision of the Hebrew and Hellenist communities in Jerusalem and [this need] was met in two different ways, respectively, by James and the presbyters and by the seven Hellenist authorities. Each of these supervisory groups would have managed the distribution of the common funds, made decisions affecting the life style of Christians, and entered into discussion about church policy as regards converts. The urging of the common assembly by the Twelve (Acts 6:3) which led to this development is the closest the Twelve ever come in the NT to appointing local leaders (Brown, 1980 323, 327-328).

In sum, Brown along with others would conclude that the heralding of the Gospel and the training of disciples was the predominant passion of the Twelve. Outside of this, community administration and decision making was left to others—the Seven and the "elders." As a result, it can be seen that, even when the issue of titles is set aside, it is hazardous to conclude that the Twelve were functioning as "bishops."

*Acts 6:2 shows Peter on behalf of the Twelve refusing administration.*

*Community administration and decision making was left to others.*

This negative response, however, should not obscure the fact that the Twelve were personally trained and commissioned by Jesus himself and that they were relied upon to systematically train others in those habits of mind and heart into which Jesus had apprenticed them. Hence, even though the Twelve were not "bishops" in name or in function, they did, nonetheless, exert tremendous influence and pastoral oversight (*episkopē*) by virtue of their preaching the Gospel to outsiders and their training insiders in the ways of Jesus.

*The Twelve did, nonetheless, exert tremendous influence and pastoral oversight.*

When the Twelve originally became disciples of Jesus, they had to surrender themselves wholeheartedly to be influenced, to be persuaded, to be guided by Jesus. In response to that self-giving which is sustained by a deep admiration of the master, Jesus was able to progressively enlarge and transform their habits of perception and of judgment such that they were grasped by the way of life which Jesus received from the Father. In the end, they could say: "No one has ever seen God; it is the only Son, who is nearest to the Father's heart, who has made him known" John 1:18).

Those who gathered around the Twelve after Pentecost had to be moved with the selfsame admiration and trust which the disciples felt for Jesus. Without a sustained admiration and trust, nothing significant could be learned or transmitted. In a sense, the Twelve deeply *knew Jesus and exemplified Jesus* by virtue of the deep transformation which they had experienced under his direction. Only to the degree that the Twelve progressively enlarged and transformed the settled instincts of the Jews surrounding them would they be able to share what they had received from Jesus. The circle is thus complete: "He who receives you receives me, and he who receives me receives him who sent me" (Matt 10:40).

*The Twelve deeply knew Jesus and exemplified Jesus.*

One can immediately see from this that some who bear the title of "bishop" today share only marginally in the pastoral authority and transforming presence which characterized the Twelve. On the other hand, many pastors and lay ministers in today's local churches who are loved and admired because of their contagious knowing and exemplifying of the way of Jesus (and who are, to that degree, the functional successors of the Twelve) do not and will not ever bear the title of "bishop." In conclusion, the issue as to whether the Twelve fancied themselves as bishops has a historical complexity and a pastoral importance in today's church which defies easy answers.

## Application to the Churches Today

On the basis of everything that you have discovered, what applications would you make regarding the "offices" and "ministries" in your church today? Generate a few spinoffs and write them down here and in the margins.

## Further Readings for Case Five

Bishops' Committee on the Liturgy
    *Study Text III: Ministries in the Church.* Washington, D.C.: United States Catholic Conference Publications Office, 1974.

Brown, Raymond E.
    *Priest and Bishop: Biblical Reflections.* New York: Paulist, 1970.

    "*Episkopē* and episkopos: The New Testament Evidence," *Theological Studies* 41:322-338, 1980.

    *The Churches the Apostles Left Behind.* New York: Paulist, 1984.

Bruce, F. F.
    *Peter, Stephen, James, and John: Studies in Early Non-Pauline Christianity.* Grand Rapids: Eerdmans, 1980.

Burtchaell, James Tunstead
    *From Synagogue to Church: Public Services and Offices in the Earliest Christian Communities.* Cambridge: University Press, 1992.

Campenhausen, Hans von
    *Ecclesiastical Authority and Spiritual Power in the Church of the First Three Centuries.* Stanford: University Press. Tr. by J.A. Baker from 1953 German orig., 1969.

Cooke, Bernard
    *Ministry to Word and Sacraments.* Philadelphia: Fortress, 1976.

Kelly, George A.
    *The New Biblical Theorists: Raymond E. Brown and Beyond.* Ann Arbor: Servant Books. [well-argued apologetic against modern biblical scholarship as represented by Brown], 1983.

McBrien, Richard
    *Catholicism.* Minneapolis: Winston. pp. 569-602, 1980.

Schweizer, Eduard
    *Church Order in the New Testament.* London: SCM Press. Tr. by Frank Clarke from the 1959 German orig., 1961.

Tanquerey, Adolphus
    *A Manual of Dogmatic Theology.* New York: Desclee. Tr. by John J. Byrnes from the 1904 Latin orig., 1939.

## CASE SIX

# Collaboration as the Hallmark of Peter's Authority

During the former broadcasts of Televangelist Jimmy Swaggart, one often saw a ten-foot tall, free-standing placard which looked something like this:

*According to Swaggart, the Roman Catholic hierarchy is the leading hinderance to the Gospel of Jesus Christ.*

According to Swaggart, the Roman Catholic hierarchy is the leading hinderance to the Gospel of Jesus Christ. Swaggart's position here ought not to be too surprising. Most Protestants over fifty were raised with a strong dose of warnings against the soul-threatening dangers of substituting an infallible pope for the infallible bible. Swaggart represents the anti-Catholic position that emerged from the Reformation of the sixteenth century.

*According to some Catholics the unbroken line of popes is what makes "the true church."*

On the Catholic side, there are priests and lay people who routinely believe that the key element which makes Roman Catholicism "the true church" is the unbroken line of popes that began with the apostle Peter. In a recent visit to a rural church in northwest Ohio, I noted that the parish bulletin had an entire page devoted to "A Look at Church History." The bulletin began:

> Jesus Christ established only ONE Church, the Catholic Church, nearly 2,000 years ago. He did this by making St. Peter the first

Pope and giving His twelve Apostles the authority to rule and teach in His Name. The authority of Jesus still remains in the world today. It has been handed down through the centuries to other Catholic Popes and bishops. In all, there have been 263 Popes in the Catholic Church. Their names and the years they reigned as Vicar of Christ have been recorded in history.

A month later, I stopped to pray in a Russian Orthodox church in Cincinnati. I left this church with another bulletin. The heading, in this case, was "Origins of Orthodoxy." This bulletin stated:

> Jesus Christ founded his church through the Apostles. By the grace received from God at Pentecost, the Apostles established the Church throughout the ancient world. St. Paul founded the Church of Antioch; St. Peter and St. James, the Church of Jerusalem; St. Andrew, the Church of Constantinople; St. Mark, the Church of Alexandria; St. Peter and St. Paul, the Church of Rome. The Roman (or Western) church separated from the True Church in the year 1054 after changing the Creed and wrongly claiming supremacy of the Bishop of Rome (Pope) over the other bishops. Drifting further from its origins, the Western church was then shattered into a myriad of sects by the Protestant Reformation.

It is clear that the Orthodox Christians regard papal claims as one of the leading causes of the Latin Church's breaking away from "the True Church"—the Orthodox Church. Orthodox Christians, therefore, perceived the papacy as lacking a biblical foundation long before the Protestant reformers began making their objections.

*Orthodox Christians regard papal claims lacking a biblical foundation.*

Catholics have traditionally regarded Matt 16:18 as securely specifying Jesus' intention to establish the papacy as an enduring aspect of Christianity. The *Baltimore Catechism* helped to form the faith of most Catholics forty years or older (myself included). In this catechism's treatment of Catholic belief regarding the Church, one finds the following text and illustrative diagram:

Q147. Did Christ give special power to any one of the apostles?

A147. Christ gave special power in His Church to Saint Peter by making him head of the apostles and the chief teacher and ruler of the entire Church.

It would seem that people would find it difficult to object to this simple and compelling argument. But people do object. Swaggart's book, *Catholicism and Christianity*, frames the question as follows: "Did Jesus give Peter the keys to the church, making him the first in a long succession of popes, as claimed by the Catholic Church?" His response begins as follows:

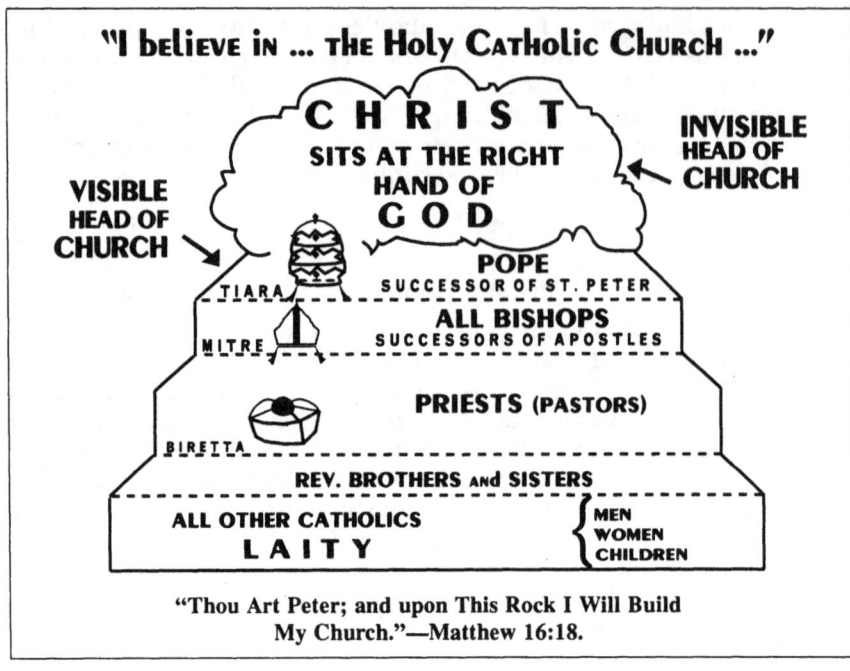

First, and foremost, we know that Christ is the head of the church (Ephesians 1:22). Peter was never head of the church, nor is any other man—only Christ. Second, Peter himself said that Christ was the true cornerstone (1 Peter 2:4-8).... I think it is obvious, from even a cursory investigation of Scripture, that the disciples did not take our Lord's words ("... upon this rock I will build my church," Matthew 16:18) to mean that He was appointing Peter to be their pope. A short time later they asked Jesus (in Matthew 18:1) who among them would be the greatest. If Jesus had previously stated that Peter was to be their pope, the disciples would have automatically assumed that he was the greatest among them. Of course, this was not what Jesus was saying when He made this statement (Swaggart: 25).

Swaggart's opening argument goes nowhere because it fails to correctly present Catholic belief. Even the diagram on the preceding page clearly presents Christ as "the invisible head of the Church" while the pope, in so far as he is the Vicar of Christ, is the "visible head of the church." Swaggart's second argument, however, does have some merit. Nonetheless, many will be tempted to dismiss Swaggart out of hand on the basis that he is no biblical scholar and that he is too eager to discredit Catholicism.

*Swaggart's opening argument fails to correctly present Catholic belief.*

Meanwhile modern Catholic biblical scholars have themselves taken a much more nuanced approach to Matt 16:18. Had Swaggart bothered to take up the Catholic Biblical Commentary, for instance, he would have discovered that informed Catholic scholars have stopped imagining that they can justify everything that the papacy has become by citing Matt 16:18. Relative to this and every other text, the moderate Catholic scholars who produced this representative commentary insisted that the meaning of any text must be first determined within its original context.

*The meaning of any text must be first determined within its original context.*

When this is done relative to Matt 16:13-23, it becomes evident that the presenting problem is neither "Who is the chief teacher and ruler of the entire Church?" nor "Who is my visible representative on earth?" Rather, Jesus appears concerned to learn from his disciples, "Who do men say that the Son of man is? (Matt 16:13) After hearing that the people regard Jesus as one or the other of the prophets, Jesus then turns the question directly to his disciples: "But who do you say that I am?" (16:15). Simon replies, "The Christ, the Son of the living God." In response, Jesus praises "Simon Bar-Jona" by noting that neither he nor any other "flesh and blood" person made this known "but my Father who is in heaven" (16:17). Simon is thus recognized as someone so intimate with the Father as to be inspired by him. But more. "You are Peter. . . ."

> Simon gets the name by which he is usually known in the NT; and those who doubt that Jesus spoke these words forget that the NT has no other passage in which the change of name is explained. . . . "Peter" comes from the G[ree]k *petros*, the masculinized form of the fem. noun *petra*, "rock," which represents the Aram[aic] *kēphā* (McKenzie II:92).

In effect, therefore, Simon received a nickname, "Peter," which, even in the Gospels, overshadows his given name. What did the biblical scholars preparing this commentary say was the force of this nickname?

*The reason why Peter is called the rock is the faith that he has just shown in his confession.*

> In the context, the reason why Peter is called the rock is the faith that he has just shown in his confession. He has made known the faith of the disciples; and it is upon faith in Jesus as the Messiah that the group Jesus has formed will endure. Peter is the speaker and example of this faith (McKenzie II:92).

Even the moderate Catholic scholarship of the Jerome Biblical Commentary, therefore, says nothing about Jesus making Peter "chief teacher and ruler of the entire Church." Moreover, by allowing that it is Peter's personal faith in Jesus as the Messiah which is the foundation of the future church, Catholic scholars effectively reaffirm the judgment of most early Church Fathers and of Protestant scholars as well. Where, then, is the foundation for seeing Peter as the "chief teacher and rule of the entire church"? This can be discovered only when Peter's whole way of acting within the church is explored in its entirety.

## Purpose

Even with this relaxation of the former hard-line apologetics surrounding Matt 16:18, most Catholics are not willing to say that the papacy has no foundation whatsoever. What foundation does exist, however, must be based upon an investigation of how and when the Christian Scriptures present Peter as exercising leadership within the early church. The purpose of this Case Study, consequently, is to enable you to conduct such an investigation. This biblical exploration will allow you to retrace how Catholic and Protestants scholars alike have come to a shared assessment of Peter's function within the early church. Such a study, in its turn, has repercussions when it comes time for Catholic, Orthodox, and Protestant Christians to assess the origins and function of the papal ministry within the universal church.

*The purpose of this Case is to assess Peter's function within the early church.*

Before getting started, you are again invited to record your initial perceptions to three questions. By recording your spontaneous judgments now, you will be providing yourself with a declaration of your preliminary understanding of the issues. After completing the Case Study, you will then be able to reread your initial reflections and gauge to what degree you have been broadened or transformed by your inquiries. The three questions designed for this purpose are as follows:

1. Do the Christian Scriptures assign Peter a unique office or title which elevated him above the other apostles? _____ If so, name it and explain it.



2. If the Christian Scriptures do not assign Peter a unique office or title, do they nonetheless present Peter as the most distinguished and noteworthy apostle? _____ Does Peter then have what the Orthodox Christians like to call a "primacy of honor"? _____ Explain yourself here:



3. Do the Christian Scriptures present Peter as being the final court of appeals when it came time for making binding decisions governing the whole church? _____ As such, did Peter then exer-

cise a "primacy of power" within the early church? _____ Explain yourself here:

At this time, if you are so inclined, take your Christian Scriptures in your hands and pray that the Spirit of God may guide you in rightly understanding the truth about Peter within the early church.

Translation = _____
Starting time = _____ (100-200 minutes needed)

## Initial Word Studies

1. Word studies of the Christian Scriptures are revealing. Examine the following table indicating total occurrences of certain names within the Christian Scriptures.

| Occurrences | Name |
|---|---|
| 972 | Jesus |
| 569 | Christ |
| 162 | Paul |
| 161 | Peter |
| 093 | John the Baptizer |
| 050 | Simon [=Peter] |
| 036 | John [the Apostle] |
| 021 | James [the Apostle] |
| 017 | Saul [=Paul] |
| 013 | Andrew [the Apostle] |
| 012 | Thomas [the Apostle] |

Based on this alone, what can one say about the "preoccupation" of the Christian Scriptures with Simon Peter in contrast with the other names mentioned?

2. Examine those places wherein the names of the Twelve are given: Mark 3:16-19, Matt 10:2-4, Luke 6:13-16, Acts 1:13. What pattern shows up relative to who is named first?

What significance might this have?

3. Some persons mistakingly think that Jesus changed Simon's name to Peter. The Christian Scriptures, however, testify that Jesus himself continued to use "Simon" (e.g., Matt 17:25, Luke 22:31) even after Matt 16:18. In point of fact, therefore, it is more precise to think that Jesus gave Simon a nickname that he used along with his regular name. Examine the text (listed below) wherein each of the Gospels inform their readers of Simon's nickname. In each case, decide "who," "when," and "why" Simon get his nickname and fill in the following table:

*The Gospels do not offer a uniform picture as to when and why Jesus gave Simon a nickname.*

| Source | Who from? | When? | Why? |
|---|---|---|---|
| Matt 16:18 | | | |
| Mark 3:16 | | | |
| Luke 6:14 | | | |
| John 1:42 | | | |

Examine the variations in your data carefully, and try to provide some explanation as to why you think Matt 16:18 is not found in any of the other Gospel accounts.

## Peter's Failures

4. While Peter is prominently featured in all four Gospel accounts, it has not gone unnoticed that, in many instances, it is precisely the failures of Peter which are featured. Within the Gospel according to Mark, for instance, the following are the more serious failures specifically attributed to Peter:

   a. Jesus rebukes Peter twice at Caesarea Philippi (8:27-33)
   b. Peter is singled out as sleeping in the Garden (14:37)

c. Peter vehemently declares that he will not deny Jesus (14:31) but then goes on to deny him three times (14:66-72)

*Matthew and Luke try to soften Peter's failures.*

Both Matthew and Luke take over the basic content of Mark's Gospel, but, both Matthew and Luke try to soften or even reverse the force of Peter's failures. Let's take each of the above instances in turn.

(a) Read Mark 8:27-33. If you lived in the community that had only Mark's Gospel, what would you say was the response of Jesus to Peter's declaration, "You are the Christ"?

Mark's account uses the same verb *epitima* ("rebuke, reprove, censure") three times in the account. The RSV, in an attempt to soften the force of Jesus' dissatisfaction with Peter's profession, deliberately translates the Greek term with the mild, "he warned them" (Mark 8:30). The NRSV tries to rectify this linguistic fudging by substituting, "he sternly ordered them" (8:30). Check to see whether your translation uses the same English verb in each of the three uses of *epitima*:

*The RSV, in an attempt to soften the force of Jesus' dissatisfaction with Peter's profession, resorts to linguistic fudging.*

1st use: "he *warned* them to tell no one" (8:30)
2nd use: "Peter . . . began to *rebuke* him" (8:32)
3rd use: "seeing his disciples, he *rebuked* Peter" (8:33)

In the first case, the rebuke must be puzzling. Earlier in the Gospel, Jesus silences those demon-possessed from making him known (1:34, 3:11). Now the disciples themselves are likewise rebuked and ordered not to make his identity known. Would the explanation for this rebuke be found in the fact that Peter's understanding of Jesus' identity is defective? How so? As seen in what immediately transpires, Peter definitely perceives Jesus as a victorious Messiah. Jesus, in contrast, perceives himself as moving toward official rejection by the temple establishment. Jesus' rebuking of Peter, therefore, signals Jesus' dissatisfaction with Peter's understanding of who he is.

Now read aloud Matt 16:13-23. Notice the vast difference! Write your observations here:

If Mark left the impression that Jesus was somehow dissatisfied with Peter's judgment, Matthew's insertion of 16:17-19 has the effect of giving the reader the impression that Jesus is mightily impressed. But not for long. One moment Simon is praised as "solid-rock," but, in the next moment (16:23), Simon is censured as a "Satan" (who, in Matthew's Gospel, is the one who tempted Jesus in the desert in 4:1-11). The "solid-rock" has now become the "stumbling-rock."

*Simon is praised as "solid-rock," but, in the next moment Simon is censured as a "Satan."*

Reflect upon this: Jesus made many enemies due to the nature of his ministry. He never called any of his enemies "Satan." Judas, one of the Twelve, identified Jesus to his enemies with a kiss (Matt 26:49). Even then, however, Jesus did not rebuke Judas as "Satan." Why does Peter and Peter alone receive this rebuke?

(b) Peter is also presented in a bad light when he is singled out by Jesus as failing to watch and pray with him. According to Mark's Gospel, Jesus deliberately took Peter, James, and John aside with him into the garden called Gethsemane. When he returned to find "them" sleeping, Jesus addresses his complaint only to Peter saying, "Simon, are you asleep? Could you not watch one hour? Watch and pray that you may not enter into temptation . . ." (Mark 14:37f). What do you detect here?

*Jesus reverted back to calling him "Simon" when he singled him out for failing to watch and pray with him.*

The attentive reader will note that Jesus, instead of addressing Peter by his nickname ("Rock"), has reverted back to calling him "Simon." By so doing, Jesus conveys his acute disappointment with Peter who, just a few hours earlier, had boasted, 'Even though they all fall away, I will not' (14:29). Despite this boast, Simon is incapable of joining Jesus in his anguished prayer. Mark thereby prepares his readers for the upcoming flight and the three-fold denial of Peter—failures that might have been adverted had Peter prayed for strength in the face of "temptation" (14:38).

Matthew makes only small changes in Mark. Luke, in contrast, carefully edits Mark's narrative so as to give quite another impression. Read Luke 22:39-46. Note your observations here:

Luke leaves the impression that all the disciples entirely entered into the prayer of Jesus. To begin with, Luke omits any mention of Jesus taking Peter, James, and John to be with him. According to Luke, Jesus withdrew himself from all his disciples by "a stone's throw" (Luke 22:41 only). When Jesus returned, he "found them sleeping *for sorrow*" (Luke 22:45). By adding the words italicized, Luke leaves the impression that the disciples had so deeply sympathized with Jesus that they were exhausted by their grief (and not, as in Mark, by the late hour). Nonetheless, Luke did not omit having Jesus ask, "Why do you sleep?" (22:46), but only once. Mark has Jesus doing this three times thereby emphasizing the inability of Peter to enter into Jesus' anguish.

*Luke leaves the impression that the disciples had so deeply sympathized with Jesus that they were exhausted by their grief and that in the garden they remained physically close to him when he was crucified.*

(c) When Jesus was arrested, Mark reports, "And they [his disciples] all forsook him, and fled" (Mark 14:50). Matthew repeats this (Matt 26:56). Luke, in contrast, entirely deletes this from his Gospel, probably because it reflects so badly upon the character of the disciples. While Jesus is being executed by the Romans, therefore, Luke notes that "all his acquaintances and the women who had followed him from Galilee stood at a distance" (Luke 23:49). According to Matthew and Mark, only "the women" (Mark 15:40, Matt 27:55) risked following Jesus to the place of his crucifixion. Luke's addition here of "all his acquaintances" appears to be calculated to leave the impression that just as his disciples remained emotionally close to him at the Last Supper (Luke 22:28) and in the garden (Luke 22:45), so too, after his arrest, they remained physically close to him when he was crucified.

Even though Luke deliberately alters Mark's record regarding these things, he does not go so far as to omit or even to substantially alter Mark's vivid portrait of Peter's denying Jesus. In some ways, Luke even intensifies Peter's personal betrayal by having Peter deny Christ three times in the very courtyard (Luke 22:63) where Jesus is being detained. After the third denial, the cock crowed "and the Lord turned and looked at Peter" (Luke 22:61). Mark and Matthew report that Jesus was being questioned inside by the high priest while Peter, in the courtyard outside, was being questioned by the servant girl. The contrast here is between Jesus affirming who he is while, at the same time, Peter is outside denying who he is.

Luke, however, does leave out Mark's indication that Peter "began to curse" (Mark 14:71, Matt 26:74) during his third denial. Whom did he curse? From the context, the Greek text implies that Peter resorts to cursing Jesus (Gundry: 890) so as to better dispel any hint that he, Peter, has any sympathy for him. The RSV, embarrassed at this, conspires to save Peter yet more shame by adding words not found in the Greek: "he began to invoke a curse *on himself*" (Mark

*Luke could not stomach Mark's portrait of Peter as cursing Jesus.*

14:71). The NRSV, aware of what the RSV translators had done, has removed the added words (shown in italics). Luke, keenly aware of Mark's meaning, chose the course of dropping the entire phrase from his Gospel. Luke, consequently, could allow that Peter denied Christ three times but could not stomach Mark's portrait of Peter as cursing Jesus and swearing a false oath (Mark 14:71). In order to better judge the worth of your own translation, look up the opening words of Mark 14:71 and note them here:

No community likes to think of its leading member in an unfavorable light. Most Americans, for instance, do not want to know that George Washington broke written treaties with Native Americans and slaughtered them when they refused to vacate their own lands. Likewise, Americans prefer to forget that President Nixon deliberately lied, over a period of months, when he repeatedly and publicly denied reports that American planes were systematically bombing civilian populations in North Vietnam. And, more recently, many Americans still want to believe that President Reagan was neither responsible nor knowledgeable regarding either the sale of arms to Iran or the siphoning off of profits from these sales for the illegal covert aid to the Contras in Nicaragua. With even greater force, when someone acts reprehensibly in life, it is customary to speak well of them after death.

Given all this, how does one explain how Mark, writing shortly after the death of Peter, not only refrains from presenting him as a model of fidelity and holiness, but, on the contrary, shows him to have miserably failed Jesus?

### Improving the Image of the Disciples

A close reading of the Synoptics discloses additional instances where Matthew and Luke edited Mark's narratives so as to improve the image of the disciples. As an optional exercise, interested persons might compare Matt 20:20-28 and Luke 22:24-27 with the original Mark 10:35-45; compare Matt 16:6-12 and Luke 12:1 with the original Mark 8:15-21; compare Matt 26:40-46 and Luke 22:45-46 with the original Mark 14:37-42. Persons wishing to consider all the instances of this program of deliberately improving the image of Peter and the other disciples can do so by consulting the Brown and Weeden volumes listed at the end of this chapter.

What does it mean that Matthew and especially Luke deliberately tone down the failures of Peter, but even they could not find it within themselves to entirely pass over in silence Jesus' rebuke of Peter as "Satan" and Peter's denial that he even knew Jesus? What could be gained by their repeating such an embarrassing image of Peter?

*Matthew and Luke tone down the failures of Peter, but even they could not pass over in silence Jesus' rebuke of Peter as "Satan" and Peter's denial that he even knew Jesus?*

## Peter's Authority According to Matthew

5. Up to this point, we have three indications that Peter had a place of predominance within the churches which produced the Gospels: (1) he was consistently named first when the twelve were listed; (2) he was featured more often than any other disciple within the Gospel narratives; and (3) he was, in Matthew's eyes at least, given the nickname "Rock" by Jesus due to his faith in him as the Messiah (Matt 16:18). This last indicator needs to be considered with more thoroughness.

In no Gospel other than Matthew's does Jesus ever expressly use the term "church" (*ekklēsia*). Matthew uses it three times: once in Matt 16:18 and twice in Matt 18:15-18. The first text is already familiar to you. Go on now to carefully read the second. What importance does this second text have relative to defining Peter's role within the church of Matthew?

Matt 18:15-18 specifies the progression to be used in cases of fraternal correction: (1) initially, the offended party goes alone and tries to patch things up; (2) then, if this fails, the offended party brings along one or two others to support his claim; (3) finally, as the last resort, the offended party brings the grievance before the whole community, "the church." Once the church hears the case and renders a judgment, the offending party who "refuses to listen to the church" and stubbornly holds him/herself as blameless must be shunned "as a Gentile and a tax collector" (18:17).

The reader immediately notes here that this rule suggests an early origin since the offending party is shunned as "a Gentile and a

*In no Gospel other than Matthew's does Jesus ever expressly use the term "church."*

tax collector"—classes of persons who were presumably full and equal members of Matthew's community. (see Matt. 21:31, 28:19)

The reader might also note that Peter was assigned no role in this process of public reconciliation. If Peter was understood as "ruler of the entire church" by Matthew, wouldn't it be expected that the final court of appeals should not be "the whole community" but "Peter"? _____ Since this is not the case, what do you conclude from this?

*"Binding and loosing" represents what a master of Torah does when he judges that certain conduct is permitted or not permitted.*

Pushing this text even further, note that Matt 18:18 effectively functions to enforce the authority of the process just described. In effect, the community decision in a grievance case is binding not only on earth but "in heaven" (i.e., in God's eyes) as well. This "binding and loosing" represents a Jewish metaphor used to characterize what a master of Torah does when he judges that certain conduct is permitted or not permitted on the basis of God's revealed Torah. The Pharisees, for instance, considered that a pious Jew was bound not to eat "with tax collectors and sinners" (Matt 9:11). Jesus, for his part, regarded himself as "loosed" (i.e., free) to do exactly this on the grounds that a physician is permitted to visit the sick and that God desires "mercy and not sacrifice" (i.e., acts of loving kindness and not compliance with formal ritual) (Matt 9:13).

*The right to bind and to loose was promised to Peter. Later, however, "binding and loosing" are spoken of as part of the collective judgment of the entire community.*

After Jesus' death, who had received the authority of "binding and loosing" within the community? Peter? Yes! Just read Matt 16:19. Here the right to open and to close, to bind and to loose, to judge the grievances of disputing parties from the vantage point of God, was promised to Peter alone. Two chapters later, however, "binding and loosing" are spoken of as part of the collective judgment of the entire community (without any special reference to Peter). If Matthew's community embraced both 16:19 and 18:18, what special authority for "binding and loosing" did Peter have within Matthew's church?

## Peter's Functioning in the Jerusalem Church

So far the image of Peter within the Gospels has been mixed. Peter appears to be a spontaneous leader—frequently taking the initiative before the others. His initiatives, however, sometimes earn high praise as the "trusted rock" and sometimes severe criticism as the "stone for stumbling." It remains to be seen how Peter is presented in Acts.

6. Read Acts 1:15-26. Did Peter call the brethren together? _____ Does Peter does not make the appointment of Judas' replacement all by himself? _____ Does Luke give us the impression here that Peter is "ruler" of the entire church but that, being a nice guy, he prefers not to exercise this role but to involve the whole community in decision making? _____ From this text alone, what image/role does Luke want us to have of Peter?

*Peter does not make the appointment of Judas' replacement all by himself.*

7. From your recollection, who called the community together in Acts 6 when the Hellenists raised a complaint against the Hebrew-speaking members of the church? _____ Who ordained the Seven? _____ Check your recollection by reading Acts 6:2 and 6:6. Were you correct? _____

While doing Case Three, you discovered the importance of having the Hellenists themselves decide who among them was "full of the Spirit and of wisdom" (Acts 6:3). At this point, however, it remains to discern what significance should be given to the fact that the Twelve laid hands upon the Seven (as opposed to having Peter do it alone). What does this say about Peter's status relative to the other Twelve when it came to ordaining?

*Neither does he alone lay hands upon the Seven.*

8. While doing Case One, you traced Peter's religious transformation and noted the bold pastoral initiatives he took relative to Cornelius and his household (Acts 10). Later, when Peter arrived back in Jerusalem, you also discovered that he was "criticized" by members of his own community saying to him, "Why did you go to uncircumcised men . . . ?" (Acts 11:3). What does this say about the way that the very church which Peter founded saw him as "an authority"?

*Nor imagine he does not have to respond to public criticism.*

132 \ *Exploring Scriptural Sources*

9. Finally, read Acts 15:1-22 and notice what role Peter plays during this church synod in Jerusalem. The scene opens up in Antioch. Who is stirring up trouble there? _____ Note the presenting problem deals with whether Christians are "bound" to be circumcised or whether they are "loosed" (free) in this matter. Why doesn't the Antioch community simply meet together and settle the issue for themselves? Why does a delegation have to be sent to Jerusalem?

*The delegation from Antioch is not sent to Peter alone.*

To whom is the delegation sent? _____ Note that the apostles are distinguished from the elders and that the delegation from Antioch is not sent to Peter alone. What does this say about "who" has the authority to bind and to loose within the Jerusalem church?

Who attends the synod? _____ Note the order in 15:6! Luke does not consider it important to note who convened the synod. Why not?

*Decisions of the highest order were to be arrived at by the "apostles and elders" only after a free and open discussion.*

Note that the synod had an open hearing. Barnabas and Paul undoubtedly "declared all that God had done with them" (Acts 13-14). They were opposed by "some believers who belonged to the party of the Pharisees" (Acts 15:5) who were convinced that Jesus' Exclusion Principle ought to be faithfully maintained. These "believers" thought that, if Gentiles were to be admitted, they were first required to become Jews through training and circumcision. Then Acts says: "And after there had been much debate, Peter rose and said to them" (15:7). What does this say about the process whereby decisions of the highest order were to be arrived at by the "apostles and elders" there assembled?

Alas, is this now the time for Peter to make a final declaration? _____ Let's see. Peter effectively recalls again his own experiences in Acts 10—experiences which, it will be remembered, the Jerusalem community seemingly assented to (11:18). Here again, the bottom line is that the Gentiles who have heard the Word have demonstrated receiving the same Spirit the Jewish believers did. Hence, Peter can raise the question: "If God doesn't distinguish, why should we?" The response: "And all the assembly kept silence" (15:12). What does this imply? Did Peter command that silence? Or was it his stature and/or logic which brought the objectors to hold their tongues?

Then Barnabas and Paul finish their story (15:12b). It would appear now that the story that they began in 15:4 was cut short when "some believers . . . rose up" and objected to offering baptism to Gentiles. In any case, "after they finished speaking" (15:13), James takes the floor. His address makes reference to "Symeon" which is the Aramaic form for "Simon." In effect, Luke uses this device to suggest that James addresses the assembly in Aramaic. Note that James does not use "Kepha," the Aramaic form of "Peter." In effect, James' formal address does three things: (a) he appeals to Simon's experience which first led to the baptism of Gentiles; (b) he cites a confirming prophetic text which suggests that the Lord will rebuild Israel so that "the rest of men may seek the Lord" (Amos 9:12); and (c) he puts forward a compromise resolution. In what sense, a compromise?

*Then James addresses the assembly in Aramaic and puts forward a compromise resolution.*

James' resolution backs away from the complete freedom advocated by Peter and Paul in favor of establishing a middle way: the Gentiles who join the Jesus movement are to keep three prescriptions which Jews traditionally required of Gentiles who wished to settle and live among them. These prescriptions would require that Gentiles abstain (a) from food offered to pagan gods (Num 25:2, 1 Cor 10:20ff), (b) from marriage with kin (Lev 18:6-18), and (c) from eating animals which have been strangled or still contained blood (Lev 17:8-14).

*The compromise resolution received the approval of the apostles and elders with (syn) the entire church.*

Given the fact that James makes the final resolution which carries the day (see Acts 15:22), what must be said regarding the authority and function of James within this synod?

At a later moment in Acts, Paul will visit Jerusalem and be received by "James and the elders" (21:18). Therefore, what one finds in Acts 15, relative to the predominance of James and his functioning as the presiding elder seems to be the permanent state of affairs in the Jerusalem church.

We have now seen the main lines of our Case Study. Having abandoned the inadequate appeal to a single text (Matt 16:18), our approach has been to examine the clues found throughout the Christian Scriptures relative to the office and functioning of Peter. In so doing, we have noticed both Peter's predominance and his ambiguity within the synoptic Gospels. In Acts, we have noticed some of his prominent initiatives within the early church but have also noted that he functioned collaboratively and consultatively at every point. In the end, therefore, we can return to the Baltimore Catechism question and invite you to provide a new answer in harmony with what you have discovered.

Q147. Did Christ give special powers in His Church to any one of the apostles?

*Having abandoned the inadequate appeal to a single text (Matt 16:18), our approach has been to examine the clues found throughout the Christian Scriptures relative to the office and functioning of Peter.*

10. Look back now upon your initial responses to the three questions at the beginning of this Case Study. Have you changed your mind? _____ If so, note that here:

11. What startling discoveries did you make while exploring this Case Study? Describe them for yourself here:

12. Did this Case Study raise any fundamental questions for you while you were completing it? If so, note them here so that you can return to them at a later moment?


Completion time = _____
Total time used on this Case = _____ minutes

You have now completed the sixth Case Study. Not all the texts regarding Peter have been explored; however, those you have examined are sufficient to convey a clear impression as to how Peter exercised his authority within the early church. In a moment, your conclusions will be reflected upon more completely. At this time, however, set aside everything, rest, and, once you are renewed, come back for the analysis.

## Analysis

By way of bringing together the vast amount of material on Peter found in the Christian Scriptures, the following short catechism has been prepared.

**1 Q**: Does Matt 16:18 serve to demonstrate that Jesus made Peter the head of the apostles and the chief teacher and ruler of the entire church?

**A**: When Protestants and Catholics were fierce antagonists, both sides resorted to the practice of citing "proof texts" by way of demonstrating the truth of their respective positions. Now that the heat of the Reformation has partially subsided, many Protestants and Catholics have been willing to sit down and reconsider the role of Peter as expressed within the whole of the Christian Scriptures. Within this new atmosphere, Catholic scholars no longer think it necessary to hold that any single New Testament text (such as Matt 16:18) serves to demonstrate that the papacy, as it was in the sixteenth century or as we have it today, was somehow established within the first century. Protestant biblical scholars, on the other hand, have acknowledged that Peter was the most prominent disciple among the Twelve and that he played a key role in shaping the development and the decisions of the Jesus movement after the Resurrection.

*Catholic scholars no longer think it necessary to hold that any single New Testament text serves to demonstrate that the papacy, as it was in the sixteenth century or as we have it today, was established within the first century.*

The Catholic and Lutheran participants of the official United States dialogues held during 1971 to 1973 to discuss the papacy endorsed the following statement:

> Any biblical and historical scholar today would consider anachoristic [i.e., out of its historical setting] the question whether Jesus constituted Peter the first pope, since this question derives from a later model of the papacy which it projects back into the New Testament. Such a reading helps neither papal opponents nor papal supporters. Therefore terms such as "primacy" and "jurisdiction" are best avoided when one describes the role of Peter in the New Testament. Even without these terms, however, a wide variety of images is applied to Peter in the New Testament which signalizes his importance in the early church (Empie: 13).

*However, a wide variety of images is applied to Peter in the New Testament which signalizes his importance in the early church.*

**2 Q:** What, then, is the force of "upon this rock I will build my church"?

**A:** When this text is no longer distorted by virtue of being read outside of its proper context within Matthew's Gospel, three things become evident:

(1) Simon is nicknamed "Rock" immediately after having identified Jesus as "the Messiah." Apparently, Matthew wanted to present Simon as the first to arrive at this central insight which, in due time, would serve as the foundation for the church. Even given the fact that the other Gospels seem to be unaware of Peter as having received his nickname due to this event, most scholars have been willing to grant that there may be some historical foundation behind Jesus having regarded Simon as "Rock" due to his stubborn faith in him.

(2) Even in Matthew Gospel, however, it would be hazardous to imagine that Peter was understood as having been elevated to the role of being the chief teacher and ruler of the entire church. The power of "binding and loosing," for example, was promised to Peter in 16:19, but, when that same power is described in operation in 18:15-19, the whole church is perceived as "binding and loosing" without any specific role being assigned to Peter. Furthermore, since not only Matthew's Gospel but the entire Christian Scriptures are silent regarding any "successor" of Peter, it must be assumed that, even if Peter were the final court of appeals at some point, this function appears to have been taken over by the entire community of Matthew and not by any single member.

(3) While Matt 16:18 serves to highly commend Peter's judgment, the narrative which follows serves, just as strongly, to indicate that Peter's judgment was not to be completely trusted. Jesus says to Simon, "Get behind me, Satan! You

*Matthew wanted to present Simon as the first to arrive at this central insight which, in due time, would serve as the foundation for the church.*

are a hinderance to me; for you are not on the side of God, but of men" (18:23). Even if we did not have Mark's Gospel, therefore, we would have to assume that Matthew's church did not perceive Peter's image as "Rock" as exempting him from moments in which he would display deep-seated misjudgment, cowardice, and betrayal. .

*Even if Peter were the final court of appeals at some point, this function appears to have been taken over by the entire community of Matthew.*

**3 Q**: What is the strongest case that can be made for Peter having had a certain "primacy of honor" according to the Gospel accounts?

**A**: When the names of the Twelve are listed, Peter's name always appears first (Mark 1:16 and parallels.). Peter is referred to more times within the Christian Scriptures than any other apostle. While some accounts of the resurrection appearances indicate that Jesus first appeared to Mary Magdalene and the women, there is a tradition that Jesus first appeared to Peter (see I Cor 15:5 and Luke 24:34). Peter is frequently presented as functioning as spokesmen for the Twelve (e.g., Acts 2:14).

Moreover, Peter is remembered as having taken bold initiatives, not only during his period of training under the direction of Jesus, but within the early history of the church as well. These initiatives are honored by the writers of the Christian Scriptures even when they are accompanied by some subsequent failure. Thus, as we have just seen, Peter is the disciple who received both the strongest commendation and the strongest rebuke from Jesus (Matt 16:13-23). Peter was the only disciple who dared to follow the guards that arrested Jesus, but, this bold initiative led to his threefold denial of Jesus (26:58, 69-75). So, too, in the episode unique to Matthew, Peter is presented as the only disciple who dared to get out of the boat to come to Jesus walking on the water. Weak in faith, however, Peter ends up sinking (14:18-31). According to Luke, Jesus prayed at the Last Supper especially for Peter "that your faith may not fail; and when you have turned again, strengthen your brethren" (Luke 22:32).

*Matthew's church did not perceive Peter's image as "Rock" as exempting him from misjudgment, cowardice, and betrayal.*

In sum, the Gospels highlight Peter as being the exemplary disciple who risked more, loved more, failed more. Thus, one can conclude that the Gospels do accord Peter a certain "primacy of honor" which all Christians are invited to take into account.

*The Gospels do accord Peter a certain "primacy of honor" as the exemplary disciple who risked more, loved more, failed more.*

**4 Q**: What does Acts demonstrate regarding the functional authority which Peter exercised within the Jerusalem church?

**A**: At every point, Acts features Peter as exercising his authority with consultation and collaboration. For example, Peter suggests that Judas' place be taken by another but does not presume to make the choice himself (Acts 1:15-26). Peter acts collegially with the Twelve when assembling the Hellenistic branch of the Jerusalem church for the purpose of resolving their grievances. Peter does not presume to select the Seven nor to ordain them by himself (Acts 6:2-6). When Peter takes the pastoral initiative relative to Cornelius and his household, he does not consider himself beyond criticism nor does he mandate that everyone in the Jerusalem church must approve of his activity. Rather, he painstakingly tries to win their approval by leading them to sympathetically enter into the experience of being led by the Spirit as he was (Acts 11:1-18).

*Acts features Peter as exercising his authority with consultation and collaboration.*

Acts makes it plain that, during the synod of Jerusalem, no one looks to Peter to make a decision by himself or to act as the final court of appeals when the community is divided. Here again, the synod itself, composed of both apostles and elders, appears to endorse the principle that consensus is to be arrived at through free speech and open persuasion. Peter adds his voice to the deliberations without implying that his rank or status somehow entitle him to bypass this process. Acts also makes it clear that Peter does not regard the process as a mere consultation which awaits his decision at the sole authoritative norm. In fact, during the synod, James appears to be the presider and the one who is looked to for drawing the divided church into a compromise solution which will gain the acceptance of all (Acts 15:15-21).

*No one looks to Peter to make a decision by himself or to act as the final court of appeals when the community is divided.*

In sum, Acts presents Peter as both an effective pastor and a prophetic leader within the church precisely because, when it came to decisions which had a bearing upon what God expected of his church, consultation and collaboration were the hallmarks of the discernment process. At no time does Acts present Peter or anyone else in leadership as being entitled to make decisions binding upon all without such consultation and collaboration. In the final analysis, it might even be supposed that this style of leadership within the early church reflects Jesus' own style when he admonished his disciples saying, "Whoever would be great among you must be your servant" (Matt 20:26 and par.).

*At no time does Acts present anyone as being entitled to make decisions binding upon all without consultation and collaboration.*

**5 Q**: Does the church of Rome have a certain primacy in the Christian Scriptures?

**A**: The Christian Scriptures are entirely silent when it comes to describing any special importance or primacy attached to the church of Rome. And, since the texts of the Christian Scriptures represent the principal writings drafted from 49 to 110 CE, it must be supposed that, during this entire period, the primacy of the Roman Church was not yet established. If any church is to be perceived as having a primacy of honor during the first century, it would rather be the Jerusalem church which was founded by the Twelve apostles and which continued to be the Mother Church from which many other churches traced their foundation. The Jewish uprising followed by the Roman destruction of Jerusalem in 66-70 CE, however, led to a dispersion of the Jerusalem church.

Following this, various urban churches (esp. Rome, Alexandria, Antioch) served as unifying centers within the regions where their influence was felt. Relative to the Roman church, the agreed statement of Lutherans and Catholics has this to say:

*The Scriptures are entirely silent when it comes to describing any special importance or primacy attached to the church of Rome.*

> In the period following the New Testament era, two parallel lines of development tended to enhance the role of the bishop of Rome among the churches at the time. One was the continuing development of the several images of Peter emerging from the apostolic communities, the other resulted from the importance of Rome as a political, cultural, and religious center (Empie: 16).

One can say, therefore, that the image of Peter in the Scriptures did evoke in subsequent generations of Christians a certain "trajectory" which contributed to the formation of the papacy. The story of this development, however, goes way beyond the early church and accordingly must be left aside for Volume Two of these Case Studies.

*The image of Peter in the Scriptures did evoke in subsequent generations of Christians a certain "trajectory" which contributed to the formation of the papacy.*

**6 Q**: Will the papacy always be unacceptable to Protestants?

**A**: Not necessarily. For Fundamentalists such as Jimmy Swaggart who are driven to uncritically repeat the Protestant condemnations of the sixteenth century, there will undoubtedly never be any acceptable role or function for the papacy in the church of Jesus Christ. For many discerning Protestants, however, many or most of the objections to the papacy during the time of the Reformation no longer apply. Within the context of the official Lutheran-Catholic dialogues here in the United States, for example, the Lutheran participants acknowledged that "our Lutheran forefathers rejected the late medieval papacy precisely because in their judgment it was obstructing the gospel" (Empie: 32). Now, however, that the bishops of Vatican II have asserted that "this Magisterium is not superior to the Word of God, but is its servant" (Dei Verbum sec. 10) and that the excessive notions of papacy promoted after Vatican I have been moderated, the Lutheran participants have shown a remarkable willingness to reconsider whether some future recognition of the papacy might not be possible:

*For many discerning Protestants, most of the objections to the papacy no longer apply.*

> Lutherans increasingly recognize the need for a Ministry serving the unity of the church universal. They acknowledge that, for the

*Lutherans grant the beneficial role of the papacy at various periods of history.*

exercise of this Ministry, institutions which are rooted in history should be seriously considered. . . . Lutherans can also grant the beneficial role of the papacy at various periods of history. Believing in God's sovereign freedom, they cannot deny that God may show again in the future that the papacy is his gracious gift to his people. . . . The one thing necessary, from the Lutheran point of view, is that papal primacy be so structured and interpreted that it clearly serve the gospel and the unity of the church of Christ and that its exercise of power not subvert Christian freedom (Empie: 21).

## Application to the Churches Today

On the basis of everything that you have discovered, what bearing does this have upon the Roman papacy today? How does the role of Peter serve to sanction or to challenge the ways that decisions are sometimes made within the local and universal church? Be very specific. Write your ideas here:

## Further Readings for Case Six

Brown, Raymond E., et al.
> *Peter in the New Testament: A Collaborative Assessment by Protestant and Roman Catholic Scholars.* Minneapolis: Augsburg, 1973.

Burgess, Joseph A., et al., eds.
> *Building Unity: Ecumenical Dialogues with Roman Catholic Participation in the United States.* New York: Paulist, 1989.

Empie, Paul C., et al.
> *Papal Primacy and the Universal Church: Lutherans and Catholics in Dialogue V.* Minneapolis: Augsburg, 1974.

Fiorenza, Francis Schüssler
> *Foundational Theology: Jesus and the Church.* New York: Crossroad. Esp. pp. 60-192, 1984.

Gundry, Robert H.
> *Mark: A Commentary on His Apology for the Cross.* Grand Rapids: Eerdmans, 1993.

Granfield, Patrick
> *The Limits of the Papacy.* New York: Crossroad, 1987.

Kaufman, Philip F.
> *Why You Can Disagree and Remain a Faithful Catholic.* Bloomington, IN: Meyer Stone, 1989.

McBrien, Richard
> *Catholicism.* Minneapolis: Winston. Pp. 829-842, 1980.

McKenzie, John L.
> "The Gospel According to Matthew," *Jerome Biblical Commentary.* Ed. by Raymond E. Brown et al. Englewood Cliffs: Prentice-Hall. II:62-114, 1968.

Rahner, Karl, et. al.
> *Unity of the Churches: An Actual Possibility.* Tr. by Ruth C.L. Gritsch and Eric W. Gritsch from 1983 German orig. Philadelphia: Fortress, 1985.

Swaggart, Jimmy
> *Catholicism & Christianity.* Baton Rouge, LA: Jimmy Swaggart Ministries, 1986.

Weeden, Theodore J.
> *Mark—Traditions in Conflict.* Philadelphia: Fortress, 1971.

# CASE SEVEN

# The Transformation Effected by Baptism

*In the eyes of my parents, the transformation effected by baptism was near-magical.*

In the eyes of my parents, the transformation effected by baptism was near-magical. As my mother's belly began to swell, my parents were in awe at the mysterious power of God "for thou didst form my inmost parts, thou didst knit me together in my mother's womb" (Ps 139:13). During this time, they were naturally anxious that I be born strong and healthy. To effect this, my dad stayed home evenings during the final months and set aside his passion for slow-pitch softball. He insisted on taking over all my mother's strenuous activity, e.g., lifting the baskets of wet clothes, mounting the basement stairs, and carrying them out to our backyard where they could be dried on white cotton clotheslines. Daily they lived in constant anticipation of my birth. Then, on a lazy Saturday morning in mid-August, the birth contractions began. My dad rushed my mother to our local hospital and, after three hours of a bittersweet ordeal, I was born strong and healthy into the world.

But then a new drama began. My parents were now anxious that I be baptized as soon as possible. Thus, on the first Saturday following my birth, they took me to Holy Cross Church and presented me to the pastor for baptism. Psalm 51 rang in their ears: "I was brought forth in iniquity, and in sin did my mother conceive me" (Ps 51:5). They were sure that some dark, foreboding evil menaced my everlasting soul if I, God forbid, would die before being baptized.

*My parents were sure that some dark, foreboding evil menaced my everlasting soul if I, God forbid, would die before being baptized.*

My parents stood by helplessly and nervously as the priest conducted the awesome rite in the solemn tones of the ancient Latin language which neither of them understood. By virtue of what they had been taught to believe, they regarded themselves as entirely incapable of sharing with their own child the grace and the holiness that they themselves possessed. On the contrary, they were convinced they could take care of my secular growth in wisdom and grace but that the religious domain must be entrusted to God and to his priests. After my baptism was completed, they felt a sigh of relief— my soul had been cleansed of original sin and their first-born son now had a guaranteed place in heaven. Their little one could now be distinguished from all the other unfortunate pagan babies who were not baptized as children of God and heirs of heaven.

The experience of my parents had been repeating itself for nearly fifteen hundred years. Within the first four centuries of Christianity, however, infants were not routinely baptized. The early church regarded baptism as an adult conversion rite and, as a consequence, had little reason to routinely baptize infants. And yet, for reasons that are too complex to go into here, the church of the late fourth century began to actively promote earlier baptisms. In part, this novel pastoral practice was initiated by way of countering the growing tendency among the children of Christians to postpone their own baptism (and the required conversion of life) until such time as they were certain that they had no more wild oats to sow. Augustine of Hippo (d. 430) expanded upon the patristic notion of an "original defect" and developed his theory of original sin partly in order to stimulate such early baptisms. Thus, the adolescent and child baptisms of the late fourth century gradually gave way to the infant baptisms of the fifth century.

*The early church regarded baptism as an adult conversion rite and, as a consequence, had little reason to routinely baptize infants.*

Once no active preparation and no conversion of life was expected of those being presented for baptism, it became only a matter of time before the custom originated of having every infant baptized within the octave of its exit from the womb. In those special cases where an infant was born prematurely or sickly, baptism was administered immediately. During the entire middle ages, consequently, only infant baptisms were practiced save for those scattered occasions when adults converted from another religion (usually Judaism). With the emergence of the Reformation, however, everything within the church was called into question as the reformers rigorously compared the rites and rituals to the simplicity of faith and practice of the early churches.

*During the entire middle ages only infant baptisms were practiced save for those scattered occasions when adults converted.*

Luther insisted that every sacrament depends for its efficacy upon the faith of the recipient. "I may be wrong on indulgences," declared Luther, "but as to the need for faith in sacraments I will die before I will recant." This emphasis upon faith, for Luther, was not the medieval sense of faith as the assent to revealed dogmas but the wholehearted surrender to the living God. Thus, if God ordained that certain rites be performed, submission to God meant that these rites ought to be performed with the confidence that God uses them as privileged moments in which he might transform those who surrender themselves to him. Luther was equally adamant that while faith was the essential disposition required for the efficacy of every sacrament, this faith itself was a free gift which God gave when, where, and to whom he willed.

*Luther was adamant that faith was the essential disposition required for the efficacy of every sacrament.*

Luther's notion of faith and the efficacy of the sacraments functionally challenged the traditional notion in his day whereby the priest has special supernatural powers whereby the rites he performed were efficacious in and of themselves. When it came to baptism, therefore, Luther's own principle of the necessity of faith split the reformers. Some reformers (who came to be known as the Anabaptists) insisted that an infant is not capable of faith, hence, cannot properly profit from any rite, baptism included. Furthermore, the absence of any clear mandate for infant baptism within the Christian Scriptures strongly favored the discontinuation of any practice that had no divine warrant. Luther, in contrast, strove to bend his principles to favor the continued practice of infant baptism.

*When it came to baptism Luther's own principle of the necessity of faith split the reformers.*

Contemporary Baptists do not baptize their children after birth but wait until such time that they clearly manifest the spiritual regeneration and the conversion of life which is the doing of the Holy Spirit. Baptists take their children to church on Sunday and enroll them in bible schools in order to expose them to the Word of God and instruct them in godly living. However, they deliberately wait until their children are "born again" or "regenerated" by an inward experience of the Holy Spirit before they consider having them baptized. Among Baptists, therefore, baptism administered by the total immersion in water functions as the outward sign of what the Spirit has already done in the person by virtue of inward grace manifested prior to the rite.

*Baptists wait until their children are "regenerated" by an inward experience of the Holy Spirit before they consider having them baptized.*

Lutherans, in contrast, routinely practice infant baptism on the grounds of Luther's own thinking on the subject. At times, Luther endorsed the medieval notion whereby a baptized infant was perceived as having implicit faith which was metaphorically spoken of as "a sleeping faith" which gradually "awakened" as the child advanced in years. At other times, Luther shifted his focus of attention to the living faith of the sponsor or godparents which served as a guarantee of the faith into which the infant would be nurtured through the years. In either case, Luther was persuaded that "he who believes and is baptized will be saved" (Mark 16:16). This divine promise Luther and Lutherans regard as applying to all who have been baptized, children included.

*The purpose of this Case is to explore the origins and nature of baptism as it was understood by its first-century practitioners.*

## Purpose

The purpose of this Case Study is to explore the origins and nature of baptism as it was understood by its first-century practitioners. Special attention will be given to the role of the Holy Spirit in baptism. As a result of this Case Study, you will discover the essential nature of baptism and come to recognize how Catholics, Lutherans, and Baptists each try, in their own way, to express this essential nature.

Before getting started, you are again invited to record your initial perceptions to three questions. By recording your spontaneous judgments now, you will be providing yourself with a declaration of your preliminary understanding of the issues. After completing the Case Study, you will then be able to reread your initial reflections and gauge to what degree you have been broadened or transformed by your inquiries. The three questions designed for this purpose are as follows:

1. Do you recall that Jesus ever baptized anyone? _____ Whom? _____ Why?

2. Did Jesus instruct his disciples, at any time, to baptize? _____ When?

3. Does the early church understand the Holy Spirit to be received before, during, or after the rite? _____ Explain.

At this time, if you are so inclined, take your Christian Scriptures in your hands and pray that the Spirit of God may guide you in rightly understanding what the early generations of Christians understood and practiced regarding baptism.

Translation = _____

Starting time = _____ (100-150 minutes needed)

## An Initial Word Study

1. What did the Greek verb *baptizein* ("to baptize") word "baptism" mean outside of its religious context? Take a guess.

### Whether Jesus Pioneered the Use of Baptism

*Jesus did not explain baptism as part of his public teaching nor did he practice baptism himself.*

2. When one traces the ministry of Jesus in the Synoptic accounts of the Gospel, one finds that Jesus' ministry is routinely presented in terms of a heralding the nearness of the Kingdom of God and of training his disciples to live according to the standards of excellence which anticipate this future reign. All the Gospel accounts agree that Jesus did not explain baptism as part of his public teaching nor did he practice baptism himself. From this data alone, what conclusions can be drawn?

*The Gospels present three divergent pictures of when and why the disciples used baptism.*

All the Gospel accounts agree that Jesus himself was baptized by John in the Jordan. Beyond this, however, the Gospels present three divergent pictures: (a) John's Gospel presents Jesus and his disciples as having temporarily employed baptism as part of their early public ministry; (b) Matthew's Gospel presents Jesus as not authorizing baptism until the time of his post-resurrection appearance in Galilee; and (c) Luke never presents Jesus as authorizing baptism; yet, the early church, from Pentecost onward, makes repeated use of baptism. Each of these divergent pictures will be examined in turn.

According to John's Gospel, Jesus is presented as explicitly practicing baptism (John 3:22, 26) and, as a result, the Evangelist informs the reader that "Jesus was making and baptizing more disciples than John [the Baptizer]" (4:1). But immediately thereafter, the Evangelist corrects himself saying "Jesus himself did not baptize, but only his disciples" (4:2). Even in John, however, it would appear that the practice of baptism was a temporary expedient "for John had not yet been put into prison" (3:24) and was subsequently discontinued.

---

#### Note on the Greek Terms for Baptism

The noun "baptism" (*baptisma*) occurs twenty-two times in the Christian Scriptures. The verb form, "to baptize" (*baptizein*), occurs 125 times. The root meaning of both the noun and the verb is "to immerse in water." As such, it does not principally refer to a specific religious rite but to the common experience of submerging dishes, clothes, hot iron, etc., in ordinary water.

Since the Christian Scriptures almost always (save in Mark 7:4 and Luke 11:38) uses this term to designate a religious rite, English translators have gotten into the habit of transliterating the Greek, a practice which obscures the commonplace origins of this term. Since many churches have abandoned immersion, the transliterating also serves to obscure the fact that during the first century period, baptism was administered by submersion (immersion) of the whole body in water.

From this point onward, John's Gospel makes no further reference to either Jesus or his disciples baptizing. Moreover, while John reports many appearances of Jesus after his resurrection, none of these encounters includes a commission to his disciples to baptize.

According to Matthew's Gospel, Jesus does not even begin his ministry until "John had been arrested" (Matt 4:12); hence, Matthew's chronology does not allow any period in which both John and Jesus could be presented as both baptizing disciples (as in John 4:1). At the very end of the Gospel, however, Matthew presents Jesus as appearing to his disciples in Galilee after his resurrection and commissioning them to "make disciples . . . baptizing them" (Matt 28:19). This direct commission to baptize is unique to Matthew's Gospel.

*Matthew presents Jesus as appearing to his disciples after his resurrection and commissioning them to baptize.*

According to Luke, Jesus is entirely silent about baptism both before and after the resurrection. The early church, however, is presented as employing baptism as part of the conversion rite of those "cut to the heart" (Acts 2:37) by Peter's preaching on Pentecost. From that point onward, members of the Jesus movement routinely used baptism by way of admitting new members into the circle of Jesus' disciples.

*According to Luke, Jesus is entirely silent about baptism both before and after the resurrection.*

3. The Gospels are first and foremost church manuals designed for believers and not historical records designed to give curious outsiders a "neutral" biography of Jesus. Consequently, modern readers must allow that each of the inspired Evangelists selected and editorialized upon the remembered events of Jesus' life so as to faithfully address the issues and pastorally guide the practice of their respective churches. Nonetheless, the present topic of inquiry naturally raises the modern historical question as to whether Jesus ever baptized anyone or whether he commissioned his disciples to do so. Which of the Gospel accounts would you surmise best approximates the historical situation? _____ Explain your response.

John received his nickname "the Baptizer" due to the rite of immersion which accompanied his prophetic ministry. Even from the vantage point of Christian documents, John appears to have made a deep impression on the Jews of his day and to have attracted many disciples.

It is not unthinkable that Jesus would have been attracted to John's preaching and to John's baptism. If one reads between the lines of the Gospels, it is also not unthinkable that John may have

*John received his nickname "the Baptizer" due to the rite of immersion which accompanied his prophetic ministry.*

*All four Evangelists situate the beginning of Jesus' public ministry as directly following upon his baptism by John.*

been instrumental in drawing Jesus out of his seclusion in Nazareth. In any case, all four Evangelists situate the beginning of Jesus' public ministry as directly following upon his baptism by John. Matthew, aware of the implications of this beginning, may even have been mildly embarrassed at the fact that Jesus was baptized by John as opposed to having John accepting baptism from Jesus (Matt 3:14f). John forestalls this embarrassment by having John the Baptist describe his entire purpose for baptizing as being directed toward discovering him "on whom you [John] see the Spirit descend" (John 1:33) and, subsequently, revealing this "Lamb of God" to Israel (John 1:29, 35).

It is also not unthinkable that John the Baptizer might have been instrumental in having some of his own disciples going over to Jesus (John 1:35-37). This would help to explain why these disciples might have been so ready to adapt John's baptism for their own use following the death of Jesus. On the other hand, it must be acknowledged that, according to the Synoptics, Jesus gets no help from John but finds his own disciples among the fishermen of Galilee—far from the place where John's disciples operated.

It is also not unthinkable that some of John's disciples might have regarded him as either the Messiah or Elijah—titles which John the Evangelist seems particularly determined to show that John rejected (John 1:20f, 25). In contrast, Matthew's Gospel does not hesitate to have Jesus pointedly explaining to his disciples that John was "Elijah" (Matt 11:14, 17:13; Mark 9:19, Luke 1:17). On the other hand, many of the people, according to the Synoptics, thought of Jesus as another "John the Baptist" (Matt 16:14; Mark 6:15, 8:28; Luke 9:8, 19). Herod, who had beheaded John, even appears to have judged that Jesus was "John the Baptist . . . raised from the dead" (Matt 14:2, Mark 6:16, Luke 9:9). As for the Baptist himself, despite the incident during Jesus' baptism, Matthew and Luke seems content to present John as still uncertain as to Jesus' identity even at the time he was in Herod's prison (Matt 11:2, Luke 7:19).

*Many of the people thought of Jesus as another "John the Baptist."*

In cases such as this where the historic details are at variance with each other, scholars generally favor the Synoptic accounts over John due to their smaller degree of theological overlay. Nonetheless, it cannot be entirely ruled out that Jesus and his first disciples did temporarily baptize while in Judaea (Brown, 1966: 155). If this tradition were known by the early disciples of Jesus, however, it remains unclear why it would never have been appealed to in Acts or in the letters of Paul when the baptismal practice and theology of the early churches were being hammered out. Moreover, if the tradition had remembered Jesus as having discontinued practicing baptism, this might have been used as a potent argument against the disciples sub-

*Jesus and his first disciples did temporarily baptize. It remains unclear why it would never have been appealed to in Acts or in the*

## The Transformation Effected by Baptism / 149

sequently taking it up again after his death. When baptism is taken up, needless to say, the disciples never have to deal with their recollection that either they or Jesus had formerly abandoned the practice. Hence, when all the evidence is considered, it would seem safest to surmise that baptism never formed an integral part of Jesus' ministry.

As for Matthew's presentation of the resurrected Jesus as commissioning his disciples to "make disciples of all nations, baptizing them . . . , teaching them . . . (Matt 28:19f), here too one has to deal with the possibility that this represents the developed understanding of Matthew's community but not the expressed wish of the historical Jesus. The association of "baptizing" with "making disciples of all nations" might recall the early discoveries which you made relative to the origins of the Gentile mission in Case One. What relevance might this association have when it comes to deciding what historical weight should be given to Matt 28:19f?

Separating out the history from the Gospel traditions is a process which will never be complete or definitive. For the sake of the church, however, consider what would happen if we could not be historically certain that Jesus practiced baptism himself or gave his disciples an explicit mandate to do so. Does this mean that the foundation for the church's continued use of baptism would be in danger of disappearing? _____ Explain yourself here:

*What would happen if we could not be historically certain that Jesus practiced baptism himself or gave his disciples an explicit mandate to do so?*

4. When ordination was treated in an earlier Case Study, you discovered that Jesus did not have to specifically mandate ordination since the ritual of ordination was already practiced within Judaism prior to Jesus. When suitable conditions arose, consequently, it was to be expected that the leaning of hands would be adapted as the proper Jewish mode whereby persons being publicly designated for ministry would have their identities transformed. Even without any specific mandate, therefore, might it be possible that the early church began the use of baptism in precisely the same way? _____ Explain yourself here:

*None of these practices within Judaism suffice, in and of themselves, to explain the origins of Christian baptism.*

The Jewish tradition in which the disciples of Jesus were rooted did have various occasions in which immersion in water was used. In Case Four the use of water was shown to be one step toward removing ritual impurity. Meanwhile, somewhere during the first century, the Pharisees began using water immersion as part of the initiation practice for Gentile converts. Following upon the discovery of the Dead Sea scrolls, scholars also discovered that regular immersion in water played an important role for the Jewish settlement at Qumran (c. 150 BCE to 70 CE). None of these practices within Judaism suffice, in and of themselves, to explain the origins of Christian baptism. When one looks at the Gospel accounts themselves, none of these practices is highlighted. Rather, the Gospels focus their attention upon the practice of John the Baptizer. All the Gospel accounts agree that the ministry of Jesus began only after he was baptized by John in the Jordan. To reconstruct how the early church understood its own use of baptism, therefore, one must first take a look at the importance that it assigned to John's baptism. To this task our attention now turns.

## The Baptism of John

5. Attentively read Luke 3:3-14. According to Luke, what condition had to be fulfilled before John would baptize a person?

How should one understand the phrase "preaching a baptism of repentance" (3:3)?

How does the repentance necessary for the reception of baptism effect the "forgiveness of sins" (Luke 3:3)? [Need a hint? See Ps 32:5.]

Does Luke tacitly suggest that the "forgiveness of sins" was already available to Jews through the preaching and baptism of John without any reference to Jesus? _____ How do you explain this?

*"Forgiveness of sins" was already available to Jews through the preaching and baptism of John without any reference to Jesus.*

Now look carefully at how Luke makes use of "the words of Isaiah the prophet" as a way of accounting for why John, at that time and in that place, was preaching a baptism of repentance for the forgiveness of sins. Luke cites Isa 40:3-5. Any Jew, however, would have understood the impact of this prophetic expectation within the wider context of Isaiah. Read Isa 40:1-11. What do you discover?

Luke cites Isa 40 by way of suggesting that John's message of hope and forgiveness parallels that of the former prophet who prepared the people for the return of their Lord during the Babylonian exile (which ended in 538 BCE). When the Lord comes, however, Isaiah warned that he will come as a "devouring fire" (Isa 33:14). Only "he [she] who walks righteously and speaks uprightly" (Isa

---

### Note on Isaiah

In the first part of Isaiah (ch. 1-39), one finds a collection of the oracles which the prophet addressed to the people of God or the king between 740 and 700 BCE. Isaiah opens his work with God's lamenting the fact that his people have tried to appease him with empty religious observances rather than offer him the justice and integrity which he requires of them. See Isaiah 1:1-20. Over and over again, the Lord, speaking through the prophet, warns that he will withdraw his protection from Israel and allow them to be eaten up by their enemies unless they return to his ways.

The fortieth chapter of Isaiah transports the reader some two centuries forward into a time after the destruction of Jerusalem. It is now 550-540 BCE. The people of Israel are in exile in Babylon, and Cyrus the liberator appears on the horizon. The opening hymn of consolation directs the prophet (a successor of Isaiah?) to "speak tenderly to Jerusalem" informing her that "her [former] iniquity is pardoned." (Isa 40:2). In the wilderness (the symbolic place of purification), the prophet calls upon the people to prepare "the way of the Lord"—the way of justice and integrity. Any obstacle to the Lord's coming must be metaphorically rectified: hills and valleys must be leveled out; crooked and rough areas must be straightened and "like a shepherd" (Isa 40:11), he plans to liberate Israel from her enemies and to bring her back to the promised homeland.

33:15) can hope to dwell with and be shepherded by this God. John the Baptizer, expanding upon the same evocative metaphors, made reference (a) to the cutting down of unfruitful trees which have no use but to be "thrown into the fire" (Luke 3:9) and (b) to the great "threshing floor" wherein the wheat will be separated from the chaff which "he will burn with unquenchable fire" (Luke 3:17). Such terms vividly portray the conviction that his Jewish listeners cannot hope to escape the Lord's judgment by claiming that they are "children of Abraham" (Luke 3:8). Both in the past and in the future, the Lord requires that every Jewish life must produce "good fruit" (Luke 3:9 and par.).

*John immersed repentant Jews in water in the anticipation of the one who was coming who would immerse them in the Holy Spirit and/or in fire.*

According to Luke, therefore, John's preaching was situated within the context of the expectation of the Lord's return to earth in the near future. John immersed repentant Jews in water in the anticipation of the one who was coming who would immerse them in the Holy Spirit and/or in fire. To be immersed in God's Spirit is to habitually judge and act in harmony with his ways (e.g., Ezek 36:26-28). To be immersed in God's fire is to be destroyed by his angry judgment against them. John's preaching and baptizing, therefore, prepared God's people for this eschatological event.

*Once the baptism of John is seen as an expression of repentance then it becomes quite easy to understand the character of Peter's baptism.*

6. Once the baptism of John is seen as an expression of repentance by those who are cut to the heart through John's warnings regarding "the wrath to come" (Luke 3:7), then it becomes quite easy to understand the character of Peter's baptism. Read Acts 2:22-41 and sketch here the parallels that one finds between the two baptisms:

Peter tells those who were "cut to the heart" to "repent and be baptized" (Acts 2:38). How does the repentance called for by Peter parallel or diverge from John's call for repentance?

Peter's baptism also carries with it "the forgiveness of your sins" (Acts 2:38). Does Peter's baptism effect this forgiveness any differently from John's baptism which was also "for the forgiveness of sins" (Luke 3:3)? _____ Explain your understanding here:

## Baptism and the Spirit

7. Luke presents John's baptism as anticipating the baptism in the Holy Spirit. In Acts 2, however, the pouring out of the Spirit upon the one hundred twenty disciples at Pentecost is interpreted as fulfilling the expectation of Joel (cited in 2:17-21) whereby the Lord would pour out his Spirit of prophesy just prior to his coming. Elizabeth, it will be remembered, "was filled with the Holy Spirit" (Luke 1:41) and prophesied saying, "Blessed is the fruit of your womb" (Luke 1:42). So was her husband, Zechariah, "filled with the Holy Spirit" (1:67) resulting in a long oracle telling how the "God of Israel . . . redeemed his people" (1:68) in the past and foretelling how John would do the Lord's work in the future (1:76-79). Now Luke tells us that not just a chosen few but "all flesh" (Acts 2:17), beginning with the one hundred twenty, can anticipate this same gift.

*The pouring out of the Spirit at Pentecost is interpreted as fulfilling the expectation of Joel.*

At Pentecost, Peter's preaching of a baptism of repentance went beyond John's in so far as Peter was able to say, "You shall receive the gift of the Holy Spirit" (2:38). According to Peter, when will the people receive the Holy Spirit? When the Lord returns? _____ Before the Lord returns? _____ During the rite of Baptism? _____ After the rite of baptism? _____ Explain yourself here:

The Greek construction in Acts 2:38 probably means that the gift of the Spirit is a future event anticipated after the present mandate to repent and be baptized is fulfilled. The "promise" (2:39) of the Spirit which is defined in Acts 2:16-21 does not get directly or immediately tied in with the actual moment of immersion itself. If the gift of the Spirit came with the rite, it would have been possible for Peter to say, "Repent and be baptized . . . and receive the gift of the Holy Spirit." But he does not. Rather, he says, "you will receive the gift of the Holy Spirit" (Acts 2:38). The use of the future indica-

*The Greek construction signals that the gift of the Spirit is a future event anticipated after baptism.*

tive could be interpreted as a mild imperative. In this context, however, where the first two verbs ("repent and be baptized") are in the aorist imperative, the use of the future would appear to signal an event following the baptism. How long after the baptism one must wait, the text does not explicitly say.

Luke gives us clues respecting the association of the Spirit and baptism when he presents Jesus' own baptism. Examine Luke 3:21. Does Luke want us to imagine that Jesus received the Spirit before, during, or after his baptism? _____ What clues does the text offer?

*Luke understands the Spirit's being poured out upon Jesus as leading to prophetic action.*

The Greek construction of Luke 3:21 suggests that both the baptism of the people and of Jesus had already taken place when, while at prayer, the heavens were opened and the Spirit descended. The actual words of Jesus' prayer are not heard nor is there any hint that the prayer of Jesus was somehow causally related to the descent of the Spirit. In so far as Jesus' baptism anticipates the Spirit, it can be said that Luke 3:21 harmonizes well with Acts 2:38. In so far as Luke understands the Spirit's being poured out upon Jesus as leading to prophetic action (Luke 4:18f, 24), this also parallels the action of the Spirit at Pentecost.

8. Looking beyond the baptism of Jesus, Luke provides instances within the early church wherein one can glimpse the relationship of the Spirit and the rite of baptism. Examine each case and fill in the chart below:

| Source | Spirit received before, during, or after the baptism? |
|---|---|
| Acts 8:14-16 | |
| Acts 8:35-39 | |
| Acts 10:44-48 | |
| Acts 19:1-6 | |

What conclusion can you draw? What causal relationship (if any) does baptism appear to have with regard to receiving the gift of the Holy Spirit?

## Baptism and Community Fellowship

9. Does the baptism of John have the effect of joining those who have been converted to a stable community? _____ According to Luke, we hear nothing of this. The presumption seems to be that those who have been converted know the Torah of the Lord and, as a consequence, only have to bear the fruit of conversion as they return to their already existing communities.

Does the baptism of Peter also function in this way? _____ Why or why not? [Need a hint? See Acts 2:42-47.]


In Luke's description of John's practice of baptism, one overhears John giving specific guidance to those who have repented (3:10-14). The general expectation, however, was that they already understood Torah and had only to implement it. In the case of Jesus, however, his disciples had embraced a new tradition of interpretation of Torah which was both unique and orthodox. Thus a Jew who had accepted that "God has made him [Jesus] both Lord and Christ [Messiah]" (Acts 2:36), would want to assimilate Jesus' teaching so as to update his/her interpretation of Torah and to live it out in a fellowship of like-minded individuals. Thus, those who had been baptized "in the name of Jesus Christ" (Acts 3:38) "devoted themselves to the apostles' teaching and fellowship" (Acts 3:42). Does this mean that such persons no longer regarded themselves as Jews? _____ Does this mean that such persons no longer attended the synagogue or Temple? _____ Explain.

*Jesus' disciples embraced a new tradition of interpretation of Torah which was shared in the fellowship after baptism.*

---

### John the Baptizer and Billy Graham

The crusades of Evangelist Billy Graham offer something of a contemporary parallel to the ministry of John the Baptizer. Those who have been converted by the power of God's grace during the time of Graham's preaching of the Word are invited to come forward and acknowledge what God has done for them. After having come forward (in what many Protestants refer to as the "altar call"), Graham gathers them around himself, says a prayer over them, and then hands them over to spiritual counselors who are ready to meet with each of them personally. When it is all over, however, each us urged to go back to their own homes, to their own churches, and to live out the call which they have received from God during the time of the crusade. Here Graham makes no attempt to set them aside in a distinct fellowship, nor does he urge them to fashion themselves into a special community or church.

156 \ *Exploring Scriptural Sources*

10. In what ways was the experience of the early church surrounding baptism parallel to the experience of my parents as described at the beginning of this Case Study? In what ways would the first-century experience have been entirely different?

11. In recent years, the rites of initiation have been revised so as to better reflect the experience of the early church. Name some ways in which the current rites of baptism for adults and for infants faithfully captures aspects of the first-century experience and understanding.

The rites of initiation have also been revised so as to better reflect the particular pastoral and social needs of Christians living in the late 20th century. From this vantage point, name some aspects of first-century baptisms which have not been embraced by the new rites. Why not?

12. What startling discoveries did you make while exploring this Case Study? Describe them for yourself here:

13. Did this Case Study raise any fundamental questions for you while you were completing it? If so, note them here so that you can return to them at a later moment?

Completion time = _____
Total time used on this Case = \_\_\_\_\_ minutes

While there are many fine texts respecting baptism within the apostolic letters (e.g., Gal 3:23-28, Rom 6:3-11, Col 2:8-3:17, 1 P 1:3-2:9), these have been deliberately left aside so as to keep our inquiry manageable. You might want to glance at them, if you so desire, at another time. For the moment, however, set everything aside and rest before proceeding.

## Analysis

By way of bringing together the results of this Case Study, I provide the following set of questions and answers.

**1Q**: What are the origins of baptism as a rite of the church?

**A**: Jesus was not remembered for having performed any baptisms (John 4:2) or for giving his disciples any instructions as to the proper rite and theology to be assigned to baptism. Neither is there compelling evidence that Jesus commission to baptize found at the close of Matthew's Gospel (Matt 28:16-20) should not be understood as the inspired author's mode of ahistorically updating where the resurrected Jesus and the Spirit had led the community at the time of its being set down in writing (70-80 CE). In any case, Acts makes clear that the Jesus movement did practice baptism from the time of Pentecost onward without any specific reference to Jesus as having originated or commissioned the rite.

The emergence of baptism as part of the ministry of the early church, therefore, would seem to have its historical origins in the impact which the baptism of John had upon Jesus and the early disciples. Some scholars have tried to demonstrate that the Jewish use of proselyte baptism or that the Qumran use of repeated baptisms had an influence upon the decision of the early church to adapt this rite for their own purposes. The greater probability, however, is that the baptism of John found in all four of the Gospel accounts represents what the Evangelists regarded as the immediate antecedent of Christian baptism.

*The baptism of John found in all four of the Gospel accounts represents what the Evangelists regarded as the immediate antecedent of Christian baptism.*

**2Q**: What was the significance of John's baptism?

**A**: John's prophetic message appears to have been a call directed toward Jews to return to the ways of the Lord in preparation for his coming (along the lines of Isa 40). While Matthew summarizes John's message in exactly the same terms used to summarize the message of Jesus (namely, "Repent, for the kingdom of heaven is at hand" [Matt 3:2=4:17]), John does not appear to have dwelled upon the "Kingdom of God/Heaven." However, those Jews whose hearts were rent by his call for repentance "were baptized by him in the river Jordan, confessing their sins" (Matt 3:6). They then went back into their local communities to bear witness to their altered lives.

John's baptism served to symbolize and to intensify for Jews (a) repentance for their wayward lives, (b) commitment to return to the ways of their Father, and (c) anticipation of the coming of the Lord who would submerge them in the Holy Spirit and/or in fire (Matt 4:11). In brief, one might say that John's baptism was an adult conversion rite which accompanied John's prophetic warning and expectation.

*John's baptism was an adult conversion rite which accompanied John's prophetic warning and expectation.*

**3Q**: How was baptism understood as effecting forgiveness of sins?

**A**: Within the Jewish horizon of understanding, when someone turns back to the ways of the Lord, this act of turning (designated as *teshuvah* in Hebrew) sufficed for God to forgive and, in the much stronger sense, to forget a person's sins. The Gospel accounts never suppose that Jesus somehow brought a forgiveness to the Jewish people which was not already available to them. If anything, the ministry of Jesus served to wake Jews up to the incredible experience of turning back which the psalmist declares:

*The Gospel accounts never suppose that Jesus brought a forgiveness to the Jewish people which was not already available to them.*

> When I declared not my sin, my body wasted away
>   through my groaning all day long. . . .
> [Later] I acknowledged my sin to thee,
>   and I did not hide my iniquity;
> I said, "I will confess my transgressions to the Lord";
>   then thou didst forgive the guilt of my sin (Ps 32:3, 5).

Jesus' parable of the prodigal son even goes to the extreme of suggesting that God pines away at home waiting for the sinner's return. Then, when the sinner is in sight, God sets aside his dignity and his disappointment and rushes headlong through the street in order to throw his arms around the one whom he loves. According to the parable, the son on his way home is obsessed with the notion that he has acted so shamefully as to foreclose the possibility of pardon: "Father, I have sinned against heaven and before you; I am no longer worthy to be called your son" (Luke 15:18f). What the son fails to take into account, however, is the compassion of this father who races out to embrace his son even before he has a chance to confess his unworthiness! The very fact of the son's turning back is enough for the father to conclude "my son was dead, and is alive again; he was lost, and is

*When the sinner is in sight, God sets aside his dignity and rushes headlong through the street in order to throw his arms around the one whom he loves.*

found" (Luke 15:24). In all of this there is not the slightest hint of any act of atonement or restitution as being needed before forgiveness of sins can take place. In fact, the father's undignified racing to his son and kissing him on the cheek prevents the son from abasing himself by kissing the feet of his father and confessing his unworthiness.

> He [the prodigal] is shattered by his father's demonstration of love in humiliation. In his state of apprehension and fear he would naturally experience this unexpected deliverance as an utterly overwhelming event. Now he knows that he cannot offer any solution to their ongoing relationship. He sees that the point is not the lost money, but rather the broken relationship which he cannot heal. Now he understands that any new relationship must be a pure gift from his father. He can offer no solution (Bailey: 183).

The various Christian theories of atonement whereby sins against God cannot be forgiven unless there is some prior restitution do not find strong support in the Christian Scriptures. Perceiving Jesus' death on the cross as the supreme act of atonement which makes possible the forgiveness of all the sins of the human race is, properly speaking, a medieval development which takes its definitive formulation from Anselm of Canterbury (d. 1109). The study of Anselm's atonement theory takes us beyond the scope of this present study. Volume Three has a Case Study entirely devoted to this topic. One must be careful for the moment, however, not to superimpose this or any other atonement theory as the sole perspective of Jesus or of the early church.

Within the Jewish perspective underlying the Gospels, the forgiveness of sins (even when they are not confessed) is a consequence of the turning back (*teshuvah*) which is the prerequisite for baptism: "Return to me, and I will return to you, says the Lord of Hosts" (Mal 3:7). The rite of baptism, therefore, does not have any inherent power to forgive; baptism confirms and celebrates the forgiveness which has already been given by the Father due to the person's conversion prior to the rite.

*Forgiveness of sins is a consequence of teshuvah which is the prerequisite for baptism.*

**4Q**: Does baptism confer the Holy Spirit?

**A**: The descent of the Spirit was the not the normal or expected result of John's baptism. The same can be said for the baptism which Peter administered to the three thousand Jews on Pentecost. John expected that, when the Lord returns, he would immerse his people in the Holy Spirit and in fire (as has already been explained above). Peter, in contrast, had already experienced an unbidden and unexpected outpouring of the prophetic Spirit which, following the interpretative framework of Joel, is the gift of God "before the day of the Lord comes" (Acts 2:20 = Joel 2:31). On Pentecost the disciples gathered in the upper room at Pentecost and received this Spirit without baptism.

At no point in Acts is it expressly shown that the Spirit descends upon anyone during the rite or because the rite was performed. Nothing within the Jewish horizon of understanding would have permitted Jews to imagine that some rite had the effect of conferring God's Spirit. Simon, the magician convert, wrongly came to this conclusion and was roundly condemned (Acts 8:18-24). Accordingly, there is nothing unusual in Acts presentation whereby the gift of the Spirit sometimes arrives prior to the rite, sometimes following the rite, and sometimes entirely without the rite (as in the case of the disciples at Pentecost).

Bishop Gregory of Nyssa (d. 394) has left us with a complete set of instructions used to train those who were responsible for preparing candidates for baptism. From these instructions it is clear that no one could expect to receive the Holy Spirit without a prior conversion of life. Gregory, therefore, presented a sober assessment of the limitations of baptism:

> Baptism produces no essential change in human nature. Neither reason nor understanding, nor capacity for knowledge, nor anything else that marks human nature undergoes a change. . . . Now it is clear that when the evil characteristics of our nature are done away with [through conversion], there is a change. . . . But if the washing has only affected the body, and the soul has failed to wash off the stains of passion, and the life after initiation is identical with that before, despite the boldness of my assertion, I will say without shrinking that, in such a case, the water is only water, and the gift of the Holy Spirit is nowhere evident in the action (*Oratio catechetica magna* 40).

**5Q**: Didn't Jesus receive the Spirit due to his baptism?

**A**: Matthew may give this impression since he notes that "when Jesus was baptized, he went up immediately from [under] the water, and behold, the heavens were opened and he saw the Spirit of God descending . . ." (3:16). Luke avoids this impression by having the Spirit descend while Jesus was at prayer following his baptism (Luke 3:21). Jesus at prayer is a favorite theme in Luke, and this may help to explain his editing of Mark's account. In both cases, however, no causal link is intended between the rite of baptism and the Spirit. Put more boldly: just

---

*At no point in Acts is it expressly shown that the Spirit descends because the rite was performed.*

*The gift of the Spirit sometimes arrives prior to the rite, sometimes following the rite, and sometimes entirely without the rite.*

because the Spirit might arrive during one baptism does not thereby imply that God is committed to send the Spirit only on the occasion of baptisms.

**6Q**: Of what use then is the rite itself?

**A**: Every adult baptism in the Christian Scriptures serves to enhance and to celebrate a person's turning around and the reception of forgiveness which God had worked in the person prior to the rite (usually as occasioned by prophetic preaching). The public and experiential nature of the rite itself also served to fortify the individual and to invoke the continued assistance of the Spirit in the work of sanctification which continued long after the rite. Everything, therefore, which was said previously regarding the rite of the laying on of hands (in ordination) might be analogously applied to baptism as well.

*Adult baptism serves to enhance and to celebrate what God had worked in the person prior to the rite.*

**7Q**: How did Peter's baptizing differ from John's?

**A**: Christian theology has been tempted to see John's baptizing as a kind of preparatory rite which anticipates the fuller and richer baptizing by Peter. The Christian Scriptures, however, do not demote one in order to promote the other. In point of fact, the lines of continuity are very strong. Both rites serve to confirm and enhance the *teshuvah* and the forgiveness of sins attached thereto. Both rites are framed against the background of the nearness of the Lord's return and the beginning of a new age. The major functional difference, however, is that John sent those baptized back into their local communities to bear the fruit of their conversions. After Peter or his companions baptized "in the name of Jesus Christ" (Acts 2:38), those turning back entered into the community of believers committed to learning, celebrating, and following the interpretation and practice of Torah by Jesus. This gift of Jesus was not available within the Jewish community at large; hence, Acts rightly notes that the newly baptized "devoted themselves to the apostles' teaching and fellowship, to the breaking of bread and the prayers" (Acts 2:42).

*Linking Peter's baptizing with John's, the lines of continuity are very strong.*

**8Q**: Did baptism serve to initiate these persons into a new religion?

**A**: Since John's baptism was exclusively for Jews, it carried with it no sense of a conversion to another religion. The early church, when properly seen as a movement for and by Jews, could accordingly practice baptism without imagining that those baptized were

*Jews who were baptized recovered their true Jewish identity as beloved sons and daughters of God.*

any less Jewish as a result. In fact, the Jewish followers of Jesus believed that those Jews who were baptized recovered their true Jewish identity as beloved sons and daughters of God. When Jesus, following his own baptism, hears the voice from heaven saying, "Thou art my beloved Son/son" (Luke 3:22 and parallels), this might be thought of as representing the precise depth of experience that would be available to any Jew.

With time, however, the rite of baptism would be extended to Gentiles who, in actual fact, would abandon their ancestral gods and associated rites in order to embrace the God of Jesus. Then and only then did baptism begin to function as an initiation rite into a new religion.

**9 Q**: How did infant baptism inadvertently lead to the perception that faith and grace were received during the administration of the rite itself?

**A**: As long as adult baptisms were being performed, the miracle of grace and the gifts of the Holy Spirit were manifest in the candidates before, during, and after the rite. At this point, a certain parallel can be made between adult baptism and the rite of ordination in so far as the wisdom and the Spirit were expected to be manifest as a necessary condition prior to the administration of the rite itself.

*Claims made for adults on the basis of experience were theologically applied to children as invisible effects.*

When infant baptism became the norm, however, the same claims made for adults on the basis of experience were now theologically applied to children as well. In the case of children and, more especially, of infants, however, the effects of grace were no longer manifest prior to the rite. What sense did "conversion of life" have for an infant? Accordingly, the theology of adult baptism when applied to infants began to take on the appearance of a sacred rite which had invisible (even quasi-magical) effects. Only then did the "power of the rite" to forgive sin, to exorcise the devil, and to impart grace all have unlimited scope since they could not be either affirmed or denied on the basis of any perceived conversion of life. Augustine had to go so far as to explain to his congregation that infants who screamed out in church when cold water was poured over them during baptism were not thereby resisting the Holy Spirit.

**10 Q**: Can a credible case be made for infant baptism?

**A**: Yes. But the evidence does not and need not come from the Sacred Scriptures. For example, Jesus saying "let the little children come to me" (Luke 18:16) has little to do with authorizing baptism for infants. Rather, the case for infant baptism must reside within the experience of the church itself. For centuries, the churches that have been baptizing infants have taken note that, when parents and guardians live as Christians, their children easily and naturally assimilate from them the same habitual way of perceiving life and living the Gospel. Thus, by virtue of human bonding and childhood training, a parent or god-parent can anticipate that the faith of the church will, in due course, providentially become the faith of the child. Behind every exaggerated notion of infant baptism, therefore, stands the faith and experience of parenting.

*Behind every exaggerated notion of infant baptism, stands the faith and experience of parenting.*

Even Thomas Aquinas affirmed that manifest faith and Christian morals were the prerequisites for baptism. Thus, in the case of infants, the living faith and moral living of parents and godparents was expected to supply what was wanting in the infant. Thomas theorized that the very efficacy of the rite was in a sleeping phase for infants and only awakened gradually as Christian maturity blossomed (*Summa Theologica* III, q. 69, a. 6). Accordingly those churches which practice infant baptism ought to be careful to allow that, as far as the infant is concerned, the grace of baptism shows up experientially only years after the rite.

*Thomas theorized that the efficacy of the rite was in a sleeping phase for infants and only awakened gradually.*

A church, accordingly, must know when to discontinue infant baptism—as has been the case among many Roman Catholic communities in mainland China. Following the condemnation of the Gang of Four, the churches within China were allowed a certain restricted operation. During my visit in 1982, I made contact with the Catholic Church in Beijing. What I found was a very traditional and very courageous church which was still practicing Latin rites and using the old theological manuals (having been untouched by Vatican II). I soon discovered, however, that infant baptism was no longer practiced. When I asked why, I received an answer like the following:

> Communist propaganda in our schools, in our youth clubs, and in our media is so all-pervasive that a parent can no longer guarantee that his or her own children will grow up accepting the Gospel of Jesus Christ. Hence, under these conditions, we thought it best to discontinue infant baptisms. Accordingly, we now reserve baptism for those young people who, by the grace of God, manage to resist the atheistic propaganda around them and are ready to "take up their cross" and to follow Christ.

Even a conservative church, therefore, can reflect upon and alter its practices (when it is not blocked from doing so by a theology which blinds them to the validity of their own experience).

*Churches in China have returned to the practice of the second and third centuries wherein Christian parents did not presume to have their children baptized for much the same reason.*

These churches in China have accordingly returned to the practice of the second and third centuries wherein Christian parents did not presume to have their children baptized for much the same reason.

Infant baptism, therefore, requires not only the providential bond between parents and children for its efficacy, it also requires a climate in society which is not systematically subverting the Gospel. Some ordained ministers in the United States have confided to me that the lure of secularism and materialism in our society has reached such proportions that even professing parents in our society discover that they cannot effectively transmit their faith commitments to their own children. Even in our own society, therefore, infant baptism may have to be suspended.

*Infant baptism stands at the beginning of an extended journey of initiation which culminates in the rite of confirmation.*

**11Q**: Does the restored adult catechumenate offer yet another approach for validating infant baptism?

**A**: Yes. Another theologically and pastorally sound approach to infant baptism is to acknowledge that such a baptism stands at the beginning of an extended journey of initiation which culminates in the rite of confirmation. The churches of the second to the fifth centuries practiced an extended period of adult initiation known as the catechumenate. In 1976, the Catholic bishops approved the restoration of the adult catechumenate and had this to say:

> The rite of Christian initiation described below is intended for adults. They hear the preaching of the mystery of Christ, the Holy Spirit opens their hearts, and they freely and knowingly seek the living God and enter the path of faith and conversion (Rites: 20).

One can note here that the work of the Holy Spirit is presupposed prior to the rite.

When it came to those baptized as infants; however, the Sacred Congregation of Rites had this to say:

> The steps of the catechumenate will be appropriately adapted to those who, baptized in infancy, are confirmed only as adults. The initiation of children into the sacramental life is for the most part the responsibility and concern of Christian parents. They are to form and gradually increase a spirit of faith in the children, prepare them for the fruitful reception of the sacraments of confirmation and the eucharist. The role of the parents is also expressed by their active participation in the celebration of the sacraments (Rites: 298).

All in all, therefore, when infant baptism is practiced within the context of a modified adult catechumenate, the experience of the faithful will amply testify to the gift of God's Spirit as received prior to, during, and follow the rites themselves. As a result, one is safeguarded against making exaggerated claims for the power of infant baptism in and of itself. Its power will be seen as again experientially evident in what happens during the entire initiation process stretching from baptism to confirmation.

**12Q**: Can those churches practicing "infant baptism" recognize the baptism of those churches practicing "believers' baptism" and visa versa?

**A**: Hopefully, yes. The *Baptism, Eucharist, and Ministry* document prepared by the World Council of Churches has this to say on the topic:

> When the expressions "infant baptism" and "believers' baptism" are used, it is necessary to keep in mind that the real distinction is between those who baptize people at any age and those who baptize only those able to make a confession of faith themselves. The differences between infant and believers' baptism become less sharp when it is recognized that both forms of baptism embody God's own initiative in Christ and express a response of faith made within the believing community.
>
> The practice of infant baptism emphasizes the corporate faith which the child shares with its parents. The infant is born into a broken world and shares in its brokenness. Through baptism, the promise and claim of the Gospel are laid upon the child. The personal faith of the recipient of baptism and faithful participation in the life of the Church are essential for the full fruit of baptism.
>
> The practice of believers' baptism emphasizes the explicit confession of the person who responds to the grace of God in and through the community of faith and who seeks baptism.
>
> Both forms of baptism require a similar and responsible attitude towards Christian nurture. A rediscovery of the continuing character of Christian nurture may facilitate the mutual acceptance of different initiation practices (WCC: 4).

**13Q**: Is it any longer possible to speak of baptism as a sacrament "instituted by Christ"?

*Both infant baptism and believers' baptism require a similar and responsible attitude towards Christian nurture.*

*It no longer becomes either desirable or credible to imagine that Jesus instituted specific sacraments at specific historical moments.*

A: Yes and no. Traditional theology supposed that Jesus had a clear intention to found a church and to endow it with a well-defined hierarchy and set of sacraments. Once one leaves this world of thinking, however, it no longer becomes either desirable or credible to imagine that Jesus instituted specific sacraments at specific historical moments supported by specific biblical texts.

Contemporary theologians, therefore, have begun to take a larger view of the subject. Human encounters with the Word made flesh resulted in transformed lives and evident grace. Jesus, consequently, might be thought of as *the primordial sacrament*. The community of disciples (the church), in so far as they continued to mediate the transforming presence of Jesus in history, effectively participates in the same sacramental reality. The living church, consequently, might be seen as sacramental in its totality of operations and not just during its sacramental moments. Accordingly, Karl Rahner, the highly respected Catholic theologian has this to say:

> If we see the sacraments from the perspective of the very essence of the church, and recall what we said earlier about the possibility of a process of becoming in the essential law of the church; if, moreover, we take into account that today, in contrast to the time of the Reformation, even baptism cannot be traced back very easily to a verbal institution by the historical Jesus, . . . then we can say that the origin of the institution of the sacraments has to be understood, and also can be understood, in a way which is analogous to the institution of the church itself by Jesus. The sacramentality of the church's basic activity is implied by the very essence of the church as the irreversible presence of God's salvific offer in Christ (Rahner: 413).

*As long as God's grace abounds, sacraments will be celebrated.*

In sum, it is highly questionable today to claim either two or seven sacraments in isolation. Sacraments exists as relational realities which express the ongoing character of ecclesial bodies. At the same time as they express our encounter with the living God. The number and the forms of the specific sacraments, therefore, periodically change in order to take into account the historical and cultural character of those specific people reaching out for God's blessing. In the end, therefore, as long as God's grace abounds, sacraments will be celebrated. And, where sacraments are celebrated, they will always be mythically and historically linked to that Jesus who stands at the origins of our encounter with the living God. Beyond this, no other justification is either necessary or desired.

## Application to the Churches Today

From the time of the first century, baptism has undergone many pastoral and theological modifications. The truth remains, however, that the Christian Scriptures retain the experience and the practice of those first Christians who adapted baptism for themselves and for their messianic movement. What does this past usage say to today's contemporary churches? Where does it challenge us? Where does it confirm us? Write down your reflections here in the space available.

## Further Readings for Case Seven

Bailey, Kenneth E.
> *Poet and Peasant: A Literary-Cultural Approach to the Parables of Luke.* Grand Rapids: Eerdmans, 1976.

Bausch, William J.
> *A New Look at the Sacraments.* Notre Dame: Fides/Claretian, 1977.

Cullmann, Oscar
> *Baptism in the New Testament.* London: SCM Press, 1950.

Dunn, James D. G.
> *Baptism in the Holy Spirit.* London: SCM Press, 1970.
>
> *Unity and Diversity in the New Testament: An Inquiry into the Character of Earliest Christianity.* Philadelphia: Westminster, 1977.

Martos, Joseph
> *Doors to the Sacred: A Historical Introduction to the Sacraments in the Catholic Church.* Garden City: Doubleday. Esp. pp. 161-202, 1981.

Milavec, Aaron
> *To Empower as Jesus Did: Acquiring Spiritual Power Through Apprenticeship.* Lewiston: The Edwin Mellen Press, 1982.

Rahner, Karl
> *Foundations of Chistian Faith.* New York: Crossroad, 1982.

Sacred Congregation of Rites
> *The Rites of the Catholic Church as Revised by Decree of the Second Vatican Ecumenical Council and Published by the Authority of Pope Paul VI.* New York: Pueblo, 1976.

Turner, Paul
> *Confirmation: The Baby in Solomon's Court.* New York: Paulist, 1992.
>
> *Sources of Confirmation: From the Fathers Through the Reformers.* Collegeville: The Liturgical Press, 1993.

World Council of Churches
> *One Baptism, One Eucharist, and a Mutually Recognized Ministry: Faith and Order Paper No. 73.* Geneva: World Council of Churches, 1977.

# CASE EIGHT

# Thy Kingdom Come and/or Going to Heaven?

What can God be expected to do for his elect in the future? Will the Kingdom of God come to us on earth? Or must we wait until we die so that our souls will go to be with God in heaven?

Christians are divided on this issue. All in all, however, the responses break down into two divergent sets of expectations. Some Christians pray "thy kingdom come" while others pray that they "might go to heaven." Each of these futures needs to be explored.

*Some Christians pray "thy kingdom come" while others pray that they "might go to heaven."*

During my youth, my primary education made use of the *Baltimore Catechism*. In the very first lesson, we memorized the following:

Q3. Why did God make us?

A3. God made us to show forth His goodness and to share with us His everlasting happiness in heaven.

Within the light of this response, I was taught that life in this world is just a brief interlude leading to an eternity with God and his angels in my heavenly home. The notes to my catechism expressed it this way:

> The happiness of heaven consists in the direct vision, love, and enjoyment of God. This reward so far exceeds man's nature that without the supernatural help of God it could not possibly be attained. In heaven God gives us the light of glory, which enables us to see Him face to face. During our life on earth God gives us His grace, which enables us to live a supernatural life and to perform the actions that can earn this reward (*Baltimore Catechism*: 6).

As an eight-year old, the "vision of God" moved back and forth from being something "awesome" to being something terribly "boring." When I asked my religion teacher about this, she wisely settled for telling me that my dear mother who had died just after Christmas would be in heaven waiting for me. The prospect of being rejoined to my mother was *very* concrete and *very* appealing. I had to admit that "the direct vision, love, and enjoyment" of my mother was much more conducive to make me yearn for heaven than all the fanciful images of choirs of angels surrounding the throne of God.

*"The direct vision, love, and enjoyment" of my mother was much more conducive to make me yearn for heaven than all the fanciful images of choirs of angels surrounding the throne of God.*

But this was not all. Even though God created us with an immortal soul, and even though each of us naturally seeks happiness, not everyone gets to go to heaven after death. Hell is the other option. Heaven is reserved as the reward that God gives to those whom he judges worthy. It is as if one could say:

> He's making a list; he's checking it twice;
> He's going to find out who's naughty or nice. . . .
> He sees you when your sleeping;
> He knows when your awake;
> He knows when you've been bad or good;
> So be good for goodness sake.
> Oh, you better watch out; you better not pout;
> I'm telling you why:
> ***Christ is coming to judge you on the last day.***

Some of the familiar Christian metaphors associated with judgment have been displaced onto Santa Claus. These metaphors, however, properly belong to the Final Judge who has before him the whole of my life and will decide whether I are worthy of candies or coal (the latter, a thinly veiled metaphor for hellfire) in the next life.

As a boy of eight, therefore, my anticipation of joining my lost mother in heaven was also firmly tied to avoiding hell by being good and not committing sins. My early religious life, consequently, was lived within the feeling tones associated with the anticipation of union and the fear of loss. When the time came for me to die, I earnestly wanted to go to heaven.

Meanwhile, in another part of town, the children of parents who were Seventh-day Adventists were being nourished on an entirely different notion of what God had in store for them. For them, it was not a question of "going" somewhere after death. Rather, God had promised to come to them and to renew and purify this earth such that it would again become the paradise which God had intended for humankind from the beginning.

> The first two chapters of the bible tell of God's creation of a perfect world as a home for the human beings He created. The bible's last two chapters also speak of God's creating a perfect world for humanity—but this time its a recreation, a restoration of the earth from the ravages sin brought (Ministerial Association: 375).

Children within this community are taught to perceive the massive starvation in Ethiopia or the massive flooding in Bangladesh or the drive-by killings in America as signs of "the ravages of sin." Petty jealousy among siblings as well as the collective antagonism between nations can serve to represent the scope of the ravages of sin. When God returns, all this will be wiped away. No more genetic deformities. No more joblessness or homelessness. No more aimlessness for

*My anticipation of joining my lost mother in heaven was also firmly tied to avoiding hell by being good.*

*Children of parents who were Seventh-day Adventists were being nourished on an entirely different notion of what God had in store for them.*

youth. No more fear for the safety and welfare of their children on the part of parents and grandparents.

Basing their perspective upon Second Peter, Seventh-Day Adventists believe that the present world and its inhabitants "will be cleansed by fire" ( 2 Pet 3:6f, 12f). Rather than viewing fire as the eternal torment of the damned in hell, the fire which the Lord will bring with him on "the day of God" (2 Pet 3:12) will destroy sin and the works of sin leaving only the elect as the inhabitants of "a new earth in which righteousness dwells" (2 Pet 3:13).

> Life in the new earth will challenge the most ambitious for eternity. . . . [T]he redeemed will "build houses and inhabit them" (see Isa. 65:21). Building implies design, construction, furnishing, and the potential for remodeling or rebuilding. And from the word "inhabit" we may infer a whole spectrum of activities relating to daily life (Ministerial Association: 378).

In sum, while the Catholic boy of eight was anticipating going to an extraterrestrial location to be with his mother and God, his counterpart, in a different church across town, was being taught to pray "thy kingdom come." This latter prayer meant that God was preparing to return to earth to recreate the terrestrial paradise and the perfect society with his saints. Here are the two different sets of metaphors; the two different moods of anticipation.

In part, they overlap. The Catholic boy, had he been better informed, would have spoken about the resurrection of the body as having a enduring role within Catholic tradition. The Seventh-day Adventist meanwhile could have spoken of the souls of the redeemed as being stored in heaven with God until the time of the Lord's return to earth. Within their basic outlines, however, the two systems significantly diverge.

*Fire will destroy sin and the works of sin leaving only the elect as the inhabitants of "a new earth in which righteousness dwells" (2 Pet 3:13).*

## Purpose

The purpose of this Case Study will be to explore how the Synoptic Gospels present Jesus' own metaphors respecting what future God has in mind for those who love him.

Before beginning, you are again invited to take a measure of your present starting point. Consider the following three questions.

1. In your own upbringing, how were you trained to regard "eternal life"? Where was eternal life and what would you be doing there?

*The purpose of this Case will be to explore Jesus' own metaphors respecting what future God has in mind for those who love him.*

2. Now that you have gained some wisdom and grace beyond your childhood years, in what ways have your early expectations have been enlarged or changed? Please describe here in some detail.

3. To what degree would what you wrote above conform to Jesus' own preaching respecting God's future? _____ What key text, if any, anchors your expectations with those of Jesus? _____

At this time, take your bible in your hands and pray that the Spirit of God would guide you in understanding what future some of the early disciples expected in view of the teachings of Jesus.

Translation = _____
Starting time = _____ (100-180 minutes needed)

## An Initial Word Study

1. On the basis of the previous Case Study, it is apparent that Jesus' ministry was not immediately directed toward either the establishing of a church or the promotion of baptism. What then was the central image or metaphor which served as the basis for all of Jesus' preaching?

The central metaphor dominating Jesus' preaching was the Kingdom of God. Within the Synoptic accounts, Jesus' public ministry is summarized by saying that "he went about all Galilee, teaching in their synagogues and preaching the gospel of the kingdom . . ." (Matt 4:23). And again, when Jesus is presented as foreseeing the future, he says, "This gospel of the kingdom will be preached throughout the whole world, as a testimony to all nations; and then the end will come" (Matt 24:14).

What is the "kingdom" and how does Jesus understand it as "good news"?

*The central metaphor dominating Jesus' preaching was the Kingdom of God.*

Jesus never specifically defined the Kingdom of God. Nor do the Evangelists. In both cases, hearers would have been quite familiar with "the kingdom." Jews were entirely familiar with the notion that their Lord and God acted powerfully within history in order to forward the cause of justice and righteousness. "Kingdom," therefore, is not a place, not a title, not an office. Rudolph Schnackenburg explains:

> Israel experienced Yahweh's kingship in the historical action of its God. There is no "kingdom" and no "sphere of dominion" but a kingly leadership and reign which develops from Yahweh's absolute power and shows itself in the guidance of Israel. This original meaning, namely that Yahweh as king actively "rules," must be kept in mind through the whole growth of the *basileia* ["kingdom"] theme. God's kingship in the Bible is characterized not by latent authority but by the exercise of power, not by an office but a function; it is not a title but a deed (Schnackenburg: 13).

Jesus never specifically defined the role of his band of disciples relative to the anticipated Kingdom of God. One can surmise, however, on the basis of Matt 24:14 and other texts, that Jesus anticipated that his disciples would continue his own preaching of "the good news of the kingdom" until the new age began. These disciples, it will be remembered, had already been sent out while Jesus was with them for the purpose of proclaiming the kingdom (Matt 10:7 and par.). As a result, it is not surprising that, according to the writings of the Christian Scriptures, the early churches gave no thought to building programs, Christian schools, Christian hospitals, sports programs, political parties, and soup kitchens. All these things may, at one time or the other, be legitimate developments of the mission of proclaiming the good news of the kingdom. However, these activities

*Jews were entirely familiar with the notion that their Lord and God acted powerfully within history in order to forward the cause of justice and righteousness.*

---

### Note on "Gospel"

The RSV uses the term "gospel" to translate *evangelion* in Matt 4:23 and 24:14. "Gospel" comes from Old English and literally means "good news." Only later did this work come to mean the book what narrates the "good news of Jesus" (Mark 1:1). Jesus, consequently, was remembered by the Evangelist, not as proclaiming "the gospel," but "the *good news* of the kingdom." The NRSV appropriately uses "good news" in both places. Check your translation of these texts.

*Jesus anticipated that his disciples would continue his own preaching of "the good news of the kingdom" until the new age began.*

in and of themselves would have been perceived as having no inherent merit or justification aside from the kingdom.

Luke makes it clear that the proclamation of the kingdom continued to form the central agenda of the early church. Philip, one of the Seven ordained by the Twelve, is presented as reaching out to the Samaritans in these terms: "he *preached good news about the kingdom of God* and the name of Jesus Christ" (Acts 8:12). Likewise, Luke sometimes characterized the mission of Paul in precisely the same terms: "he entered the synagogue and for three months spoke boldly, *arguing and pleading about the kingdom of God*" (Acts 19:8). The whole of Acts closes with these words: "he [Paul] lived there [in Rome] for two whole years . . . *preaching the kingdom of God* and teaching about the Lord Jesus Christ quite openly and unhindered (Acts 28:31). According to these texts, what has priority: the kingdom or Jesus? _____ How did you decide?

*Luke makes it clear that the proclamation of the kingdom continued to form the central agenda of the early church.*

2. Word frequency charts reveal that, all in all, the term "kingdom" (*basileia*) occurs 162 times in the Christian Scriptures. This term is not inherently a religious term. For example, see the following:

In most instances, the Christian Scriptures does not just have "kingdom" but, to add clarity, use either the phrase (a) "Kingdom of God" or (b) "Kingdom of Heaven." Here is a frequency table:

| Source | To what does the word "kingdom" refer? |
|---|---|
| Matt 4:8 | |
| Matt 12:25f (2x) | |
| Matt 24:7 (2x) | |

| Source | Kingdom of God | Kingdom of Heaven |
|---|---|---|
| Matthew | 05 | 32 |
| Mark | 15 | 00 |
| Luke | 33 | 00 |
| John | 02 | 00 |
| Acts | 07 | 00 |
| Paul's letters | 08 | 00 |
| Hebrews | 00 | 00 |
| Peter, James | 00 | 00 |
| Revelations | 01 | 00 |

What conclusions can you draw from this table?

*The parables of the kingdom are curiously absent from John's Gospel.*

One conclusion that can be drawn is that most of the instances of "Kingdom of God" and "Kingdom of Heaven" are to be found in the Synoptics. In Acts and the letters of Paul, the occurrences of "Kingdom of God" decreases. In those Christian Scriptures written late in the first century, the use of "Kingdom of God" entirely disappears.

---

### The "Kingdom" in John's Gospel

John's Gospel presents Jesus as explicitly referring to the "Kingdom of God" on only two occasions (John 3:3, 5). Both of these instances are early in his Gospel and show up in Jesus' nighttime conversation with Nicodemus.

In the remainder of John's Gospel, other metaphors are used, particularly "eternal life" (17 occurrences) or simply "life" (18 occurrences). Many scholars regard these metaphors as functioning as near-equivalents for the term "kingdom." If this were the case, one might imagine that John's readers may not have had the Jewish background necessary to understand the "kingdom" language of the Synoptics and that John had to resort to using "eternal life" by way of capturing Jesus' preoccupations with God's Reign.

John, for that matter, presents Jesus as presenting long discourses focusing attention upon himself and not upon the Kingdom of God. The parables of the kingdom which are so familiar to us because of the Synoptics are curiously absent from John's Gospel. In fact, if we had to rely upon John's Gospel alone, we would never know that Jesus ever taught using parables and that these parables were seemingly his preferred mode of heralding the Kingdom of God.

**"Kingdom of Heaven" only finds its place in Matthew's Gospel.**

Another important conclusion that can be drawn from the table on the previous page is that "Kingdom of Heaven" only finds its place in Matthew's Gospel. Does this difference in vocabulary imply that Matthew was presenting Jesus as someone preoccupied with "going to heaven" (=Kingdom of Heaven) while Mark and Luke, in contrast, have Jesus advocating an earth-based kingdom (=Kingdom of God)? _____ How would one find the answer to this question?

**Matthew has only five occurrences of "Kingdom of God" whereas the text of Mark open before him already had fifteen.**

One could check all the instances in which "Kingdom" is mentioned by Matthew and compare these to those found in Mark and Luke, but this would be very time consuming. Relying on the hypothesis that Matthew wrote his account of the Gospel with Mark open before him, it seems suspicious that Matthew has only five occurrences of "Kingdom of God" whereas the text of Mark open before him already had fifteen.

What ever happened to the ten missing occurrences of "Kingdom of God" which Matthew did not carry over into his Gospel? Find out for yourself. Check the first five instances of "Kingdom of God" in Mark which Matthew omits, put a finger at that spot, and then compare it with the parallel text of Matthew. Record your results here:

| Mark (source) | Matthew (parallel) | What did Matthew do with "Kingdom of God"? |
|---|---|---|
| 1;15 | 4:17 | |
| 4:11 | 13:11 | |
| 4:26 | 13:24 | |
| 4:30 | 13:31 | |
| 9:1 | 16:28 | |

What conclusion can you draw regarding the relationship of Matthew's "Kingdom of Heaven" with Mark's "Kingdom of God"?

## The Kingdom in Jewish Expectation

3. Within the Synoptics, the term "Kingdom of God" is repeatedly used without any explanation. This can only mean that the audience for whom it was intended already had a background understanding of the future which God was planning for his people. Within the prophetic literature of the Hebrew Scriptures, one finds frequent and repeated scenarios of how, in the end-times, God would powerfully intervene in history by taking the part of his people against their foes. From the prophetic literature, one gains the impression that, "in this world," the just suffer needlessly at the hands of the wicked; "in the world to come," however, God will vindicate the just before their enemies and establish them in a kingdom which will have no end.

*Within the Synoptics, the term "Kingdom of God" is repeatedly used without any explanation.*

4. Take time out to consider the details of three prophetic passages which are eschatological (i.e., spelling out the end times). If you are pressed for time, consider only (b).

   (a) Examine Isa 64:4-8 [the prayer of longing] and 65:16-25 [the answer to that prayer]. What do you discover?

   (b) Examine Zech 14:1-11. What do you discover?

   (c) Examine Dan 7:15-28. What do you discover?

> ### "Kingdom of God" and "Day of the Lord"
>
> While the phrase "Kingdom of God" is rarely found within Jewish eschatological literature, near-equivalents are plentiful. In the reading from Zechariah, for instance, you saw that when the Lord comes at the end of history he "will become king over all the earth" (Zech 14:9, 16, 17). According to the vision of Daniel, when the Lord comes, he will destroy all evil rulers and give sovereignty and kingship to "the saints" (Dan 7:18, 22, 27; see Luke 1:52).
>
> Zechariah repeatedly emphasizes that the "day of the Lord" is coming (Zech 14:1, 3, 4, 6, 7, 8, 9, 13, 20, 21). The phrase "Day of the Lord," in this context, does not refer to either the Sabbath or that future time when God will come to establish the kingdom of the saints on earth. For those who fail to walk in the ways of the Lord, the Day of the Lord will be "their day of calamity" (Jer 46:21), "a day of distress" (Hab 3:16), "a day of downfall (Ezek 26:18, 27:27, 32:10), "a bitter day" (Amos 8:10). From the vantage point of those who will be saved or rescued by the Lord, the Day of the Lord will be "the day when the Lord binds up wounds" (Isa 30:26), "the day when I cleanse" (Ezek 36:33), "the day when the Lord gives rest" (Isa 14:3), "the day when I pay attention" (Jer 27:22), "the day when the Lord takes the field of battle" (Zech 14:3). Thus, within the prophetic literature, the expectation of the "Day of the Lord" forms a foundation for appreciating Jesus' expectation of the "Kingdom of God."

| Source | How soon? | Where will it show up? | How do these terms relate to Kingdom? |
|---|---|---|---|
| Matt 25:31-34 | | | "eternal life" (25:46) |
| Matt 19:27-29 | | | "new world" (19:28) & "eternal life" (19:29) |
| Matt 13:36-43 | | | "close of the age" (13:39, & 40) |

## Where and When is the Kingdom expected?

According to the Synoptics, Jesus preached a kingdom which "is at hand" (Matt 4:17 and parallels). According to Matthew, this proclamation was not unique to Jesus since the message of John the Baptizer could be summarized in the same terms (Matt 3:13). *How close* is this kingdom? *How soon* will it come? *Where* will it show up?

*Jesus preached a kingdom which "is at hand."*

5. To discover this for yourself, consult the four texts from Matthew listed below and record your results in the spaces provided. These texts have been chosen because they specifically relate to the end-

*Thy Kingdom Come and/or Going to Heaven?* / 179

times. They have been deliberately arranged in reverse order. Use the margins to define the terms in the right-hand column.
Now, on the basis of the clues offered in these three texts, what can you conclude about the location of the kingdom?

What can you conclude about the temporal closeness of the kingdom? Is it already present? _____ If so, how so?

Do any of these texts support the notion that a person must die so that the "soul" may enter into the kingdom? _____ Which? _____ If so, how so?

Now look at the kingdom prayer which Jesus taught his disciples: Matt 6:9-13. English translations obscure the fact that the Greek repeatedly uses the aorist imperative which anticipates a single action as opposed to repeated action. The "hallowing," "coming," and "doing" are thus requested from the Father not on a daily basis but, once for all, at the end of time. Raymond Brown translates the prayer as follows:

> Our Father who are in heaven,
> May your name be sanctified,
> May your kingdom come,
> May your will come about on earth as in heaven.

*The "hallowing," "coming," and "doing" are requested from the Father not on a daily basis but, once for all, at the end of time.*

Brown explains that "the coming about of God's will is basically the same as the establishment of His kingdom, and, indeed, as the sanctification of His name" (Brown, 1961: 194-195). If this is the case, what does the kingdom prayer say about the location and the temporal closeness of the kingdom?

Does the petition that the kingdom "come" appear compatible with the notion that Jesus wanted his disciples to pray that they might "enter" or "go to" heaven after their deaths? _____ Explain, if you can, how the original set of expectations were eventually entirely replaced by the latter?

## Delay in the Lord's Coming

*Some texts provide clues for determining how "near at hand" the kingdom was.*

6. The texts that have been examined so far do not offer any specific time or date regarding the arrival of the kingdom. Scholars have noted, however, that some texts do appear to provide clues for determining how "near at hand" the kingdom was. Read, for instance, Mark 9:1 and 13:30, and decide what upper time limit you would be inclined to set based on these texts. Write your conclusions here:

Mark 9:1 has been taken over by both Matthew (16:28) and Luke (9:27) into their Gospels. Within the missionary discourse of Matt 10, however, one finds a saying unique to Matthew. This saying seems to envision that the Son of man (the final judge of Matt 25) will come *even before* the mission to Israel is completed. The text reads as follows:

> For truly, I say to you, you will not have gone through all the towns of Israel, before the Son of man comes (Matt 10:23b).

*Even when the arrival of the kingdom was expected soon, care was taken to declare that no person knows exactly "of that day or that hour."*

7. In each of the cases referred to, it might be noted that, even when the arrival of the kingdom was expected soon, care was taken to declare that no person knows exactly when: "of that day or that hour," no one knows, not even the angels in heaven, nor the Son, but only the Father" (Mark 13:32 and parallels). Such a text most probably had the purpose of silencing speculation regarding any specification of the actual day. Both then as well as today (especially as we approach the year 2000), it would appear that the churches will have to deal again and again with individuals who do claim to know "that day or that hour or that month or that year." The disruption of lives occasioned by such "inspired" projections will be enormous.

The Gospel of John hints that some of its own members may have gone through some such crisis when the apostle John died and the Lord still had not returned. John's Gospel, which was completed near the end of the first century, hints at this crisis in these terms:

> Jesus said to him [Peter], "If it is my will that he [John] remain until I come [again], what is that to you? Follow me!" [As a result] the saying spread abroad among the brethren that the disciple [John] was not to die [before the return of the Lord]; yet Jesus did not say to him that he was not to die, but, "If it is my will that he remain until I come [again], what is that to you [Peter]?" (John 21:22-24).

What appears to be the logic of this argument?

While John's Gospel does not repeat any of the sayings found in the Synoptics regarding "how close" the kingdom might be, John's community does appear to have had a tradition that Jesus would return in glory prior to the death of John. Hence, the logic of the Gospel was not to deny that Jesus had ever made such a prediction; rather, the entire construction is put into the conditional, "if it is my will" (John 21:22). Thus, when John died, his community had to understand that it was not in accord with his will that John should be alive when he returns. Raymond Brown, the world-renowned Catholic expert in John, dubbed this logic as "casuistry to show that Jesus' promise was not absolute" (Brown, 1967: 74).

*John's community had a tradition that Jesus would return in glory prior to the death of John.*

8. Within Second Peter, a pseudapostolic letter compiled in the early second century, one finds hints of yet another crisis created by predictions of the end-times. In this case, however, the focus is not on the return of Jesus but on the coming of the Lord-God on the day of the Lord. Here is the text divided to make for easier reading:

> Scoffers will come in the last days . . . saying:
>> Where is the promise of his coming? For ever since the fathers [Abraham, Isaac, etc.] fell asleep, all things have continued as they were from the beginning of creation.
>
> [A] They deliberately ignore this fact:
>> [1] that by the word of God heavens existed long ago and an earth formed out of water and . . . the world that then existed [at the time of Noah] was deluged with water and perished;

[2] but by the same word the heavens and earth that now exist have been stored up for fire, being kept [intact] until the day of judgment and destruction of ungodly men.

[B] But do not ignore this one fact, beloved:

[1] that with the Lord one day is as a thousand years. . . .

[2] The Lord is not slow about his promise as some count slowness, but is forbearing toward you, not wishing that any should perish, but that all should reach repentance (2 Pet 3:3-9).

What is the implied logic of this argument?

*According to Second Peter, if the Lord delays his coming, it is only by way of mercifully extending the period to "reach repentance" through the spread of the Gospel.*

This text needs unpacking. To begin with, the scoffers appear to be Jews (or Jewish Christians) who deny the Day of the Lord on the grounds that no significant change has taken place since Abraham. The countering argument is that great change has taken place. When? To begin with, massive change took place at the time when God, by his Word, created the heavens and the earth (Gen 1) and, later, when God destroyed the earth by water (Gen 7). Once this former destruction is granted, then it follows that the future destruction of the ungodly by fire will be equally certain. The Day of the Lord is coming! From the Lord's perspective, however, this "day" could be a thousand years. In effect, according to Second Peter, if the Lord delays his coming, it is only by way of mercifully extending the period to "reach repentance" through the spread of the Gospel. The upshot of this text is to use ancient biblical history to refute the scoffers and, at the same time, to extend the key metaphor of the "Day of the Lord" to embrace an indefinite period devoted to repentance. Within this framework, the feverish anticipation of a quick return is cooled—at least for the first thousand years following Jesus.

9. Has the Lord as yet returned with his angels to establish the Kingdom of God on earth? _____ If not, then it must be granted the Gospel accounts themselves contain an early enthusiasm for the messianic age which has not yet come to pass. Cosmic, collective, and personal evil still continue. Weeds are still growing among the wheat. The great Day of the Lord has not arrived. Was the early church then mistaken about these things? _____ Explain.

10. What is the source of the perspective which shifts the collective and this-worldly hope to the early church to that of a private and other-worldly judgment of the individual soul after death? Account for this as fully as you are able.

## Jesus' Struggle with Evil

11. The last point that needs to be considered is the impact of exorcisms upon Jesus' contemporaries. In Jesus' day, there was no biological science which diagnosed diseases as due to microbes, to vitamin deficiencies, or genetic disorders. In Jesus' day, an ordinary experience of a fever or a headache overtook someone with no known cause and passed away just as mysteriously. All of the irregularities in life which caused human suffering were considered by Jesus' contemporaries as due to demonic influence.

*Jesus performed numerous exorcisms without any use of lengthy rituals.*

Jesus performed numerous exorcisms. None of these involved the lengthy rituals associated with ancient magical exorcisms or with medieval Christian exorcisms. Nor do we find the Gospels describing

> ### Note on a Philosopher's Exorcism
>
> Any public speaker making a deep impression on his contemporaries had to effectively deal with hecklers of various kinds. Appollonios of Tyana, a contemporary of Jesus, went about the Greek cities preaching wisdom and moral reform. He made a deep impression on his contemporaries and gathered to himself many disciples. The following account portrays how he dealt with a demonically possessed lad who began as his antagonist and ended up as his disciple:
>
>> And when he told them to have handles on the cup and to pour over the handles—this being the purer part of the cup since no one's mouth touched that part—a young boy began laughing raucously, scattering his discourse to the winds. Apollonios stopped [teaching] and, looking up at him, said, "It is not you that does this arrogant thing, but the demon who drives you unwillingly," for, unknown to everyone, the youth was actually possessed by a demon, for he used to laugh at things no one else did and would fall to weeping for no reason. . . . Thus, when Apollonios began staring at it, the phantom in the boy let out horrible cries of fear and rage, sounding just like someone being burned alive or stretched on the rack. . . . But Apollonios spoke to him angrily such as a master might to a cunning and shameless slave, and he commanded him to come out of him. . . . But the young boy opened his eyes, as if from sleep, and . . . he threw aside his fancy soft clothes and, stripping off the rest of his luxuriousness, came to love poverty and a threadbare cloak and the customs of Apollonios (Flavius Philostratus, *The Life of Apollonios of Tyana* 4.20).

the victim as spewing vomit or causing objects to fly across the room as in the case of the Hollywood version of "The Exorcist." According to the Gospel, wherever faith in Jesus was evoked by his preaching, healings and exorcisms followed (as explained earlier in Case Four). In each instance, these were accomplished with little effort and little fanfare on the part of Jesus.

*Within the ancient world, erratic and malevolent conduct was attributed to demonic influence.*

Within the ancient world, erratic and malevolent conduct was attributed to demonic influence. Thus, in the Synoptics, the man "crying out [night and day] and bruising himself with stones" (Mark 5:5 and par.) is diagnosed as possessed by "an unclean spirit" (Mark 5:2, 13). According to Luke, Judas Iscariot was driven by Satan to betray Jesus (Luke 22:3)—conduct unimaginable for a man in his right mind. According to Mark, Jesus repeatedly had to take firm action to silence possessed individuals who interrupt his teaching (Mark 1:23, 34).

Healings and exorcisms are not unique to Jesus. Within both the Jewish and pagan literature of the first century, prophets and rabbis, philosophers and magicians, were also known to have evoked a deep faith which manifested itself in healings and exorcisms. Exorcisms, therefore, do not set Jesus apart as bizarre but allow him to take his place as one who "taught them as one who had authority" (Mark 1:22).

*The disciples of Jesus were sent out to herald the Kingdom of God, and healings and exorcisms accompanied their mission.*

Within the Gospel accounts, healings and exorcisms are not limited to Jesus. On the contrary, the disciples of Jesus were sent out to herald the Kingdom of God on their own (Matt 10 and Luke 9), and healings and exorcisms accompanied their mission. According to Luke, Jesus additionally sent out "seventy others" (Luke 10:1) who returned to him reporting their success in these terms: "Lord, even the demons are subject to us in your name!" (Luke 10:17)

Against this background, read Matt 12:28 (=Luke 11:20) within its context. What does it mean that Jesus' exorcisms are being interpreted as *a sign* that "the kingdom of God has come upon you"?

*According to Matt 12:28, the exorcisms of Jesus constitute something of the arrival of the kingdom.*

The Synoptics overwhelmingly represent the Kingdom of God as a future expectation. In the case of Matt 12:28, however, one gains the impression that the exorcisms of Jesus constitute something of the arrival of the kingdom. How would you explain this?

12. Your investigation began with a word study and ended with a consideration of exorcisms. Your purpose was to come to an understanding of the central theme of Jesus' preaching. In the end, therefore, if you would be guided by the teaching of Jesus as presented in the Synoptics, how would you express *in your own words* the "good news of the kingdom."

13. On the basis of your conclusions, would you say that my early Catholic formation regarding "going to heaven" or the Seventh-day Adventist's anticipation of "a new earth" was closer to what Jesus taught about the kingdom? _____ Explain.

14. What startling discoveries did you make while exploring this Case Study? Describe them for yourself here:

15. Did this Case Study raise any fundamental questions for you while you were completing it? If so, note them here so that you can return to them at a later moment?

    Completion time = _____

    Total time used on this Case = \_\_\_\_\_ minutes

Rest now and set your materials aside. When you are refreshed, come back and examine the analysis which follows.

## Analysis

The following questions and answers are prepared in order to bring together the Synoptic understanding of Jesus' message regarding the kingdom.

**1 Q**: What was the central message of Jesus to his contemporaries?

**A**: "Repent, for the kingdom of heaven is close at hand" (Matt 4:17 and par.).

**2 Q**: What is meant by the "Kingdom of Heaven"?

**A**: Matthew makes use of the phrase "Kingdom of Heaven" as his preferred equivalent for "Kingdom of God."

The anticipation of the Kingdom of God has deep roots within the prophetic tradition of Israel. The prophets looked forward to a time when God would forgive Israel their sins of infidelity and come to their aid against their enemies. After so doing, Jerusalem and the temple would be rebuilt, the exiles would all be gathered together, the holy ones who had fallen asleep would be brought to life, and God would come to permanently dwell with his people, thus securing their blessings and happiness forever.

Jesus stood within and marginally transformed these prophetic and eschatological expectations when he proclaimed the Kingdom of God. Jesus heralded the coming of God and invited the Jews of his day to set their own houses in order such that they might greet him when he arrives. Meanwhile, Jesus passed over in silence all of the customary threats which the prophets directed against the Gentiles. For Jesus, the mood associated with God's arrival is not first and foremost God's vengeance upon his enemies (the Gentiles) but God's mercy and blessings extended toward all those who follow his ways. This becomes especially clear in Jesus' vision of the final judgment. Embracing the image of "the Son of man" which is especially dominant in Daniel and Enoch, Jesus expected the Final Judge to come and take his throne while his angels gathered all nations (Jews and Gentiles included) and separated them "as a shepherd separates the sheep from the goats" (Matt 25:32). The Final Judge does not place all Jews on his right and all Gentiles on his left—as some of Jesus' contemporaries might have supposed. Rather, those who practiced righteousness and mercy will then be blessed by "inheriting the kingdom prepared . . . from the foundation of the world" (Matt 25:34). Those who failed to practice justice and mercy, however, will be cursed and sent for destruction into the "eternal fire prepared for the devil and his angels" (Matt 25:41).

*For Jesus, the mood associated with God's arrival is not first and foremost God's vengeance upon his enemies but God's mercy and blessings extended toward all those who follow his ways.*

The Kingdom of God, therefore, makes use of and transforms Jewish metaphors in order to evoke God's future victory over all the enemies of human well-being—personal and social brokenness, sin, injustice, suffering, oppression, and death.

**3 Q**: Did Jesus expect the Kingdom of God to arrive during his lifetime or during the lifetime of his disciples?

**A**: This question cannot be definitively settled. The Gospel accounts represent the faith and expectation of the community following Jesus and do not represent the personal memoirs of Jesus. This questions, consequently, must be transformed to ask, "Did the early churches expect that the Kingdom of God would arrive during the lifetime of the disciples?"

To this latter question, one can answer a qualified "yes." Some of the early churches were comfortable in remembered Jesus as having said, "There are some standing here who will not taste death before they see the kingdom of God come with power" (Mark 9:1). Such a precise time-frame placed on the lips of Jesus would indicate that some second-generation followers of Jesus regarded the imminent expectation of the Kingdom of God to be part and parcel of Jesus' teaching. With the death of the last apostle, however, third-generation disciples were forced to moderate and revise their assessment of God's timetable relative to the return of Christ and the full inbreaking of the Kingdom. John 21:23f and 2 Pet 3:3-13, consequently, would appear to be attempts by third-generation disciples to deal with the disappointment felt when the imminent expectations were frustrated.

**4 Q**: Did Jesus expect the Kingdom of God to arrive on earth or did he expect that those who died would be transported to heaven?

**A**: Both Jesus and his early disciples expected that God's final saving activity would take place on earth. The Jesus prayer, "thy kingdom come, thy will be done on earth as it is in heaven" (Matt 6:10) makes it clear that this earthly realm, distorted as it is by injustice, brokenness, and sin will be the precise realm to which the Father is bringing his saving activity.

Even when Christians perceived that God's transforming intervention in this world did not come soon, they fully expected that they would experience God's coming after death, thanks to the resurrection of the dead (see, e.g., 1 Thess 4:13-18). The Greek notion of the natural immortality of the soul (an idea which receives no explicit role in the Sacred Scriptures) furthermore made it possible to envision that the souls of the just would be transported to heaven after separation from the body in death and live

*The Kingdom of God makes use of and transforms Jewish metaphors in order to evoke God's future victory over all the enemies of human well-being.*

*Followers of Jesus regarded the imminent expectation of the Kingdom of God to be part and parcel of Jesus' teaching.*

*Jesus and his early disciples expected that God's final saving activity would take place on earth.*

among the angels until such time that the Lord would gather them to himself and return with them when he came to establish his kingdom on earth.

With time, however, many believers began to focus almost exclusively on their hope in joining the angels and saints immediately after death. The prospect of accompanying the Lord and of enjoying his kingdom following the resurrection of the dead seemed very remote. This revision had the effect of playing down the Jewish perspective that God functions where and when we need him, namely, within the murkiness of human and cosmic history. Furthermore, the Greek notion of the natural immortality of the soul tended to supplant the original Jewish hope that those who "sleep" in the earth would be raised to life on the last day. Finally, the Greek tradition of exalting the things of the soul while downgrading the things of the body (especially sexuality) tended to short circuit the Jewish balance that always existed between flesh and spirit.

*The Greek notion of the natural immortality of the soul tended to supplant the original Jewish hope that those who "sleep" in the earth would be raised to life on the last day.*

The Jewish perspective (as contrasted with the Greek) declares that the image and likeness of the Creator resides within the whole person (flesh and spirit) and that human nature was created *to live with God in the Garden* (i.e., in the nature world and not with the angels in heaven). Genesis also finds it congenial for God to have the "tree of life" planted in the Garden itself thereby declaring that Adam and Eve, had they proved faithful, would have been offered the fruit of this tree and to "live forever" (Gen 3:22). The perspective of Genesis is far removed from the Greek notion that eternal motion and eternal life can only be achieved by a spiritual soul living in the realm of eternal objects and ideas.

The incorporation of Greek metaphors into the Jewish eschatology of Jesus was wisely and fittingly accomplished so as to accommodate Gentile converts to the church. With time, however, the Greek emphasis on the soul tended to subvert the rightful importance that the things of the flesh and the things of the earth have in the eyes of God. Accordingly, it is not without foundation that many current pastors and theologians blame the current crisis regarding sexuality and ecology as flowing from the displacement of Jewish balance by Greek spiritualization. Thus, when it comes to our present day, many wise pastors have tried to readdress the imbalance of our immediate past by returning to the wisdom found within the Jewish metaphors of the kingdom which Jesus embraced as his own.

*The Greek emphasis on the soul tended to subvert the rightful importance that the things of the flesh and the things of the earth have in the eyes of God.*

**5 Q**: Can the promised kingdom be equated with personal salvation?

**A**: Not entirely. The value and the dignity of the regenerated human person is central to the Gospel; however, the Kingdom of God embraces and goes beyond "personal salvation." The history of Christianity demonstrates that to the degree that the message of the kingdom has been reduced to personal salvation (the reception of grace or salvation by faith), Christians have, to the same degree, neglected their engagement in working with God to transform the political, social, and ecological structures of their society and their world.

The Catholic bishops of the Vatican II were aware of this neglected engagement when they were drafting the *Pastoral Constitution on the Church in the Modern World* (Latin title: *Gaudium et Spes*). In the face of an excessive religious individualism, the bishops wished to recall to mind the social and global future God has in store for his peoples. In part, the bishops declared:

> For after we have obeyed the Lord, and in His Spirit nurtured on earth the values of human dignity, brotherhood and freedom, and indeed all the good fruits of our nature and enterprise, we will find them again, but freed of stain, burnished and transfigured. This will be so when Christ hands over to the Father a kingdom eternal and universal: "a kingdom of truth and life, of holiness and grace, of justice, love and peace" [Preface for the feast of Christ the King]. On this earth that kingdom is already present in mystery. When the Lord returns, it will be brought into full flower (*Gaudium et Spes*, sec 39).

In this same document, the Catholic bishops spoke of atheism "as one of the most serious problems of our time" (*Gaudium et Spes*, sec.19). The bishops identified the origins of atheism within "a violent protest against the evil in the world" and identified believers as having "more than a little to do with the rise of atheism" (*Gaudium et Spes*, sec. 19). On this very sensitive point of self-criticism, the bishops elaborated:

> To the extent that they [believers] are careless about their instruction in the faith, or present its teaching falsely, or even fail in their religious, moral, or social life [to implement this faith], they must be said to conceal rather than to reveal the true nature of God and of religion (*Gaudium et Spes*, sec. 19).

The Catholic Church is not alone in its recognition that the Gospel of "personal salvation" has led to a neglect of the social and global ramifications of the Kingdom of God. Parallel state-

*To the degree that the message of the kingdom has been reduced to personal salvation, Christians have, to the same degree, neglected their engagement in working with God to transform the political, social, and ecological structures.*

*The Catholic Church is not alone in its recognition that the Gospel of "personal salvation" has led to a neglect of the social and global ramifications of the Kingdom of God.*

ments can be found in the official statements of the World Council of Churches and of most Protestant denominations as well. Among many Catholics and Protestants, however, these statements have not taken root and the narrow doctrine of "personal salvation" continues to guide their instinctive spirituality.

**6 Q**: Does the promised kingdom lead to passivity?

**A**: No. Jesus never for a moment suggested that heralding God's future promises gave him the luxury of tending to his own personal salvation and leaving the rest of the world go to hell. Just to the contrary, Jesus openly and courageously confronted the forces of evil in his day. These forces took the shape of distorted forms of religion which served to bind and weaken the human spirit. These forces also took the form of demonic powers bent upon ruining God's personal and collective future for humankind.

*Jesus openly and courageously confronted the forces of evil in his day.*

The spiritual freedom that Jesus gave to his disciples took the form of training them to interpreting the Torah such that God's purposes would be actually served. When confronting the Temple priests and their supporters, Jesus observed that "tax collectors and harlots go into the kingdom of God before you" (Matt 21:31). This doesn't mean that they are corrupt sinners. On the contrary, it may well mean that nearly all of them were pious individuals faithful to their assigned religious duties; yet, many tax collectors and prostitutes had a better sense of what it meant to seek justice and to serve God's cause. Accordingly, Jesus cut his disciples free of their interpretation of Torah and assured them that God in heaven would endorse what they collectively decided to "bind and loose" on earth (Matt 18:18-20).

*Being religious in the footsteps of Jesus means confronting the forces of evil which cause needless suffering, oppression, and disease.*

Regarding those powers of evil which bring spiritual and physical brokenness, Jesus trained his disciples to confront these forces in the confidence that God intends them to be brought under his dominion. In a word, God opposes needless suffering. When Jesus is presented as expelling demons, healing the infirm, and training his disciples to do likewise, Christians learn from this that religion can never lead to passivity in the face of evil. Rather, being religious in the footsteps of Jesus means confronting, according to ones capacity and state of life, the forces of evil which cause needless suffering, oppression, and disease. In the end, therefore, far from being reduced to idle waiting, Christians are urged by their Father to begin now the process of anticipating his coming by struggling against evil in the name of Jesus. Then, when the Lord returns in power, he will find out which of his servants was ready and watching and working for his coming (see, e.g., Matt 24:45-51 and Luke 12:32-40).

**7 Q:** Why do so many Christians continue to think in terms of salvation in terms of the soul experiencing bliss in heaven after separating from the body at death?

**A:** Like myself, many Christians were brought up within the medieval perspective that envisioned "salvation" as dying in the state of grace such that one could be judged worthy to enter heaven. Today, this notion of salvation is still widespread and worthy of adherence; yet, it falls short of expressing Jesus' vision of God's future. The expectation of a blissful existence for the soul after death overplays an individualistic notion of salvation and downplays the rightful expectation that the realm of creation (our body, our culture, our environment) also awaits the promise of God's redemption. Hence, the biblical images of the new heavens and the new earth are needed in order to align our expectation that God's initiative in the world goes way beyond a narrow notion of "saving souls" and fully extends to the binding up and healing of body and soul in the full range of its personal, social, and ecological existence. The hope for a universal human solidarity and a society built upon justice for the weak and dispossessed, therefore, enters into the core of God's vision to which Christians are committed.

*The expectation of a blissful existence for the soul after death overplays an individualistic notion of salvation and downplays the rightful expectation that the realm of creation awaits the promise of God's redemption.*

Great care must be taken, therefore, that those other-worldly visions of the future which have, with authentic integrity, been fashioned and played out by medieval Christians do not serve to obscure God's future by promoting a false-gospel of quiet resignation to the exploitation by powerful elites and of blissful indifference to the social, economic, and environmental blight which currently afflicts many of God's children. As the bishops of Vatican II rightly noted: "Far from diminishing our concern to develop this earth, the expectancy of a new earth should spur us on, for it is here that the body of a new human family grows, foreshadowing in some way the [messianic] age which is to come" (*Gaudium et Spes*, sec. 39).

**8 Q:** Do the Christian Scriptures provide accurate representations of the future?

**A:** Jesus' preaching of the Kingdom of God uses very graphic and evocative images. It is to be expected that today's preachers would continue to conjure up images of the future which stir the hearts and minds of their hearers. Martin Luther King's address, "I Have a Dream" given during the march 1963 march on Washington amply represents how kingdom hopes must be tailored for different times and different peoples. As for the specific images within the Sacred Scriptures, however, *it would be deceptive and misleading to pre-*

tend that these were somehow exact depictions of precisely when and how the kingdom will arrive.

The Jewish prophets were stirred by the Spirit of God to say "no" to the particular injustice and oppression of their day. They did so in the firm reliance that God was passionately shouting "NO" with them. However, there is no single, consistent scenario for the future to be found therein. Within the collected apocalyptic poems of Isaiah, for instance, there are times when the Egyptians are slated for utter destruction (31:3) and times when the Lord "will send a savior to protect and deliver the Egyptians" (19:20) such that, in the end, they too will receive his blessing: "Blessed by my people Egypt" (19:25). Similarly, there are times when Isaiah speaks exclusively of "your offspring [Israel]" (43:5) as being gathered into the kingdom; at other times, the prophet (or someone speaking in his name) says that "the nations of every tongue" (66:18) will be so gathered by the Lord. Those churches which imagine that the bible contains a single and unified scenario for the arrival of God's kingdom have not been able to deal squarely with either the character or diversity of the many scenarios which have been inspired by the same Spirit.

*There is no single, consistent scenario for the future to be found in the prophetic literature.*

The same holds true for the kingdom parables of Jesus. At one moment, those unfit for the kingdom are "thrust into the darkness outside" (Matt 8:11); at another moment, the worthless are "cut down and thrown on fire" (Matt 6:20, 13:30, 13:50). In the Book of Revelation, the unfit are, in one of the five futuristic scenarios, pressed to death in "the great wine press of the wrath of God" (Rev 14:19). In effect, therefore, this multiplicity and diversity of images stands as a warning to the attentive reader that such images are reliable and predictive *when and only when* they are *not* being understood as presenting the step-by-step historical details of God's future.

*Diversity of prophetic images stands as a warning that such images are reliable when and only when they are not being understood as step-by-step historical details of God's future.*

Even more emphatically, those clues regarding the time when the kingdom will arrive must also be interpreted metaphorically. Whenever people are crushed by famine, by oppression, by catastrophic loss, God's intervention can and must be felt as "close at hand." In point of fact, however, Christians must continually assert that "of that day or that hour no one knows, not even the angels in heaven, nor the Son, but only the Father" (Mark 13:32).

*Whenever people are crushed by famine, by oppression, by catastrophic loss, God's intervention can and must be felt as "close at hand."*

Likewise, it seems impossible to know, on the basis of the biblical materials, whether the Kingdom of God will arrive suddenly or progressively. Even the bible must allow God to be God.

The tragic danger of searching for God's activity in the bible is that it frequently robs Christians of the skills necessary to find the clues of God working in history. Every Christian, for example, would take the exodus events (Exod 1-13) as divinely inspired and divinely guided. But how about the advent of *peristroika* in the former U.S.S.R. and the release of new energies in Eastern Europe? Might not these events have more than a little to do with God's engagement in human history? Many of those in the church have a clear idea of what God did in the distant past and a clear idea of what God will do in the uncertain future, but no idea of what God might be doing right under their very noses. It would be tragic, therefore, for Christians to be so stuck within the imagery of the Holy Scriptures as to be unable to read the signs within their own times. *God acts in history and not in books.*

> *Many have a clear idea of what God did in the distant past and a clear idea of what God will do in the uncertain future, but no idea of what God might be doing right under their very noses.*

**9 Q**: In the end, what does it mean to believe in God?

**A**: To believe in God means different things to different people in different times and different circumstances. In God there may be no change; but, we humans do change and as we change we find our God meeting us where we are today and not where we were yesterday or a year ago. Hence, what it means to believe in God has nearly a fresh answer for every momentous shift that we experience in our personal and social lives.

> *To believe in God has nearly a fresh answer for every momentous shift that we experience in our personal and social lives.*

Relative to the future, however, one can perhaps say that there are two kinds of persons and two kinds of belief:

(a) The first kind consists of those who (while they may believe many things about God and be very pious) have settled in and accepted the murkiness and brokenness of personal, social, and ecological situations. Essentially, they have developed settled habits of accommodation and avoidance when it comes to systemic evil. When confronted with evil, they turn the other way or move out of the neighborhood. They act against evil only when it is the last resort by way of protecting themselves and those whom they love. In the end, however, they judge that they are powerless and that the ravages of evil from generation to generation cannot be markedly reduced.

(b) On the other hand, there are those others who have suffered from the brokenness of personal, social, and ecological situations who do not flee or accommodate. In the beginning, more often than not, they find no one able or willing to champion their cause. They turn to God in their distress. In their anguished prayer, they do not find any escape or pious consolation; rather, they find their God suffering with them and urging them to take action. By and by, they develop the settled habit of resisting all forms of accommodation. They find within themselves an unaccountable courage to exert themselves in the face of evil. Even should they be crushed, they would still loudly protest in the name of God, or in the name of Jesus, or simply in the name of humanity (as exemplified, for example, by Oskar Schindler).  In the end, such persons are driven by a compulsion to light one candle rather than to idle stand by and curse the darkness.

For those who pray, they know that this compulsion comes from God.  For those who cannot pray or who have never learned to pray, they explain their compulsion as coming from some Power, some Force, some Mystery which quietly bubbles up in their reflective moments. In any case, they yield to this Presence and, submitting themselves to this dangerous and wonderful journey, they are inexorably lured toward a better future which, in the present dire circumstances, may well appear (to most onlookers) to be beyond hope and beyond redemption.

At times, the forces of evil may triumph—but they know that this is temporary.  To believe in God, for them, means the certainty that the future is, in some mysterious way, in God's hands.  Having harmonized their personal energies with this God, they know they are 'preparing the way of the Lord' (Mark 1:3 and par.).  This is the faith; this is the hope; this is the love exemplified by Jesus and the saints.

*To believe in God, means the certainty that the future is, in some mysterious way, in God's hands.*

## Application to the Churches Today

On the basis of what you have discovered regarding the Synoptic picture of Jesus' anticipation of God's future, what does this say to you and to the contemporary church?

**Postscript**: Over the years, Christians have become accustomed to the Eucharistic acclamation: "Christ has died, Christ has risen, Christ will come again."  There have also been new Christian hymns which celebrate the expectation of the Kingdom of God.  In what follows I provide two such hymns.  The first in from North America; the second from South Africa.

## I Will Not Die

I will not die before I've lived to see that land;
Firm as the earth, God's own promise.
I'll not let go [of life] until I've held it in my hand;
That word of hope, and gentle laughter.

I will not rest until his dawn is in my eyes;
That fragile light, new like morning.
I will not sleep before I'm awakened to that sunrise;
And all the world knows his glory.

> For his right hand has delivered us from death;
> He has regarded our tears,
> She who is goodness and grace.

And I will breath in that mighty wind of justice;
I'll know my name and rise up singing.
And I will call until my words bring on the thunder;
Washed in that rain, then I'll know him.

He will stand up for the poor and the needy;
He'll break the chains that bind God's people.
For she is home for the lost and the desperate;
Her strong hand goes before us.

> For his right hand has delivered us from death;
> He has regarded our tears,
> She who is goodness and grace (1990: Team Pub.)

## Freedom is Coming

Oh freedom is coming (3 times)
Oh yes! I know! (3 times)

Oh Jesus is coming (3 times)
Oh yes! I know! (3 times) (South African Hymn)

Oh freedom is coming (3 times)
Oh yes! I know! (3 times)

## Further Readings for Case Eight

Baum, Gregory
  "Eschatology," *An American Catechism.* Chicago Studies 12/3:304-311, 1973.

Brown, Raymond E.
  "The Pater Noster as an Eschatological Prayer," *Theological Studies* 22:175-208, 1961.

  *Jesus: God and Man.* Milwaukee: Bruce, 1967.

Cone, James H.
  *Martin & Malcolm & America: A Dream or a Nightmare.* New York: Maryknoll. [two prophets; two different eschatological visions], 1991.

Congregation for the Doctrine of the Faith
  *Letter on Certain Questions Concerning Eschatology.* Vatican: Polyglot Press, 1979.

Küng, Hans
  *Eternal Life? Life After Death as a Medical, Philosophical, and Theological Problem.* Tr. by Edward Quinn from the 1982 German orig. New York: Doubleday, 1985.

Ministerial Association
  *Seventh-day Adventists Believe . . . : A Biblical Exposition of 27 Fundamental Doctrines.* Washington, D.C.: General Conference of Seventh-day Adventists, 1988.

Myers, Ched
  *Binding the Strong Man: A Political Reading of Mark's Story of Jesus.* Maryknoll: Orbis, 1988.

Neusner, Jacob
  *Messiah in Context: Israel's History and Destiny in Formative Judaism.* Philadelphia: Fortress, 1984.

Nickelsburg, Jr., George W.E.
  *Resurrection, Immortality, and Eternal Life in Interestamental Judaism.* Cambridge: Harvard University, 1972.

Perrin, Norman
  *Rediscovering the Teaching of Jesus.* New York: Harper & Row, 1967.

Prusak, B.P.
  "Heaven and Hell: Eschatological Symbols of Existential Protest," *Cross Currents* 24/4:475-491, 1975.

Robinson, John A.T.
> *Jesus and His Coming.* Philadelphia: Westminster, 1979.

Russell, D.S.
> *The Method and Message of Jewish Apocalyptic.* Philadelphia: Westminster, 1964.

Schnackenburg, Rudolf
> *God's Rule and Kingdom.* Tr. by John Murray from the 1963 German orig. New York: Herder and Herder, 1963.

Weiss, Johannes
> *Jesus' Proclamation of the Kingdom of God.* Tr. by R. H. Hiers and D. L. Holland from the 1982 German orig. Philadelphia: Fortress, 1971.

# APPENDIX

# Paul's Practice of Honoring Women

*The equality of discipleship extended to Gentiles marvelously caught on while the equality of discipleship extended to women floundered.*

History shows that the equality of discipleship extended to Gentiles marvelously caught on while the equality of discipleship extended to women floundered. Why did this happen? Were the Jewish disciples of Jesus' day more open to sharing their "chosenness by God" with Gentiles before they were willing to extend religious opportunity to the women in their own courtyards? One might think so.

Many scholars and many women finger Paul as the culprit who reversed the agenda of Jesus. Jesus, as we have seen, was solidly for women (Case Four) and cool toward any Gentile mission (Case One). Did Paul, accordingly, turn these priorities on their head? No and yes. There is not enough space here to work this out in detail. I would, however, like to briefly sketch a few details in order that one might see something of the complexity of the issue.

To begin with, Paul's authentic letters point in the direction of an equality of discipleship ("neither male nor female" Gal 3:28) that was not just a pious theory with Paul. Within the Hellenized urban centers which Paul visited, a somewhat greater freedom was allowed for women within public life. Accordingly, Paul actively associated women with himself as co-workers in his missionary toil. Mary, Tryphaena, Tryphosa, and Persis are specifically named by him as having "labored hard" among the Romans (Rom 6:6, 12). Euodia and Synthche are named as having "contended side-by-side" (Phil 4:2f) with him. Paul acknowledged missionary teams such as Priscilla and Aquila, who were founders of house churches. In this case, the woman (Priscilla) is named before the man, thus indicating her superior status as a "fellow-worker" (Rom 16:3f; 1 Cor 16:19; Acts 18:2, 18, 26; 2 Tim 4:19). Priscilla, moreover, is identified by Luke as having finished Apollos' training in the "way of God" (Acts 18:26); hence, her role can never be limited to domestic tasks so as to free her man for his missionary endeavors.

*Paul actively associated women with himself as co-workers in his missionary toil.*

*English translations contribute to obscuring Paul's acknowledged reliance upon female co-workers.*

English translations, here again, contribute to obscuring Paul's acknowledged reliance upon female co-workers. At the end of his Letter to the Romans, Paul specifically acknowledges Junias (a woman) as both "fellow prisoner" and "apostle" (Rom 16:7). The RSV, however, would never let a non-scholar know it. Compare for yourself the RSV translation with my own literal translation prepared from the Greek (italics added):

> Greet Adronicus and Junias, my *kinsmen* and my fellow prisoners; they are *men of note* among the apostles (Rom 16:7 RSV).

> Greet Adronicus and Junias, my *kinsfolk* and my fellow-captives, who are *noteworthy* among the apostles (Rom 16:7).

A much more decisive text in the authentic Pauline letters is the one which declares, "Women should keep silence in the church" (1 Cor 14:34). Some scholars think that 1 Cor 14:33-36 is a later addition to Paul's letter. They conclude this on various grounds: (a) In some ancient manuscripts, 1 Cor 14:34-35 is found after verse 40; (b) When one reads 1 Cor 14 as a whole and follows the internal logic in the text, 1 Cor 14:33-36 does appear to break the flow; and (c) If 1 Cor 14:33-36 is interpreted to mean that Paul is silencing women, then this would openly contradict what Paul said earlier in 1 Cor 11:2-5 about the active participation of women in the community's prayer and prophesying. Needless to say, if this evidence taken together is seen as demonstrating that 1 Cor 14:33-36 represents a non-Pauline addition made by a copyist to his text, then this cannot be used for interpreting the mind of Paul and the role of women in the Corinthian community.

*Some scholars think that 1 Cor 14:33-36 is a later addition to Paul's letter.*

On the other hand, still other scholars have allowed that 1 Cor 14:33-36 is authentic but that it can be interpreted such that it harmonizes with 1 Cor 11:2-5 and presents an argument against those who would try to silence women. When read in this light, Paul opens by quoting the men of Corinth who are saying, "Women should keep silence." In just a moment, however, Paul turns their anti-woman bias against them. Here is how it goes:

*On the other hand it can be interpreted such that it presents an argument against those who would try to silence women.*

> [Some of you men are saying:] As in all the churches of the saints [in Jerusalem?], women should keep silence in the churches. For they are not permitted to speak, but should be subordinate, as even the Torah says. If there is anything they desire to know [about Torah], let them ask their husbands at home. For it is shameful for a woman to speak in church.

> [Now I this I say:] WHAT? Did the word of God originate with you [the men], or are you [the men] the only ones it has reached? (1 Cor 14:33b-36)

The implied answer to the two final rhetorical questions is emphatically "NO"—God has given his word and his prophecy to both women and men. This being the case, women have the right to speak, to prophesy, and to discuss in the church just as much as the men. Thus, after the disjunctive conjunction ("What?"), the argument of the men is roundly defeated. For those who care to look, this same Greek construction occurs in 1 Cor 11:20-22.

The objections heard in 1 Cor 14:34, however, were not entirely dispelled by Paul's offensive. In fact, these same objections appeared with greater force in the first Letter to Timothy. Nearly all scholars acknowledge that this letter was written "in Paul's name" after his death by way of putting greater order into those communities claiming Pauline origins. Relative to women, this letter entirely subverts Paul's authentic thought in favor of bringing all women into conformity with the standards of polite society:

> Let a woman learn in silence with all submissiveness. I permit no woman [wife?] to teach or to have authority over [to dominate?] a man [her husband?]; she is to keep silent [as her husband instructs her]. For Adam was formed first, then Eve; and Adam was not deceived, but the woman was deceived and became a transgressor (1 Tim 2:11-14).

We have no way of knowing what crisis generated 1 Timothy or, once circulated, how it was received. It is hard to imagine that women immediately stopped reading and interpreting and discussing Torah with the men as soon as the letter appeared. The text implies that some women were teaching men (e.g., as in the case of Prisca and Aquila training Apollo in Acts 18:26). After all, one does not forbid something unless it was actually being done.

As the text goes on, the logical affirmation of patriarchy is heard: Adam was number one! Then Eve. Eve was deceived! Adam was not. The message drawn from the Genesis narrative is clear: Men are the superior according to the order of creation; hence, they are the God-ordained rulers over women. Furthermore, Eve was deceived; hence, all women are unreliable teachers. Men alone ought to teach. Needless to say, the anonymous authorship of 1 Timothy knew quite well that there was not a single saying of Jesus or of Paul which could be used to bolster the silencing of women. So what was to be done? Subvert both Jesus and Paul by using a specious argument garnished from Genesis.

From this woefully incomplete sketch, one can glimpse that Paul ran with the message of Jesus and took it far beyond anything Jesus could have envisioned in his own milieu. Paul openly associated with capable women as co-workers and apostles with him in the work of the Lord. Paul openly advocated the right of women to speak and to prophesy in the churches.

But it didn't last. Ideological and theological subordination eventually defeated Paul's practice of the equality of discipleship. The record of this defeat is most clearly found in the letters of Timo-

---

*The first Letter to Timothy subverts Paul's authentic thought in favor of bringing all women into conformity with the standards of polite society.*

*There was not a single saying of Jesus or of Paul which could be used to bolster the silencing of women.*

*Ideological and theological subordination eventually defeated Paul's practice of the equality of discipleship.*

thy and Titus. Most scholars agree that, while these Pastoral Epistles are attributed to Paul, they were in fact written by someone writing in his name sometime after the turn of the second century. Nonetheless, the fact that these letters were received as Pauline letters served to impose upon Pauline theology a new agenda. As a sample of this new pseudo-Pauline agenda, examine the advice given to older women when teaching young-women in the churches:

> Bid the older women . . . train the young-women to be lovers-of-men, lovers-of-children, sensible chaste, domestic [home-workers], kind [good], being subject to their men [husbands and fathers], lest the word of God be cursed [by Gentiles?] (Tit 2:3-5).

The new agenda here is the old agenda of subservience and patriarchy. The young women are not being trained to know and to interpret Torah. Rather, the old women are teaching the younger women to be subject to the discernment of the men. The fact that the training is women-to-women insures that it takes place in the courtyard where women will have no contact with the agenda occupying the men. In those churches wherein the letters of Timothy and Titus were read and honored, one can be certain that all the Marys were back in the kitchen. Men alone "sat at the feet of Jesus," and women, if they were especially lucky, might learn a few things from their husbands when they came home.

*In those churches wherein the letters of Timothy and Titus were read and honored, one can be certain that all the Marys were back in the kitchen.*

The implied motive for this reversion to patriarchy is found in the last line (2:5b): women in traditional roles make the word of God more appealing and acceptable to Gentiles and Gentile converts. In effect, therefore, this might lead one to believe that the Pastoral Epistles do represent an eagerness on the part of the men to share their "chosenness by God" with Gentiles while withdrawing this same religious opportunity from the women in their own courtyards.

Learning is liberating. Once Mary (who represents many women in Luke's church) began to hear Torah for herself "at the feet of Jesus" and then began to acquire the art of applying it to her own life, she established herself as *a disciple* equal with the men. She could never go back to her former position of trusting that the men in her life entirely knew and understood all those things (which were formerly beyond her grasp). More importantly, she could never go back to thinking that she need only obediently submit to masculine direction to assure herself that she was entirely in harmony with what God would have her be and have her do. If every Jewish man gained his independence and his stature before men and before God by virtue of learning to read and to interpret Torah for himself, why should this same rule not apply also to women?

*Mary could never go back to thinking that she need only obediently submit to masculine direction.*

*Even in the first century, there was no single answer as to what roles and responsibilities were to be given to women.*

In the end, therefore, the religious issue of what roles and responsibilities are to be given to women in the church does not have an easy answer. Even in the first century, there was no single answer. The churches following Luke's Gospel undoubtedly favored women more than did those following Matthew's Gospel. And those communities which were guided by the authentic letters of Paul must have functioned quite differently from those who had taken it upon themselves to first implement the agenda of the Pastoral Epistles.

During the third century, the Pastoral Epistles had gained acceptance everywhere as "authentic." Even this, however, did not obscure the fact that "Paul" was not able to cite a single word or event in the life of Jesus which supported the agenda of silencing women. Thus, wherever the Gospels were being preached and interpreted by men, careful listeners heard something more. They heard Jesus addressing the good news of the Kingdom of God in terms which capture the experience proper to women. They recalled that Jesus healed women saying, "Your faith has saved you." They softly blushed when Jesus took the side of voiceless women and shamed the men (even his own disciples) when they tried to obstruct their good deeds. Thus, both yesterday and today, the dangerous memory of Jesus continues to haunt the church and to expose the weak underside of the Pastoral Epistles.

*The dangerous memory of Jesus continues to expose the weak underside of the Pastoral Epistles.*

> No one puts new wine into old wineskins; if he does, the wine will burst the skins, and wine is lost, and so are the skins (Mark 2:22, Matt 9:17, Luke 5:37f).

www.ingramcontent.com/pod-product-compliance
Lightning Source LLC
Chambersburg PA
CBHW082146230426
43672CB00015B/2853